ITRAGIC
INVESTMENT

HOW RACE SABOTAGES COMMUNITIES
AND JEOPARDIZES AMERICA'S FUTURE—AND
WHAT WE CAN DO ABOUT IT

R. JAMES ADDINGTON

iUniverse®

TRAGIC INVESTMENT
HOW RACE SABOTAGES COMMUNITIES AND JEOPARDIZES AMERICA'S FUTURE—AND WHAT WE CAN DO ABOUT IT

iUniverse books may be ordered through booksellers or by contacting:

iUniverse
1663 Liberty Drive
Bloomington, IN 47403
www.iuniverse.com
844-349-9409

ISBN: 978-1-5320-7081-5 (sc)
ISBN: 978-1-5320-7082-2 (e)

Library of Congress Control Number: 2019903420

Print information available on the last page.

iUniverse rev. date: 02/11/2021

To all my relations and to future generations.
And in memory of Imani-Nadine Hairston Addington.
This is my accountability to you.

CONTENTS

ACKNOWLEDGMENTS

This manuscript was incubating for several years. It emerged bit by bit, piece by piece. The emergent pieces changed as I edited and rethought what I was expressing. I always experienced a sense of urgency regarding this witness; however, the urgency was tempered by the need to clearly articulate the body of work that was emerging. My passion has been to speak clearly, persuasively, and as relevantly as I can.

I have spent the past twenty-seven years training and organizing for racial justice and community well-being. This is the primary existential database that animates this witness. However, it rests on the foundation of a lifetime of engagement in social justice organizing, training, and advocacy—stretching back to the civil rights movement, work in South Phoenix and Chicago's inner-city neighborhoods, as well as stints in rural villages in places as disparate as Jamaica, Venezuela, Nigeria, India, and the Philippines.

I am especially indebted to all my fellow organizer-trainers at Crossroads Antiracism Organizing and Training for their commitment, skill, and guidance in this work. The patience, sensitivity, and skill of people like Robette Dias, Jessica Vasquez-Torres, Anne Stewart, Debra and Michael Russell, Derrick Dawson, Jo Ann Mundy, Fernando Ospina, Joy and Ryan Bailey, Lori Adams, Emily Drew, Lillie Wolf, Kara Bender, Aliisa Lahti, Jyaphia Christos-Rodgers, Karen Ziech, Bill Gardiner, Mel Hoover, and many others were crucial to my ability to do this work. I regard the founder and original director of Crossroads, Rev. Joseph Barndt, as a mentor and colleague on the journey.

In 1993, the Minnesota Collaborative Antiracism Initiative (MCARI) was one of the spin-offs of Crossroads' work. In the early years of MCARI's existence, my late wife, Imani-Nadine, was its original codirector; I was privileged to be her cotrainer. Her witness and guidance were fundamental to my grasping the importance of this work and my persistence. Even now, her spirit continues to guide me. My gratitude and sense of indebtedness extends to all the colleagues who were involved in that multiyear effort—in congregations, denominations, councils of churches, community organizations, nonprofits, tribal governments, philanthropic foundations and funds, higher education, primary and secondary education, and corporations in Minnesota and North Dakota.

I wish to especially give thanks for the skill and persistence of Carmen Valenzuela, MCARI's eventual codirector and colleague, and all the colleagues involved in HEART (Higher Education Anti-Racism Training) over several years: Debra Leigh, Mary Clifford, Phyllis May-Machunda, Amy Phillips, Leon Rodrigues, Karen McKinney, Raul Ramos, and a host of others. It's also important to single out three Twin City councils of churches for their early sponsorship of MCARI: the Minnesota, Greater Minneapolis, and Saint Paul Area Councils of Churches. Their sponsorship involved the participation of dozens of individuals from congregations in the Twin Cities and across Minnesota. Without it, MCARI would have been stillborn. I wish to also express appreciation for the efforts of Lou Schoen, who was directly responsible for the involvement of these three councils.

A special word of appreciation to the Mille Lacs Band of Ojibwe and Mary Sam for the years we worked together to shape understanding, respect, and justice in the relations of the tribe with nearby communities. Those efforts were humbling, instructive, and deeply rewarding. All the people from the Mille Lacs Band and nearby communities that participated in this effort were crucial to its impact.

It is crucial to acknowledge the collegiality and collaboration of philanthropic organizations that were central to the work in Minnesota; the Saint Paul Foundation and the Otto Bremer Foundation were especially important to our efforts.

I also wish to express my deep gratitude to my artist friend Ingrid McGarry, whose creative sketches enlivened the text of this manuscript immensely.

Last but certainly not least, I want to thank my wife, Cheryl, for her constant encouragement, support, editorial assistance, and guidance. Without it, I'm not sure this work would have survived the upheavals of a busy life and its constant demands; it might still be incubating.

INTRODUCTION

BEYOND THE BLACK-WHITE BINARY

El Capitan

Years ago, when I worked for the US Forest Service in eastern Arizona, one of the larger forest fires our crew was assigned to was just outside my home town of Globe. At the time, I was a young high school grad earning money for college. The fire was on the eastern slopes of a ridge of the Pinal Mountains known as El Capitan. The fire grew quickly and soon was out of control. Consequently, the local forest ranger sent word out for additional firefighters.

Many who answered the call where young men from Globe and nearby San Carlos who were out of work and needed income (San Carlos is the location of tribal headquarters for the San Carlos Apache Nation). I was assigned a crew of eight young men, all of whom were older than me (I was nineteen). They were also all young men of color—Mexican American and Apache. We were sent to a section of the fire line to clear brush and scout for "smokes" (areas where sparks from the main fire had alighted and might ignite new areas).

As I sat with my crew in a circle on the trail, preparing to give instructions, I realized one of the men was someone I knew. Cruz Salazar had graduated from Globe High School four years ahead of me. Cruz had been a fullback on the Globe High football team. He had been All-State his senior year, a fearsome, hulking bulldozer who was almost impossible to stop. I'm sure that opposing cornerbacks and safeties dreaded the sight of Cruz barreling toward them with the ball pressed against his ribs.

When I realized that Cruz Salazar was part of my crew, I was almost overwhelmed. He was one of my heroes. As an athlete, his commitment and willingness to invest his body were legendary. And now, here I was, charged with telling him what to do. As time dims the memories, I don't really remember how my little crew did. I'm sure we fulfilled our assignment. I recall us clearing brush, digging out smokes, and working through the heat of the day. What I do remember clearly was that Cruz Salazar, someone who was an icon to me, was under my supervision.

That experience was one of many that helped me begin to grasp, slowly I'm sure, that in our nation, race matters. Certainly it mattered in Globe, Arizona, in the late 1950s. I was a young white man working for the US Forest Service, saving money for college. Cruz was a young, dark-skinned Mexican American, my senior in years, out of a job and desperate for income-producing work. While many factors flowing together accounted for our differing roles and social position, race is the one constant that especially illuminates them all. The way in which race mattered likely had nothing whatsoever to do with any particular individual's personal bias. Rather, it was about the systemic outcomes that over time gave me an advantage. On the surface, it may seem that the differences might be explained in terms of class and simple economics. On closer examination, it becomes clear that Cruz's skin color and cultural heritage placed him at a disadvantage, in this case an economic disadvantage. His race was a predictor of how likely he was to be economically disadvantaged. Similarly, my race predicted—compared to Cruz—how likely I was to have an advantage.

All this was not clear to me at the time; it is clearer now, in hindsight. However, a troubling sense of dissonance was deeply disconcerting. I had learned to understand race in terms of the traditional black-white binary. Cognitively, I had difficulty *seeing* beyond black and white; experientially, I knew the sense of dissonance was about race.

The sense of dissonance I experienced was complicated by the fact that there has always been a great deal of ambiguity regarding this matter of race and *who* is *what*. However, as anyone growing up in the Southwestern United States knows, Latino, specifically Mexican American, is indeed a racial category, from a community perspective. In years past, the Supreme Court called this perspective "common knowledge" and used it as one basis for determining who is white or nonwhite. Functionally, an identity that the census forms tell us is ethnic is also racial.

Commonly in this nation, when the conversation turns to race, it falls quickly into a familiar place: the black-white binary. It is presumed that conversations about race are about African Americans. The conversation is framed as a black-white issue. This becomes problematic because it ignores the impact of race on multiple communities of color, and it ignores our history. There are reasons, of course, why this particular binary has such power. It is important to examine them. However, it is even more important to be clear that in our history, the dynamics of race have played out in terms of *white and nonwhite,* not simply black and white.

If residents of Globe had been asked, "Is Cruz Salazar white?" the response would have been, "Of course not," regardless of what census forms or sociologists might tell us. I suspect that Cruz himself would have responded in a similar fashion. This is important because it means that race is more than black-white; it is bigger than the familiar binary. It is about who is white and who is not. Historically, this has been a matter of law and public opinion. Our legal system has defined the boundary separating white and nonwhite. However, it has been a shifting boundary. Some who might have been considered nonwhite in one generation might be legally white in succeeding generations. What has remained constant has been the two poles of the continuum: white and nonwhite.

Our Original Investment

This book will make the case that in the context of this binary (white and nonwhite), this nation self-consciously and intentionally *invested* in racial oppression. The *Merriam-Webster* online dictionary defines *investment* as "the outlay of money (or resources) usually for income or profit"; it also suggests that the term means "to involve or engage emotionally; to commit money (or resources) in order to earn a return." This sense of emotional engagement is crucial to understanding the role of racial oppression in our development as a nation.

In *Confrontation: Black and White*, Lerone Bennett Jr. suggested that enslaved Africans were like the venture capital that jump-started the American economy.[1] This is more than poetic truth. Enslaved Africans and the system that commoditized them built the nation, not simply the antebellum South. However, in order for the system to function at its best, it required more and more swaths of land and natural resources. The nation was inflamed by the vision of Manifest Destiny. Our problem was that the land we needed was occupied. The solution was to remove the occupants, by whatever means necessary. A case can be made that the history of American Indian policy can be summed up in one word: disappearance. Removal was not sufficient; tribal people needed to disappear.

Our original investment involved two separate yet deeply interconnected funds: slavery and Indian removal and disappearance. These two, in turn, were central to our development as a nation, economically, politically, and culturally. We might not be a world power today had we not invested in these "funds." They were and are foundational to national life. As investment funds, they paid strong and consistent dividends. They continue to do so.

We built a social framework that facilitated our ongoing investment in these funds. Like careful investors, we plowed the dividends of our investment back into this framework, creating a society marked by racial separation. Some have dubbed our society *American Apartheid*. The term is drawn from the history of South Africa and the domination of that nation by a white minority. It is noteworthy that our experiments with legally sanctioned segregation and the creation of American Indian reservations both informed the architects of South African apartheid. White South Africans shaped a nation marked by racial separation. This was key to the multigenerational domination by the descendants of Dutch and British colonists. In recent years, social activists in the US have been using this term as a way of indicating deep historical commonalities between the two nations. Using the term apartheid, however, is not to suggest our two histories are identical or that ordinary people's experience is the same in both nations. Each nation has a unique history; the struggle for racial justice in each is unique as well.

While our two original investment funds were intimately and continually related, the circumstances of each were unique. Enslaved Africans were purchased from traders on the west coast of Africa. Some of them had been kidnapped from their home villages; others were prisoners of war. They came from many cultures and tribes and spoke a multitude of languages. Since they were purchased and then sold in slave markets to the highest bidder, the Europeans considered them property—chattel. This was an important distinction. In nations where private property was a sign of wealth and power, the ownership of enslaved people also indicated wealth and power. Chattel slavery turned human beings into commodities that could be bought and sold and had monetary value.

When Europeans came to the Americas (whether in search of gold and other riches or in search of new lands to settle), they encountered a variety of indigenous nations with vastly differing cultures. The Doctrine of Discovery, promulgated initially by Pope Nicholas V, encouraged them to believe they had holy authority to claim land as their own that was actually occupied by groups that had been there for millennia. Thus, even when they entered into treaties with Native people, they did so from the perspective of having a legitimate claim upon the land; Native people were simply occupants, even interlopers.

Our original dual investment created a precedent. Social subordination and domination would be central to the development of the nation. We expanded the parameters of our original investment as needed, whether excluding Chinese and other Asians from immigration, denying former Mexican citizens civil rights following the Mexican War, or confining American citizens of Japanese descent in concentration camps. This investment was the price of nationhood—a price we were quite willing to pay.

Now, however, these foundations, so integral to our emergence on the world scene, have effectively snared us and jeopardize our very future. Our apartheid social framework, built by the dividends from our investment, simply cannot respond to the challenges of our day. It is insufficient for the times. From the perspective of social justice and questions of morality, we can conclude that the framework was never adequate; it was based on oppression and coercion. However, this framework, for better or for worse, conveyed us to this moment. The pressing questions concern the future. Where do we go from here and how do we get there?

The aim of this book is to tell this story and to suggest a pathway into a just and sustainable future. There is more at stake here than clarity about our past or even the proper ideological lenses for such viewing. Unless we grasp this history and its impacts on us today, we may not safely negotiate the passage before us. The future requires something more than apartheid. Regardless of how well this framework may have served some of us previously, it simply will no longer do.

Structure

This book is organized into four parts. Part 1 is an exploration of how and why race still matters in our society. It begins with an exploration of the tripolar dynamics among community, history, and race. Then we move to a careful look at the idea of race, racial identity, and racism, followed by an exploration of systemic power, the social inculcation of race (racialization), and thinking systemically about race and racism. Finally, the section explores the mythic dimension of race and the role racism plays in the nation's traditional narrative.

Part 2 takes a deeper look at our historic investment in racial hegemony. It will build on themes introduced in part 1 and take them deeper. First, we will consider historical method: how do we view the past and assess the people, places, and events that brought us to current times? We will consider a framework that helps us discern the themes and motifs present in five hundred years of European imperial-colonialism. These themes and motifs coalesced over time into a social framework whose parameters were crystalized by the time of our War for Independence. In chapter 6, we will note the impact of five foundational crops in the shaping of our nation. We will then do a more careful and nuanced examination of our nation's investment in racial domination, followed by a consideration of the benefits and dividends of this investment, in times past and in our current day.

I will use the phrase *European imperial-colonialism* when referring to Europe's multicentury efforts in the Americas. Often the terms *imperialism* and *colonialism* are used interchangeably. While both characterized Europe's American enterprise, they do suggest slightly different dynamics. The nations involved were building empires to preside over; they had imperial aspirations. Empire, alone, does not necessarily entail settlement; it means control. However, they were also colonizing and settling territory, effectively expanding their geographical base. They were establishing colonies they intended to populate.

Part 3 builds on the previous two sections and summarizes the impact of our historic investment on the nation as a whole and on those of us who are white, in particular. The section begins with an explanation of the term *white supremacy*: what does it mean and how is it being used in this manuscript? We will then explore the normalization of white identity and the echo chamber effect that centers white identity in our social experience. White identity becomes, in effect, a collective landscape, a terrain. In chapter 11, we will explore the features of this terrain; these features are the marks of our collective social identity. In the final chapter of part 3, we will explore the pathologies of white identity and the themes of historical loss and trauma and their existential significance for white people. What have we lost at the hands of race? Has something been taken from us, and are we traumatized by this loss? Clearly, generations of domination have visited loss and trauma on others; are we, who are white, also touched in a similar fashion by the same dynamics? This chapter will make the case that racism hurts white people as well as people of color, albeit differently.

Part 4 proposes the reparation of community as the portal to the future. We begin with an examination of language and its role in the dynamics of hegemony and resistance. Second, we move to an exploration of the dynamics of accountability in the formation of community, effectively reframing how the idea of accountability is typically understood. Third, we will consider antiracism as the interventions that interrupt the processes that replicate our racial past and repair the fabric of community. Finally, the book discusses the connections between racial justice and shaping sustainable, resilient communities. The conclusion will suggest some concrete directions and steps for moving beyond racial apartheid.

Approach and Method

Part of my task, as I understand it, is to connect the dots. I am not really interested in repeating the work others have done. There has been a great deal of insightful and creative work done that documents the history of race in the development of our nation. When depending on others' work, I give appropriate credit and references. I hope my contribution will be in linking the work of others together in a fashion that clarifies current impacts. I am especially interested in making some provocative suggestions regarding the impact of race on those of us who are white, our collective sense of identity and how we move into a more sustainable future as a nation.

In addition to a more traditional academic approach that entails research and documentation, I use my own experience as a filter that informs research. This is my primary research. I've spent virtually my entire vocational life as a trainer and organizer. The past twenty-seven years have been dedicated to working specifically for racial justice, with a focus on helping organizations and communities develop the capacity to overcome racial apartheid.

I do not come to this work dispassionately or without a sense of personal stake. My late wife, Imani-Nadine, was African American. Her insights, passion, and commitments deepened and intensified my own. This work gets me out of bed every day. Not surprisingly, our family crosses the color line; I am clear that the well-being of my children, grandchildren, and newly acquired stepchildren are at issue. I believe that the soul of our nation is also at issue. And I believe that our capacity to endure as a people is at issue.

Thus, I confess to strong feelings and personal investment in this work. I am unapologetic for the ways in which my commitments may color and give an edge to my writing. However, I do not believe it is helpful to begin a witness from the perspective of how things ought to be, or even that things should be different than they are. We have to begin with what is. Every experienced organizer and trainer has learned that you have to begin your work with the way things are. Then we can ask, "How did things get this way? How did we arrive at this moment?" This sets the stage for asking, "Where do we go from here, and how do we do it?"

A word about sources is also important. Readers will note that this book has a fairly substantial bibliography. Many of these sources are drawn from the literature that directly addresses the history, social impact, and continuing challenge of race. However, many of the works noted have nothing to do with race directly. They are included because they have informed and illuminated my efforts to understand the role and significance of race in our complex society.

This presumes that our work can indeed be informed by insightful work from a variety of sources, whether related directly to race or not. I have found the work of Peter Drucker, for example, on organizational dynamics and leadership very insightful and helpful. His work has helped me discern some of the organizational dynamics that promote and strengthen racial domination, as well as insights regarding effective leadership. Likewise, the work of John Gall on systems dynamics has been quite useful. Gall helped me understand the self-replicating character of systemic default settings. They both have helped me grasp the impact of race on the development of institutions and social systems. Neither of them directly addressed systemic oppression. Both of them are white men who have experienced the privileges associated with their station. However, both of them bring insights that call into question some of society's unquestioned assumptions, thereby illuminating the dynamics of race and racial oppression and suggesting alternative ways to organize relationships. The key to utilizing such work is having an analysis that has been collaboratively shaped and that includes primary input from people of color and others who have intimate experience of systemic oppression.

Comments on Resistance

This book is rooted in the history of resistance to racial oppression. It is the witness of countless communities, individuals, and organizations over many generations that has given me the courage, insight, and even language to shape this work. My hope is that this work contributes in some small way to this grand drama of resistance. I have come to believe that we as a nation must self-consciously deal in a deep and vigorous manner with the continuing challenges presented by race and racism. Frankly, I question our capacity as a nation to endure if we do not. It is this sense of urgency that impels me to write this book and offer whatever guidance it may provide in the ongoing struggle to shape human communities grounded in justice and the hope for a sustainable future.

I especially hope that social activists, community organizers, organizational developers, and educators find this book strengthens their commitment to and passion for the liberation of white people as part of the work of deconstructing the social fabric formed by our investment in racial oppression. I certainly hope that scholars who study the role of race—historians, sociologists, legal scholars, psychologists—as well as the artists of our day—writers, poets, musicians, dancers, painters—find my work helpful and perhaps provocative.

Flow and Process

Finally, a word about the flow of this book and the writing process. Two metaphors are suggestive of the way the book unfolds—scaffolding and spiraling. Each new piece of content builds on what has gone before and contextualizes what is to come, in a scaffolding-like fashion. Rather than flowing in a simple linear fashion, the book unfolds like a spiral, each turn of the spiral going deeper. This means that some subject matter will be revisited; each revisit will be at a deeper level that takes into account new contextual material and material previously covered. Each part, however, stands on its own, notwithstanding the scaffolding and spiraling effect. Each could be read or presented apart from the whole.

PART I

RACE AND WHY IT MATTERS

Introduction

Part 1 is foundational to the rest of this manuscript. It establishes baseline definitions that will be presumed in the ensuing chapters. In chapter 1, we examine community, historical narrative, and the connection between them. This focus will help us understand the mischief race has done in our nation. In chapter 2, we will explore an operational definition of race and racial assignment. In chapter 3, we will unpack the dynamics of systemic power and clarify the role they play in racial oppression. Finally, in chapter 4, we will examine the mythological roots of racial oppression. This chapter will suggest that the social dynamics that racialize and oppress communities of color are rooted in the mythic story of white superiority and are neither coincidental nor accidental. We will examine some of the ways this story plays out in everyday affairs.

The perspectives expressed are based on careful perusal of current and recent scholarship and represent the author's understanding and application of others' research. Many conclusions drawn have been influenced and shaped by the insights of fellow organizer-trainers with whom I've worked closely for over twenty years. I am, however, solely responsible for their articulation and application in this book.

1

Community, History, and Race

This examination of our historical investment and its contemporary impact begins with commentary on three interconnected dynamics: community, history, and race. We cannot speak of the impact of race abstractly. Examining its impact on the fabric of community and our nation's history gives us a deeper sense of its function than an abstract, stand-alone definition. Race cannot be understood in isolation; its social-historical impact discloses its social significance. We have to talk about its impact on community life, in all its iterations, and examine its impact on our understanding of our history.

1. Community: A Brief Commentary

Neurological research has confirmed the centrality of relationships in our sense of self as individuals. We are wired for relationship and are shaped by our relationships with others. Daniel Goleman, in his book *Social Intelligence*,[2] points out that the architecture of our brains biases us for connection with others. Humans form groups; we are a communal species. Jeremy Rifkin, in his work *Empathic Civilization,* suggests that empathy is the key human capacity that guides our participation in relationships and perhaps offers the possibility of achieving genuine global consciousness.[3]

Empathy, in this sense, is more than an emotional quality; it happens at the cellular level. Mirror neurons are the basic sensors in the brain that knit us together. According to Goleman, "they reflect back an action we observe in someone else, making us mimic that action or have the impulse to do so." Goleman further suggests they are "a neural snapshot of primal empathy in action."[4] The term *empathic resonance* names the basic human capacity for connecting with other humans and even other creatures. From an evolutionary perspective, this capacity enhanced the likelihood of survival in a dangerous world. In forming connections that knit us together in solidarity, we form communities. Individually, some may be more solitary than others, but as a species, we are marked by our communal relationships. This means that being in community is foundational to our survival—our continued success as a species.

Our sense of who is in our community is continually changing, even as our relationship to space and time changes. There has been an ongoing conversation about what it means to live in one interconnected world, as disclosed by the photos of the earth from space. Our capacity to discern systemic connections and think systemically is an outcome of our emerging post-Einsteinian worldview. We can see that the earth is knit together via systemic connections. This same imaginal capacity is pulling us beyond our traditional sense of who makes up our community. Our sense of community is expanding as we struggle with being global citizens. And so, issues of immigration, migration, and population dislocations become lively public policy debates as nations attempt to sort out national and international responsibilities. The very existence of the United Nations, unwieldy though it may be, testifies to our changing sense of who constitutes our community, who we are directly connected to.

Economic realities dramatically express the emerging global character of human community. Huge ships, laden with containers filled with products, line up in the busiest harbors to deliver goods to us produced by our neighbors on the other side of the world. Closer to home, brisk trading relationships with Canada and Mexico knit us together in deep and important ways. Every week, for example, billions of dollars in trade traverse our border with Mexico, going both ways (that's just the legal trade). Our connections with Mexico are historic and deep, perhaps more so than with any other nation. But we are intimately connected with virtually every other nation on earth. Isolation is no longer possible; five hundred years of globalization has produced an interconnected world that rests on and in a sense mirrors the deeper ecological systemic connections. Nations create policy interventions that strengthen, strain or weaken these connections; nonetheless, we remain an interconnected world.

Communication technologies, including social media, knit us together and strengthen these interconnections.

This maze of complex interconnections rests, finally, on our basic capacity as human beings to form connections. Our communal connections are life and death to us. In this sense, community (the dynamic, constantly shifting social fabric we live in) is an outcome of our neural makeup. It is fundamental to being human. But this is true not only for us; there are other communal species as well.

When we carefully examine the natural world, we can see that complex interconnectedness is ubiquitous. Human communities are not unique in this sense. In fact, we can learn a great deal about our human communities by observing the planet's ecosystems. The biomimicry movement suggests that we can learn how to shape sustainable communities by being attentive to the ecological systems of our planet.

One of the lessons from the natural world seems to be that monocultures do not survive. They lack the reservoir of creativity that characterizes multicultures. Diversity is the key to ecological health. Diverse ecosystems are adaptive; they adjust to changing times and contextual realities. They have the capacity to regenerate. They have a regenerative relationship to the ecosystems in which they are embedded. (Bioneers is one of the organizations that champions this approach to organizing society. *Original Instructions: Indigenous Teachings for a Sustainable Future,* edited by Melissa K. Nelson, lifts up the work of Bioneers and the role of indigenous knowledge in shaping its approach.[5]) The lesson in this for human communities is that diversity is key to survival. Communities that enforce monoculturalism do so at their own peril. Such communities lack the capacity for creative change; they are not adaptive. In the short term, they may well be powerful. In the long term, they do not survive.

History

The centrality of history to this conversation needs a bit of unpacking. First, in order to understand current racial dynamics, we have to look at our history. This helps us to understand how we arrived at our moment. This means that we must become historians. We must become *popular* historians of the grass roots—historians who help communities understand their history. This includes making sense of the dynamics of race. Our history as a nation helps us do that. Such an exploration of the past always involves at least three things: context, perspective, and connection.

Context. An examination of our racial history requires a larger context than simply our history as a nation. We have to remember that the United States emerged in the context of over five hundred years of the European imperial-colonial enterprise. Racism, as a social force, cannot be understood apart from this European enterprise. While its roots may well be older, the ideology of race was articulated in the context of European colonial expansion and the globalizing economics it birthed.

Perspective. Clearly, an examination of the past does not happen in a vacuum. History is always more than simply facts, such as names, dates, and events. It is also interpretation. What do these facts mean? How are they connected? What is their connection to our present moment? Interpretation requires a lens, a rational framework that makes sense of the facts. Such schemes always involve values and represent fundamental commitments and beliefs. This book develops such a perspective. We will examine our history through the lens of *racial oppression and resistance.* Chapter 5 is an expanded commentary on historical method and the implications of this particular lens.

Connection. Historical research that makes sense of the present and that has implications for our lives is existential. It reveals personal and community connections. It makes sense of our lives and provides a place to stand as we chart our pathway into the future. In this sense, it is neither abstract nor unbiased. This is one of the secrets of history as an academic discipline; scholars discover that their research has crept into their bones; a personal connection happens. Historians who focus upon a particular slice of the historical record discover that their lives are colored by their research. They begin to see connections everywhere that lead back to their focused research. In part 2, we will utilize the research some have done on the early years of our republic. Their careful unpacking of the record reveals the contemporary connections they believed are laid bare in their work.

I want to call this way of thinking about history—as context, perspective, and existential connection—historical imagination. Historical imagination brings poetic sensibilities to the intellectual discipline of social science. Octavio Paz, Mexican philosopher and writer, believed that such a sense of history bestows personal agency upon individuals. It bestows a sense of personal power and responsibility.[6]

Historical imagination is a feature of our neural bias for connecting with others. We talk about our relationships. We tell stories about our relationship journeys. As communities develop, a sense of identity also develops. This sense of identity is created, deepened, and strengthened by storytelling. We shape narratives that talk about our community's origin and destiny: where we came from and where we are going. They also evoke a sense of solidarity. They are a form of community self-talk. This sense of solidarity is a mark of empathic resonance; it is an outcome of empathic connections. It is also the medium of culture; cultures are formed in the dynamics of community self-talk.

Yuval Harari, an Israeli historian, in a recent TED Talk underscored the importance of imagination and storytelling.[7] Harari posed the question, "What explains the rise of humans?" He suggests that the real difference that sets us apart is not on the individual level; rather, it is on the collective level. We are able to cooperate flexibly in very large numbers; we form networks of cooperation. How do we do it? Imagination is the key. We can create and believe stories that we share and that interpret reality. This is historical imagination in action.

Historical imagination, in this sense, bears witness to the importance of empathic connections in shaping community identity. Historical imagination, through community self-talk, strengthens the deep sense of community and clarifies the basis upon which new members of the community are engaged. Engaging new members, of course, is critical if a community is to regenerate. When community self-talk creates walls of exclusion to community membership, the likelihood of survival is in jeopardy. Walls that exclude produce monoculture; they produce communities that live in echo chambers that normalize the status quo. Consequently, such walls produce communities versed in monologue, not dialogue. This is especially problematic if the community's stories about itself project an image of justice and inclusion, while the community's practices replicate oppression and exclusion. Indeed, this tension births the experience of dissonance, both cognitive and existential.

Race

Dissonance is a strong clue regarding the destructive power of race and racism. They produce walls of exclusion and domination. They promote the development of monocultures, thus placing the continued existence of communities in jeopardy. The social artifacts of our past ensnare us and undermine our capacity to respond to the challenges facing us. The destructive impact of racism cannot be grasped apart from a thoughtful examination of the concept of race itself. The notion of race has, in effect, been an ideological tool. This tool has been complicit in generations of hegemony, oppression, and disappearance.

We can say three things, initially, about race that contextualizes a deeper discussion in chapter 2. First, the American racial template has always been about more than the familiar black-white binary. The actual binary has been white and nonwhite. Second, in this nation, everyone has a racial assignment; no one gets to opt out. Neither do we choose our race. Racial assignment effectively creates the boundary between white and nonwhite. Third, race always intersects with other social identities; it is intersectional.

If racial identity is a social assignment rather than a biological given, how does the assigning take place? We are placed individually into the white/nonwhite binary by a variety of means. Further, the assigning process continues to operate throughout our lifetimes; it is not a once-and-for-all assignment. It is part and parcel of our socialization into society. The rules governing racial assignment are, at best, ambiguous, slippery, and complex. Assignment happens when a clerk fills out a government form that requires checking off a box. It happens when information from a hospital birth record is transferred to a state birth certificate. It happens via television, conversation among peers, family conversations, and social media. The processes that assign racial identity, interpret that identity, and teach us our assigned identity can be termed *racialization*. Racialization is a lifelong, multigenerational process.

Race is not a separate social identity, standing apart from other identities. Rather, it is constantly connecting with and impacting other assigned social identities. Many social justice activists speak of the intersection of oppressions. Indeed, there are many social identities that qualify people for discrimination and oppression. This means that a discussion of race and its impacts must also examine other socially constructed identities, such as gender, class, age, sexual orientations, appearance, and ability. These social identities invoke, reinforce, and mutually shape one another. In addition, these identities intersect and interact in me. These are not abstract and theoretical intersections.

Race has had an incredibly destructive impact on the formation of community life in our history. It has been a core organizing force. It has led to social apartheid, the formation of communities marked by walls of exclusion and communities on the margins—ghettos. Indeed, social hierarchies apparently are a feature of virtually every society. However, in our history, racial hierarchy was at the core of our national identity: the United States as a nation was racially formed. Apartheid has been such a strong feature of our history that we tend to take it as the norm. We tend to believe that monocultural communities are simply a reflection of people's natural tendency to live with their own kind. In making this assumption, we overlook the role that our government has played in fostering and enforcing, through law, apartheid communities.

Race has distorted our sense of history. The official narratives of our journey as a nation highlight our exceptionalism and minimize or dismiss the stories of every community on the margins. Thus we have inherited a stunted and distorted historical imagination that considers only a small portion of our journey. Most of us simply don't know our own history. This tends to be especially true of those of us who are white. The historical record we know (or think we know) is a story of triumphal expansion, highlighting Yankee ingenuity, hard work, and our spirit of independence. It is a story of resistance to unjust taxation and domination. We find it easy to overlook or ignore the cost of this history in human terms.

We shall return to the conversation about community and historical imagination in part 4. This brief commentary on race sets the stage for a more careful examination of the idea of race and its function in this society. We will note how race has been and continues to be an ideological tool facilitating our investment in oppression, both directly and indirectly.

2

Race and Racial Identity

In chapter 1, we suggested that the significance of race is best understood in the context of community and history. We explored, briefly, how race impacts and distorts community life and historical imagination. Now, in order to take the conversation a step deeper, we need to ask, What is race / racial identity? How have we understood race in our history? How have the dynamics of race played out in our history? What has been the function and significance of racial assignment? And finally, what is racism?

Race, a Social Construct

There is a general consensus in our time among social scientists, legal scholars, historians, biologists, and other scholars that race is socially constructed, rather than simply being a biological phenomenon. It is a multigenerational fabrication. While this may well be the current presumption in most academic circles, it is not necessarily a common understanding in the general public. Many of us still tend to use the term as if it indicates biological realities. In this view, race is simply a name assigned to biological givens that distinguish groups of humans. Racial classification is a practical way of categorizing human beings. Some believe that race may still be a useful category in population studies. Sorting humans into groupings based on their race may even seem to be an innocent activity that serves a practical purpose, perhaps like categorizing butterflies, birds, or trees.

Such presumptions, however, ignore our nation's history and the role that racial assignment has played. Our history undermines any potential usefulness race may have as a category. Categorizing people by race has been done with malice aforethought; it has never been as innocent as sorting plants and animals into groups and subgroups. It is not simply a taxonomic exercise. It is about social value and status. In order to understand this clearly, we must first explore what it means to suggest that race is a social fabrication. Who fabricated race? When was it done? What was the social-historical context? What role or function did and does this fabrication play?

Dorothy Roberts, a legal scholar at the University of Pennsylvania, has noted that, "Like citizenship, race is a political system that governs people by sorting them into social groupings based on invented biological demarcations. Race is not only interpreted according to invented rules, but, more important, race itself is an invented political grouping. Race is not a biological category that is politically charged. It is a political category that has been disguised as a biological one ... The very first step of creating race, dividing human beings into these categories, is a political practice."[8]

With these comments, Roberts captures both the artificiality and deceptive character of race as a social construct. Her commentary means that the processes that assign racial identity have to do with power; they are a political exercise in the most fundamental sense. They are not only social practices; they are a matter of law. Racial identity has and continues to be couched in law. Ian Haney Lopez has carefully documented the way that legal processes embed race in our social fabric. In his classic, *White by Law*, Lopez notes that "race is not an independent given on which the law acts, but rather a social construction at least in part fashioned by law."[9] He further quotes John Calmore regarding the role of social struggle: "Race is not a fixed term. Instead, 'race' is a fluctuating, decentered complex of social meanings that are formed and transformed under the constant pressures of political struggle."[10]

It is clear that racial distinction is and has been ambiguous. The lines separating racial groups have at times been indistinct and shifting. Calmore suggested that political struggle has been fundamental to the significance of racial identity; its social meaning is dynamic. Nonetheless, throughout our nation's history, the idea of race / racial identity has been central. Has there been anything consistent and constant in our understanding and use of the idea? We have racialized every social group that makes up our nation. None have escaped racial assignment. However, the racial assignment of some groups has been more fluid and fluctuating than others. The Irish, Italians, Jews, and many other European ethnic groups have seen their racial assignment change in response to changing social conditions. Over time, they traversed the terrain of nonwhite identity and became white (we will note this journey in more detail later). Many contemporary Americans may be shocked to learn that their ancestors were viewed as nonwhite. Political struggles, economic realities, and cultural practices all have played a part in the dynamic of shifting racial boundaries. Race may very well be a "decentered," shifting social meaning system, as Calmore suggested. Perhaps, though, what have remained constant are the parameters of the background construct—the fundamental binary of white-nonwhite. The dynamics of systemic power have maintained this binary; it is virtually self-replicating.

There are some racial groups that have consistently remained nonwhite. They constitute the background constant, a definitive part of the racial bedrock of this nation. If one's paternal grandfather is Italian and one's mother is English, one simply becomes a white American of English and Italian descent. Barack Obama, however, will forever be known as our first black president, his mixed-race heritage lifted up only when it is politically or socially advantageous to do so.

If you are black in this society, or if you are American Indian, that is your racial identity until the law and common knowledge declare you otherwise. Further, your identity places you firmly on the nonwhite side of the binary. This has been a consistent feature of our history as a nation. In principle, of course, this has been the case for every racialized group; however, the boundaries seem more deeply etched or firmly entrenched when it comes to black and Indian identity. Perhaps this is a reflection of the original racial construct in our nation: Africans in America (whether enslaved or free) and Indian people were the "other." Whiteness, as consciousness and legal identity, emerged in shaping the features of their otherness.

Jacqueline Battalora, in *Birth of a White Nation,* notes that the term "white" did not appear in law until 1681 in the colony of Maryland.[11] She further notes the legitimizing role that law plays and suggests that this statute and subsequent ones in the colony of Virginia were effectively the legal invention of white identity. They were enacted following the rupture in colonial society that resulted from Bacon's Rebellion in 1676. Nathaniel Bacon had rallied poor, working-class, white and African laborers—free and enslaved—in an effort to overthrow the governing council of Virginia. While unsuccessful, his violent effort got the attention of Virginia's wealthy elite. The subsequent legal invention of white identity created a social class distinct from Africans and Indians that was bound together by law. This new legal identity provided a basis for social solidarity. Antimiscegenation statutes constructing a wall around white identity further strengthened the bonds of social solidarity.

Typically, when we think of racial identity, we think of skin color and secondarily of other physical characteristics, such as hair, shape of face, shape of nose, and so on. Skin color, especially, has been the primary marker indicating nonwhite identity. We have often presumed that skin tone expresses an interior racial essence. The darker one's skin, the more indelibly etched is nonwhite identity. Of course, no one is actually black, although some people are dark brown, like rich chocolate. In a similar vein, it is interesting to point out that no one is white. Most of us with primary roots in Europe are pinkish or light beige. Some are very pale. No one is actually white.

We might ask, "What is the significance of naming the superior identity white and the most inferior identity black?" While we can certainly debate this, it is interesting to note that in European Christian mythology, white indicates purity, and black suggests death and evil. Darker shades of skin similarly suggest dirtiness and impurity. This is not an accident or coincidence. Our European forebears self-consciously drew on familiar mythic material to define racial identities and characteristics. Terminology that tapped into mythic history clearly indicated who the superior people were and who the inferior people were. Naming groups in this manner also inferred justification for the coercion of labor and the theft of land and resources.

Of course, all kinds of anomalies and contradictions emerge as we consider skin color and the application of racial categories. There are American Indian people who are enrolled members of Indian nations who look white. There are people who understand themselves to be black who could pass as white. Historically, the question we pondered was, "What makes someone nonwhite?" The presumed answer was, "It's in the blood!" Racial essence may be hidden or disguised, but it's still there. Therefore, we needed some kind of formula that helped us determine someone's racial identity, regardless of appearance—a way to calculate who really belonged in the white camp and who was an imposter. We needed some sort of racial identity arithmetic. This is the role of blood quantum and the one-drop rule. They functioned as legal mechanisms used to assign racial identity. Blood quantum was (and is) a bureaucratic mechanism used to deny Indian identity. It was a tool used to say who is not an Indian, based on the quantum of blood (from one tribe) one had flowing through one's veins. The one-drop rule (the rule of hypodescent) suggested that one drop of African blood (any identifiable African ancestor) made one black (for legal and social purposes).

Racial Arithmetic: It's in the Blood!

"It's in her blood!" With this comment, a friend of mine indicated why a particular acquaintance of his was able to instruct people in Native American spirituality. She, after all, "has Native heritage," he noted. She's part Native American. With this comment, my friend expressed a still current belief in race as a natural, biological *isness* that influences how we behave and what sensibilities we bring to our lives and work.

Scholars, including geneticists, are telling us that there is no evidence for race as a naturally occurring biological feature. Still, our belief in the power of the blood to determine how we do our lives and perform in society remains strong. The metaphors we've used historically to track racial identity refer primarily to blood. The popular belief has been that blood is the carrier of the essence of race. Race may be expressed physically in skin color, hair texture, or the shape of a nose, but even when it's not, its presence in the blood is determinative!

So, the one-drop rule and the mathematics of blood quantum still affect how we think about race and the decisions we make about race. Even the categories we check on census and other government forms reveal our continuing belief in race as a natural, biological phenomenon residing in our blood and genetic makeup. The addition of the category *biracial* or *mixed-race* reinforces the power of the notion and indirectly strengthens the one-drop rule.

Much of the debate around the notion of biracial or mixed-race identity has been about individuals who have white and black ancestry. It is not my intent to minimize or dismiss the importance of other ancestries. There are likely more people who claim other racial mixtures. There are historical reasons that much of the conversation focuses on children of black–white unions. Black–white relations have often defined our view of race and racial dynamics. The conversation occurs in the historical context of the one-drop rule and efforts to subordinate black Americans. This history, therefore, shapes the conversation, often in hidden ways. For some parents, the conversation has also been an effort to prevent one's offspring from being categorized as black. After all, we're very clear about the social significance of black identity.

Back to my friend and his comments regarding identity and blood. My friend is a medical practitioner trained in the scientific method. If pressed, he would likely conclude that whatever skills his acquaintance had were not a function of some mysterious quality of her blood. They are more likely related to her socialization. She may well be part of a Native community. She may be an enrolled member of a tribe. Or she may have studied Native spirituality. But her skills are not a racial characteristic rooted somehow in the chemistry of her blood!

Still, this archaic belief in the mysterious power of blood is fundamental to understanding racial ideology. Identity is somehow lodged in the blood; it's a function of the mysteries of blood chemistry. In this view, genealogy itself is carried in the blood; one's true identity is encapsulated in one's blood! Further, in this view, that which is carried in the blood controls behavior, capacities, inclinations, and intelligence. In effect, it is like a deep program that has all the instructions that shape one's life. In this context, it is easy to understand previously held notions regarding blood transfusions and some people's resistance to receiving blood donated by a person of color, especially one of African descent. The stigma of nonwhite identity indicated a deep, essential impurity, an impurity carried in the blood.

The ancient ideas of purity and pollution inform our beliefs about race. If one's racial identity is pure and therefore epitomizes humanness, then the point of indicating other identities is to illuminate impure humanity, polluted humanity. Racial ideology suggests that race mixing dilutes racial purity, thereby producing mongrelization. Historically, we presumed that racial mongrels were inferior. The gifts and skills inherent in the racially pure would be watered down and weakened. On the one hand, such beliefs justified maintaining racial apartheid; maintaining the purity of the races guarded the unique skills and characteristics each possessed. However, such beliefs also presumed that moral and intellectual superiority marked only one pure race: white.

Blood quantum, as noted previously, originally was a bureaucratic tool for erasing Indian identity. It uses simple arithmetic to calculate the "quantum" of Indian identity carried in one's blood. The US government used blood quantum rules to disqualify individuals from eligibility for Indianess, thereby disqualifying them for rights outlined in treaties. It was used to determine who was not an Indian. After three generations, Indian blood was sufficiently thinned, so that one no longer qualified as a legal Indian, from one federal perspective. Today, some Indian nations have appropriated blood quantum and used it to protect or increase tribal identity and membership. It is important to note that this is a different use of blood quantum than was originally intended by the federal government.

For example, the Mississippi Band of Choctaw Indians requires one-half blood quantum to qualify for tribal membership. There is a history that provides context for this requirement. In 1898, the Curtis Act was the US government's effort to delegitimize and dismantle tribal governments in Indian Territory (later to become Oklahoma). The federal government pressured tribes in Indian Territory to undergo allotment, according to the terms of the General Allotment Act of 1887 (also called the Dawes Act). Under the auspices of allotment, tribes had to create tribal rolls, thus determining who was "in" and who was not. Tribal rolls then determined who was allotted a parcel of land. Allotment was purportedly a tool for assimilating Indian people into the American way of life and teaching the value of private property. Perhaps even more to the point, it was a strategy for seizing any land not allotted. Allotment turned out to be a massive theft of Indian land by the federal government.

Families claiming Indian identity and heritage came out of the woodwork. The promise of land was simply too tempting. Suddenly, there were Choctaw, Chickasaw, Creek, Cherokee, and Seminole people in great numbers appearing out of nowhere. Consequently, there are people on the Dawes rolls who claimed anywhere from one sixty-fourth blood quantum to being full-blooded Indian. Many of these claimants had no history of tribal life and culture—whatever genetic heritage they might or might not have had. In some cases, poor white people ended up with land that was intended, by law, for Indian people. The connivance of federal agents facilitated this process, usually for a price. The current-day requirement of one-half blood quantum by the Mississippi Choctaw can be understood as a response to this history, in addition to any other rationale invoked. It functions as a gateway, presided over by the tribal council, to tribal membership. Tribal membership also entitles one to participate in the regular distribution of profits from the tribe's casino operation. Hence the tribe's blood quantum requirement can be understood to guard and preserve Choctaw identity and resources.

The Choctaw Nation of Oklahoma and several other indigenous nations have done away with blood quantum as an enrollment requirement. Instead, direct descent from someone on the Dawes rolls, when documented, qualifies one for tribal membership. From the perspective of tribal people, both approaches make sense, depending on how they function. Perhaps the real question is, "Who decides who is an Indian?"

When we compare the politics of blood quantum with the workings of the one-drop rule, we see clearly the process of subordination compared to disappearance. If one drop of African blood (the rule of hypodescent) makes one black, then the function of this rule is to increase and extend the black population, while protecting the purity of white identity. This is the population whose original role, in a racialized nation, was to provide cheap, subservient labor as chattel. Enslaved Africans were property. They were understood to be commodities. As such, they provided not only labor; they were an investment beyond the value of profits earned on their efforts. They could serve as collateral for a loan. They enhanced a family's wealth. They had market value! It's also a racial group whose presumed inferior nature is carried in the blood; hence, the one-drop rule provided a legal mechanism for the white collective to guard its purity and to restrict access to the property of white identity.

The one-drop rule provided a mechanism for growing the labor pool. After the United States joined Great Britain in prohibiting the transatlantic slave trade, some regions in the US accelerated the business of providing enslaved people to areas with an increasing need for labor, especially the areas that produced cotton. Virginia, especially, had a surplus of enslaved Africans. It was profitable to sell enslaved people. The one-drop rule meant, in effect, that one might even go into the business of breeding enslaved people. In addition, plantation whites were increasingly anxious about a large population of enslaved Africans. Escaped, rogue Africans were a threat! In the minds of white settlers, the threat was magnified.

Perhaps the first occurrence of such racial arithmetic in legal code was in a 1705 ordinance in the Commonwealth of Virginia. Jack Forbes, a scholar of Lenape ancestry, believes this ordinance was likely the source of blood quantum rules in later generations. He notes that the ordinance was intended to deny civil rights to any "negro, mulatto or Indian." It stated that "the child of an Indian, and the child, grandchild, or great grandchild of a negro shall be deemed accounted, held, and taken to be a mulatto."[12] This ordinance clearly expressed the unusual mental gymnastics required by racialized imaginations. It also is an indication that Virginians, at least, had already placed race firmly in their thinking about social dynamics. The ordinance foreshadows the differing functions of blood quantum and the one-drop rule. Indianess disappears after two generations; the impact of African blood hangs around for three. Apparently, nonwhite identity can be bred out!

Even though contemporary scholarship, including genetic research, the study of languages, and epidemiological studies, all suggest that race is socially constructed, much popular thinking still speaks of race as though it were natural and an essential part of humanness. We may even talk as though the term race simply indicates a convenient classification system based on biological characteristics shared by groups of people. And we still subscribe to racial arithmetic. This, indeed, suggests we believe race is more than skin deep. Many Americans believe race is an essential aspect of identity, not simply as a marker of culture but as shared biological characteristics.

The Role of Racial Designation

Racial identity is about social status and value. Thus, racial assignment is social placement. It is about social placement that is interpreted by our history. For the first seventy-five or so years, *citizen* and *white* were legally equivalent terms. Only white people could be citizens (and, of course, only white men could vote). This deep association of white and citizen continued even after the Fourteenth Amendment to the Constitution opened citizenship to people of African descent. American Indian people were not citizens across the board until the Indian Citizenship Act of 1924. This act, itself, was arguably part of the effort to make individual citizenship more important than tribal identity; coming on the heels of allotment, it was additional pressure to value property rights and to assimilate into the American way of life. On the positive side, of course, was enfranchisement: with citizenship came the vote and constitutional rights, at least in principle.

Shortly, we will look into the shaping of racial buffer zones, borderlands, and margins. They have been fundamental in our history and have been the terrain of racial fluidity. Groups whose racial assignment has changed have all been pilgrims in this racially gray area, temporary occupants in a racial no-man's-land on their way to becoming white or having their nonwhite status more indelibly etched.

When seeking to understand race, it is crucial to understand its collective character. Racial assignment is assignment to a group, a collective identity. This is clear when it comes to nonwhite identity. The mischief done by stereotypes can be attributed in large part to the fact that they refer to groups; they lead us to judge individuals based on the racial group they are part of. Abstractly, of course, we can see that this must also be true for white people. White identity is a collective identity. Here's the rub: those of us assigned to the white box don't experience ourselves as part of a racial collective. We experience ourselves simply as individuals; our collective identity is hidden from us. Lopez, referencing Barbara Flagg, refers to this phenomenon as transparency.[13] Our race is effectively transparent to us. One of the reasons why this is true is that hyperindividualism is an aspect of white identity. We are socialized to be individuals; we don't experience our collectivity. Individualism is more than an abstract idea; for us, it is an existential reality. Stereotypes lead us to presume the collective character of others. So, a conversation about race is consequently a conversation about others, not about me.

This leads to all kinds of mischief and confusion when we engage in conversation about race. In Part 3, we will explore in some depth the mischief our hyperindividualism accomplishes. One aspect of the mischief done is that we who are white find it challenging to grasp our identity as collective. We are racialized to understand identity as an individual phenomenon. Consequently, we don't think or talk about collective aspects of our racial identity, such as shared beliefs that are formed in the crucible of racialization.

If race were, indeed, a naturally occurring phenomenon, then it is simply part of the terrain of the nation's multiethnic/multicultural development. From this perspective, our history is the story of people of differing races and nationalities encountering one another, struggling with or against one another, some being forced to provide labor for others, others attacking settlers in an effort to protect traditional land. It is the grand drama of the melting pot, of multiracial America melting into the great experiment we witness today. However, this perspective does not account for the persistence of American apartheid.

If race is a social construction, then we need to ask where it came from, why it was created, and what role it played and plays in national life. These are not questions that can be answered abstractly. The answers are about us, who we have been and who we are as a nation. Our history clarifies the role of race. The history of race in other nations may provide contrapuntal context that is informative, but finally we need to examine the role of race in our history.

Ian Haney Lopez points out that our legal system has defined nonwhite identities but not white identity. White identity, in this sense, has been defined negatively. What it means to be white, historically speaking, is to not be nonwhite. Lopez points out how the courts have defined white "through a process of negation, systematically identifying who was non-white."[14] This was done in a series of decisions determining eligibility for citizenship through naturalization. They all referenced the Naturalization Act of 1790, which noted white identity as a qualification of citizenship. It seems clear that the real point of assigning some to nonwhite racial collectives is the indirect creation of white identity. What does this tell us about the function of racial identity? What does it tell us about white identity? What's the big deal about being white?

The research that documents racial disparities in virtually every arena of public life makes very clear what the advantages are in being white. Turns out that being white has been and is a very big deal. One is less apt to live with the cumulative results of daily barriers to accessing the goods and services necessary for life. Being nonwhite is a predictor of how likely one is to live in poverty, drop out of school, be unemployed, and so on. This is not to suggest that all people of color are poor, are dropouts, or are unemployed. Racial identities are collective. This is about probabilities— how likely it is that individuals encounter social barriers due to the racial group they are assigned to.

It suggests, I believe, that racial assignment is always about social domination and subordination. In the case of US history, we would have to add disappearance. Assigning American Indian identity has been tantamount to putting one on the road to disappearance. This means that race is never an innocent social grouping, as if sorting butterflies or birds. Racial assignment happens, as previously mentioned, with malice aforethought. The historical result of being nonwhite has been slavery, poverty, marginalization, negative stereotyping, and disappearance. It has meant being destined for the lowliest jobs, being turned into a marketplace commodity, living in the least desirable places, attending the worst schools, and being denied access to many public places.

This does not mean that individual white people have self-conscious mal intents relative to people of color, or even that white individuals are aware of participating in the dynamics of racial assignment. Neither does it mean that the creators of census forms and other government forms intentionally place people in problematic social contexts. It is simply to point out what the historical significance of racial assignment is and to connect that to current realities. Contemporary racial disparities are an expression of the historical function of racial assignment. They are, in effect, living legacies of our past.

When one asks, "What is the state of race relations in our city or state?" the only possible response is, "From whose perspective?" From the perspective of social dominance (that is white identity), race relations are good—as long as people know their place, stay in it, and don't make waves. From the perspective of subordination or disappearance, race relations are never good—unless one is pleased with being subordinated and "disappeared."

The Racial Buffer Zone

A curious phenomenon began to emerge in the racial dynamics of colonial society: a racial buffer zone. A buffer zone is an area separating conflicting forces; its use here is intended to suggest a social space that separated and protected white society from nonwhite communities. This "space" emerged as a consequence of the needs of the centers of power. It served the interests of white supremacy. White society needed ways to pressure and divide tribes and to parcel out work that was not being done by enslaved Africans. The process effectively assigned social value that was qualitatively distinct to those who were neither tribal nor enslaved but, also, not white. It served as a protocol for dealing with nonwhite groups, a space, so to speak, in the racial equation.

Many indigenous people of mixed heritage chose to maintain their tribal affiliation and cultural identity, in spite of pressure from white communities to identify with their Euro heritage. In the context of beliefs about blood and racial identity, such individuals were known as "mixed bloods." Those who lost tribal identity as a consequence of the dynamics of removal found, for the most part, that the white mainstream was not open to them. They inhabited the margins of white society—as Melungeon, Caramel Indians, Yellow Hammers, Brass Ankles, Turks, and Redbones. In Western Canada, the Metis people occupied this space. In many cases, the white political and economic elite used mixed-blood families to undermine the cultural integrity and political power of tribes. Federal Indian agents often designated mixed-blood individuals as tribal leaders and dealt with tribes through them, thus providing a disproportionate amount of power to these individuals. This, of course, served the interests of the federal government. Such mixed-blood leaders were sometimes influential in the treaty-making process, as whites sought to dispossess and concentrate Native people.

In Louisiana, being creole meant not being black, albeit not white. Another familiar term sometimes used was *mulatto,* referring to people of African and European heritage (and sometimes with Indian ancestry as well). The terms *quadroon* (one-fourth African blood) and *octoroon* (one-eighth) were frequently used derivations (by white society). Prior to the Civil War, there were several large communities of free Africans spread across the South and the Atlantic states. Many of these were comprised primarily of mixed or mulatto families.

Similarly, in the Southwest following the Mexican War, being Mexican meant not being Indian but also not being white. Although federal law recognized Mexicans as white at the time of the Treaty of Guadalupe, communities did not. When the new US territories—gained via the treaty—became states, Mexican people living in the new states quickly lost their white identity.

Racialization also introduced and strengthened the politics of skin tone in mulatto communities. It effectively placed a value on having European heritage. To white communities, such mixing carried the taint of "mongrelization." However, in relation to enslaved Africans and tribal communities, a mixed heritage often bestowed social advantage. Battalora speaks of this as in-between status, as being "not really but sort-of-white status."[15] It was a space to be journeyed through on the way to social acceptability (i.e., white identity). Thus, the buffering dynamic effectively became a sociological purgatory, a space to occupy while working to become white.

It is interesting to note that those occupying the zone who were of sub-Saharan African descent were not destined to ever become white, no matter the effort expended. In the lexicon of the one-drop rule, they had black blood. However, those individuals who were able to pass, as a consequence of light skin and straight hair, might successfully access white identity. This is in contrast to the Irish, Jews, Italians, and others who, as a group, traversed the buffer zone into white identity. In the one case, an entire social group gains a new racial designation; in the other, individuals effectively become white by hiding their racial identity and passing from one racial identity to another.

This buffer zone phenomenon expressed an understanding about race that simultaneously strengthened the white side of the white/nonwhite binary and broadened the parameters of the nonwhite side. New groups were assigned to the buffer zone when it served the interests of the white collective, even when that interest consisted simply in protecting our property: white identity. When an entire group of people was racialized in this manner, it involved how they were talked about, thought about, and treated by the rest of society. Thus, racial assignment was always about access to power and privilege—that is, to the systems and institutions of colonial and postcolonial society. Even though class, gender, and even ethnicity might relativize access, race nonetheless remained fundamental. Life in colonial times was hard for everyone; mortality rates were high, and life expectancy was low. Social labels that moderated the dangers were coveted. Race was such a label.

The emergence of the buffer zone also presented an opportunity regarding old, multigenerational prejudices. Groups that had known persecution in Europe owing to social identity might well find themselves under a cloud of suspicion in colonial society and consequently assigned to the buffer zone, their racial identity effectively nonwhite. This included Jews, Roma, and others who had for centuries occupied well-defined margins in European societies.

At the time of independence, the locus of race was the dynamics among African, Indian, and white people. From the perspective of the new nation, racial considerations were about nonwhite people: Africans, whether slave or free, and Indian tribes. Even then, however, social realities with regard to race were becoming more complex and more nuanced as new state governments wrestled with a new racial reality: free people of color who were neither enslaved nor tribal.

Race and Racism: A Summary

In summary, we can say that race is more than the traditional black-white binary; the actual binary is and has been white and nonwhite. Race is a social construct: the result of a fabrication process that is multigenerational and that shapes racial identities that often have indistinct and ambiguous boundaries. Racial identity is effectively a social assignment—an assignment that expresses and replicates the dynamics of social dominance, subservience, and disappearance. It is an assignment that has economic, political, and cultural aspects. Racial identity always and constantly intersects and interacts with other socially constructed identities. This is most significant in relation to other social identities that qualify people for exclusion and oppression: gender, class, sexuality, age, ability, and so on. This means that race in our society is and has been ubiquitous. It is a social constant that at times has almost become a national obsession. It is embedded in the fabric of society.

What then can be said about racism? If race is indeed socially constructed and embedded, and if it involves social dominance and advantage, then we can say that racism is systemic. It is present in the structural dynamics that constitute our society. It is seen in forms of social exclusion that benefit some and disadvantage others based on an assigned social identity, a racial identity. Power is the central issue. Power dynamics are at the heart of racism but not just power in general. Racism is the misuse of systemic power. One well-known way of putting this is that *race prejudice plus the power of institutions and systems equals racism.*[16] This way of defining racism suggests that it is always more than individual action flowing from personal prejudice and racial bias. Racism centers one racially defined group and marginalizes all others, with ever-shifting boundaries and relativized benefits and disadvantages.

Conversations about racism tend to focus on relationships between and among individuals. They tend to presume that racism is a matter of personal prejudice and, perhaps, the behaviors that flow from individual prejudices. This definition suggests that we need to focus, instead, on the institutions and systems of society and the way they function in relation to groups of people—groups with racial designations. We need to examine how institutions and systems operate in relation to the white-nonwhite binary.

If we are to get a handle on the mischief done in the name of race, then we need to look more carefully at the matter of power—in particular, systemic power. In chapter 3, we will explore the dynamics of systemic power with regard to race.

Systemic Power is like an Iceberg

3

Systemic Power and Race: Collusion by Design

Seeing Clearly: My First Glasses

When I was in second grade, my parents discovered that I was quite nearsighted (a condition I likely inherited from my mother). At the time, my family lived in Kingman, Arizona. There was no optician in our little desert town. Consequently, getting glasses meant a trip to Las Vegas, Nevada, the nearest city large enough to have several opticians.

So, one warm late September day, my parents took me to Las Vegas to get my first pair of lenses. I still remember walking out of the optician's shop wearing my new glasses. I was blown away! I could actually see individual leaves fluttering on the trees! The detailed sharpness everywhere I looked was simply mind-blowing. As the years passed, my nearsightedness grew worse; by the time I was a teenager, I was extremely myopic and required rather thick lenses. Consequently, I developed a strong appreciation for the role that corrective lenses play. They make it possible for those who are myopic to see clearly! Things that otherwise are simply a fuzzy blur are sharply defined. Seeing clearly makes activities possible that otherwise would not be. This also helped me understand and appreciate the role of braille for those who are without sight or legally blind. Braille functions like corrective lenses in the sense that it is a language facilitating discernment and communication. Braille enables one to see with one's fingertips!

Doing social analysis is a bit like wearing corrective lenses or utilizing the braille system. The analytic screen used enables one to see. Things that were previously an indistinct blur, or even invisible, are sharply defined and discernable. Of course, corrective lenses can also distort what we see. A carefully done prescription is necessary. Similarly, a carefully crafted analytic screen can allow us to discern social dynamics and their interrelationships more clearly, or with less distortion. "Carefully crafted" means being intentional about the values used in shaping the screen and choosing carefully the language employed. The screen I find most helpful in discerning racial dynamics in society was developed and refined by Crossroads Antiracism Organizing and Training over a number of years. It provides a multidimensional view of race and its reverberations and ricochets across society. It is a screen drawn from the crucible of historical and sociological research on race that is available to us.

The Crossroads' analytic screen discloses that racial dynamics are iceberg-like. There are those racial outcomes we can clearly see and even measure that are above the surface, so to speak. However, even though they are visible and quantifiable, they are, in effect, only the tip of the iceberg. Much more lies hidden beneath the surface of our "social sea." Just beneath the surface, in the meltwater area, lie dynamics that are visible if one looks closely. However, like an iceberg, most racial dynamics lay hidden, deep down, far beneath the surface. Like an iceberg, the hidden dynamics are the most dangerous. They are virtually invisible without a lens that helps us see connections and relationships. In order to apply the iceberg analogy, we must first look more carefully at systemic power. What does the term mean? How does it function in relation to race, in particular?

Systemic Power: A Focused Definition

Systemic power is the legitimate/legal ability to access and/or control those institutions sanctioned by the state.[17]

Power is at the heart of the dynamics that produce social exclusion. That includes those rooted in race as well as those rooted in other socially constructed identities. The question is, "What is meant by power in reference to social exclusion?" When we view power systemically, the definition above becomes a helpful jumping-off place. It turns out that the dynamics of access and control noted in the definition are multigenerational and reflect intentional design.

The definition further suggests that institutions are the locus of systemic power. What is the role that institutions play in society? They provide access to the resources, products, and services necessary for living, and they also facilitate collective action. Systemic power is fundamentally about the ability to access as well as control the institutions that are sanctioned and endorsed by society, and thus are seen as legitimate. These are those institutions whose products and services society in general affirms. In this sense, legitimacy has simply to do with the social permission to be. How is such permission granted? Perhaps at the most fundamental level, it is granted legally; it is a matter of legal recognition. This involves the endorsement of various levels of government. The process of incorporation, for example, has to do with governmental recognition that includes tax status (whether an entity is not for profit or for profit, etc.). In this conversation about systemic power, we are especially concerned with the recognition that is bestowed in the granting of legal sanction by governing authorities. Such recognition provides organizational form that infers legitimacy. The sense of legitimacy such sanction conveys is especially important in grasping how systemic power functions in relation to race.

Access is a consequence of the rules embedded in institutional design. These rules reflect who the institution is in business to serve, both originally and contemporarily. Access is about who gets in. In the case of public institutions, it reflects both the impact of current law and the deep, self-replicating intentions built in at the time of original inception. Access, thus, is a very important feature. The ability to access the resources that institutions make available can be a matter of life and death, health or illness, economic stability or poverty.

Control is a bit different. Not everyone who can access an institution's goods and services is in charge of the institution. Control is about institutional design and operation. The dynamics of control are about who makes the rules that govern institutional life and mission, has the authority to change the rules, oversees how the rules are carried out, defines the roles of institutional life, and shapes the accountability relationships within the institution. The dynamics of control are sketched out in a typical organizational chart. The boxes of the chart clarify the functional hierarchy.

A well-known role in every institution is gatekeeping. The personnel who are charged with administering the dynamics of access can be termed gatekeepers. This is their function, regardless of the position they occupy. Gatekeeping determines who gets in and is served by the institution.

Gatekeeping also manages institutional relations with sanctioning authorities. Control is about shaping how gatekeeping happens. In fact, most personnel in any given institution have some gatekeeping responsibilities. The lines of accountability help clarify who are the frontline gatekeepers and who are the overseers of the entire process. In a bank, for example, a teller is a frontline gatekeeper; a loan officer is a little further up the ladder of gatekeeping but is also on the frontlines. A branch manager is an overseer in the sense that she is accountable to those above her for all the gatekeeping processes in the branch—that is, all the processes that determine who can access the resources and services of the bank.

Access and control in this sense are central to a clear understanding of systemic power and how it operates. It is also important to be clear that these dynamics go on in all institutions, most notably those that are legally sanctioned. Thus, we can say that power is about the way access and control function in the legitimate, sanctioned institutions of society. Indeed, they are at the heart of social exclusion.

Sanctioned institutions operate within and are partially shaped by law. Sanction is reflected in the legal codes of society. Some of the central rules that govern institutional life are promulgated by governing authorities and couched in legalese. The process of legalization, itself, invokes a multigenerational sense of legitimacy. The same is true of the manner in which access and control happen. They invoke a generalized sense of legitimacy that reflects the values of the dominant group in society.

When laws change and, consequently, new rules are promulgated, they may very well run smack into embedded core institutional values regarding who most legitimately can access society's institutions. For example, the Civil Rights Act of 1964, in principle, opened up access to goods and services in public institutions for all Americans, especially those who previously had been excluded by Jim Crow laws. The new rules contradicted original design and intent. Even after many years, one result of this contradiction is that many institutions, perhaps even most, serve white people advantageously. White privilege is a systemic outcome. Historically, white people designed the systems in our society. Institutions, if they are sanctioned and thus legitimate, must fit into these systems. Consequently, there was a time when virtually all institutions intentionally served white people or the interests of white society. One consequence is that the weight of history tends to trump the actual language of the law. Historical momentum conveys a certain sense of legitimacy, even when it contradicts contemporary rhetoric regarding justice and fairness. This view of systemic power means that social exclusion—and in particular, racial exclusion—is not merely a matter of individual prejudice and bigotry. It is an outcome of systemic design.

We think of our nation as the land of liberty, justice, and freedom for all—of equality of opportunity, where all people can presume fair treatment and equality before the law. When institutions and systems function in a manner that contradicts these core ideological beliefs, it is a flagrant misuse of power. This misuse occasions cognitive dissonance. It somehow doesn't fit with our public understanding of our nation.

There is more to be said, however. When we view advantageous access and control from the perspective of our history and the original intent of our systems and institutions, disparate access is clearly legitimate, whether legal or not. The weight of history conveys an underground sense of legitimacy, especially to all who benefit from traditional systemic practices. This hidden sense expresses the inertial momentum bound up in the original trajectory of our social systems and the institutions they bind together.

There are some who suggest that the solution is putting more people of color in charge of administering institutional life. At first blush, this may indeed seem sensible. However, it underestimates the power of institutional culture and the historical trajectory of social systems. A change in who administers power does not change the structure of power itself. Michelle Alexander in *The New Jim Crow* notes, "The reality is that existing hierarchy disciplines newcomers, requiring them to exercise power in the same old ways and play by the same old rules in order to survive."[18] Substituting people of color for white people in institutions does not automatically change the way institutions function. In fact, many institutional gatekeepers and some executives are people of color. Converging expectations embedded in institutional culture tend to replicate the same systemic dynamics.

The Iceberg Effect: The Oppression of People of Color

To apply the iceberg metaphor, we begin with the part of the iceberg we can see. The most visible part of the iceberg, the part above the surface of the sea, can be termed the systemic disempowerment and oppression of people of color. It is oppression expressed in measurable disparities. The fact that they are measurable makes them visible. These include the impact of race in criminal justice: stop and search rates, arrest rates, felony versus misdemeanor charges, incarceration rates, sentencing disparities, and parole and probation disparities. They also include academic achievement gaps, dropout rates (secondary and college), college enrollment, poverty rates, utilization of public assistance programs, employment/unemployment rates, home ownership, access to affordable housing, homelessness rates, access to mortgage loans, access to credit, health care access, health insurance, disease incidence, mortality rates, involvement in the child welfare system, and out-of-home placement rates, to name a few. These disparities reveal the impact of race in society.

For people of color, the misuse of systemic power fosters and replicates disadvantage and oppression. These oppressive disadvantages are accompanied by a daily dose of microaggressions: linguistic slights, rudeness, being ignored, presumptions regarding ability, who is listened to in meetings, and assumptions about drug use. Such a daily experience of microaggression often results in elevated levels of stress hormones, such as cortisol. As a consequence, there are predictable health impacts. These oppressive disadvantages and their assault on one's sense of self and general well-being are rooted in systemic, rather than simply interpersonal, dynamics. They are rooted in the misuse of systemic power. They infer whose institutional participation is legitimate and valued, whose presence is seen, and whose presence is overlooked. In spite of exceptional individuals who may be very visible in society, racial disparities are associated with discreet racial groups.

The visibility and quantifiability of these outcomes do not explain or interpret them. We may be tempted to look at the communities themselves for the source of these disparities. That is, we may be tempted to do a deficit analysis. We may conclude, *This is just the result of broken families, lack of motivation, laziness, mental illness, intellectual capacity, poor education, a culture of poverty, and so on.* This is simply stereotypical thinking masquerading as social analysis.

Racial disparities and disproportionalities are a bit like a snapshot of a moving train. They are accurate for a moment in time. However, they are also regionally and locally specific. While we can break them down nationally, such a picture is not necessarily replicated in particular regions or localities of the nation. One of the striking and disconcerting things about racial disparities is that many tend to change slowly, and some even worsen, while others improve.

For example, the sociologist David Williams, professor of public health at Harvard University, in a recent TED Talk (May 2, 2017) pointed out that in 1978, for every one dollar in income for whites, there was fifty-nine cents for blacks. In 2017, this was still the case. In terms of wealth, for every one dollar held by whites, blacks had six cents, and Latinos had seven cents.[19] The racial features of income and wealth accumulation have not changed much in several years when comparing African American, Latino, and white families.

Professor Williams notes that most Americans simply do not know about these and other racial disparities. While this may well be true in specifics, I do not believe it is true in general. Racial disparities have been in the news frequently for well over twenty years. Several books and other publications have drawn attention to snapshots of racial disparities. While many white Americans may well claim ignorance about these disparities, there is a sense in which such claims are a bit mendacious. Our ignorance is, I have come to believe, a form of cultivated historical amnesia, even though the historical arc is rather short. Thanks to the internet, up-to-date information that is regionally specific is readily available. We shall examine more carefully this historical amnesia in chapter 12.

I have chosen not to include detailed studies regarding racial disparities; for those who are interested, there are many studies readily available that detail disparities and disproportionalities based on race. For white people, continuing to claim "not knowing" is a reflection of the continuing reality of white dominance: the white collective dominates and therefore can get away with feigning ignorance. I use the word feigning in reference to us as a collective. Individually, we believe it when we claim not to know, but in general, the matter of racial disparities is known. We may debate their causes, but we know of their existence. They have been a constant theme in the difficult conversations about race for many years.

One of the important considerations to note is that public conversation about race and racism tends to be limited to the measurable disparities we have noted. Frequently, the conversation highlights the ways that some communities of color fare better than others. The white collective has found it beneficial to designate some groups as model minorities. Such designation strengthens long-standing stereotypes about racial groups, including (indirectly) the white collective. Typically, however, the conversations do not examine the explicit and subtle pressures that help to maintain measurable disparities; neither do they examine how the *model minority* viewpoint contributes to the ongoing processes of racialization. We will return to this matter a little further along.

The Iceberg Effect: White Privilege and Advantage

When we look beneath the surface of the iceberg, we can see, in the meltwater, the source of the visible and measurable social outcomes noted in the previous commentary. We can discern systemically produced advantages for white people. We can term this advantages *white privilege*. These advantages have nothing to do with personal merit; they are not earned. They are unrelated to conversations about "what I have earned, or what I deserve based on my personal efforts or skills." Rather, they are about advantageous access to the sanctioned institutions of society based on an artificial social identity: race. They are about the way that social systems provide, protect, and preserve advantageous access. While law may well require equal access, in fact, those of us who are white can presume advantageous access (clearly, some of us have better access than others; class distinctions, after all, are real). A shower of micro affirmations accompanies access; these include such behaviors as being greeted warmly, being treated politely, and often not being asked for identification when paying with a check. This leads white people to experience themselves as normative. To be white in this society is to embody society's norms, including beauty, assumed work ethic, assumed truthfulness, as well as assumed skill and authority. We inhabit normative land. We don't have to be exceptional to be accorded respect and civility.

Such advantageous access is misuse of systemic power. This misuse, rather than the deficits of any particular community of color, underlies and promotes the ongoing racial disparities in our society. The misuse of systemic power means that access and control of the legitimate systems and institutions of society must be front and center in the discussion of racial oppression.

The Iceberg Effect: Internalization of the Race Construct

At an even deeper level, not even visible to the naked eye, lies the most dangerous part of the iceberg. This is the part of the iceberg that houses the mythology of racial superiority and inferiority and all the social message systems that broadcast these messages and attach them to our psyches, including racial stereotypes, jokes, and language that is racially coded. This also includes the experience of microaggression or microaffirmation. This is the arena of socialization that promulgates the racial rules and social roles that we all learn by virtue of living in this society. This is social programming. It is the internalization of the race construct. What is the program internalized? In the case of people of color, it is the *internalization of racial oppression*. For white people, it is the *internalization of racial superiority*. Here is the real racial nightmare, for here is where racialization imprisons and hurts us all. Here is where racism, as the misuse of systemic power, is fostered and nurtured.

Many, if not most, conversations about racism tend to focus on individual behavior and beliefs. They typically do not probe the social systems that foster and disseminate the ideology of race and racial bias. Individual belief systems and the behavior flowing from them are systemically engendered. None of us lives in a vacuum, and none of our individual beliefs arise spontaneously out of nothing. We are immersed continuously in a bath of collective conversations and a shower of information. Our belief systems are formed and reformed in this daily barrage. Further, our beliefs are not simply abstract ideas divorced from bodily reactions and feelings. Rather, they invoke strong feelings and physiological reactions. Consequently, individual beliefs and behavior are indeed part of the systemic misuse of power.

However, since the misuse of power is baked into our systems and institutions—in effect, a default setting—it is always more than individual belief and behavior. In fact, it does not depend on individual beliefs and behavior. Well-intentioned individuals of fine character routinely participate in the misuse of systemic power by virtue of their involvement in the daily operations of institutional life, especially those operations that shape and express access or control.

The exercise of systemic power in this sense is psychological violence. When access to institutional processes and resources is prevented or restricted based on a fabricated social identity, it is violence done at a deep, intimate, most personal level. It is an assault on self-confidence and an attack on personal resolve. Racial assignment evokes the daily experiences of relative affirmation or social subjugation (micro affirmation or microaggression). The exercise of systemic power turns racial assignment into a self-fulfilling prophecy.

Perhaps the most troubling aspect of the exercise of systemic power is it duplicitousness; these days, it does not openly express racial animosity. This makes the assault on self-confidence especially pernicious. When racial animus is direct, as was the case with Jim Crow laws, it feeds the deep underground resolve that shapes collective resistance. When racial animus seems absent or is, at best, fleeting and ephemeral, it isolates individuals and undercuts collective resistance.

Racism, as the misuse of systemic power, is ubiquitous. It is woven throughout our history and is with us today in all the systems that shape institutional and cultural life. The social architecture cumulatively shaped by systemic power is what is meant by the term *white supremacy*. In chapter 5, we'll examine the multicentury motifs that together have shaped this architecture. The work of deconstructing the myriad default settings that hold this architecture in place requires more than social organizing. It also requires remythologizing. The interiority of the architecture—its spirit— must be transformed. We must fashion and live into a new story regarding our identity as a nation and as communities. The fashioning of this story is the unifying focus of part 4 of this book. In order to weave a new story, we must understand deeply the terrain that birthed the old. This is the work of part 3. We will visit the terrain of *white racial identity* in order to grasp, clearly and deeply, its contours, features, and the pillars that maintain it.

The myriad default settings that maintain the social architecture of white supremacy are, like all systemic processes, self-replicating. Consequently, those whom the edifice serves can be or can feign cluelessness. For those of us who are white, it is as though we are uninvolved and therefore not responsible for the psychic assaults generated by the exercise of systemic power.

To set the stage for our later exploration of the interiority of white supremacy, we need to first understand the arena of mythology: symbols, rituals, and stories. A brief exploration will help us discern the mythic significance of the power dynamics that constitute white supremacy.

4

The Mythological
Underpinnings of Race

Why does race continue to bedevil us? What is the binding force that maintains the socio-psychic architecture of white supremacy? In one form or another, this disturbing question continues to intrude into our national life decades after the most obvious legal supports for racial apartheid have been deconstructed.

This question has forced me to examine the deep story of white superiority that continues to animate our collective life, albeit at times surreptitiously. Belief in white superiority is a clue to the power of race. It is mythic. It invokes powerful narratives that are buried deeply in our social fabric. To understand this, we have to dig deeper than political organization and economic arrangements. We need to examine the social symbols, public rituals, and ceremonies that maintain, reinforce, and refresh the narrative. Such examination will take us to a place we normally don't visit when it comes to race and racial oppression—the realm of mythology.

This brief exploration of mythology and its relationship to current social realities is informed by the work of several individuals and groups. It is important to give props to a few. I have been especially helped by the work of Octavio Paz, Gloria Anzaldua, Cherríe Moraga, Toni Morrison, James Baldwin, Kelly Brown Douglas, Steven Newcomb, Rudolfo Anaya, August Wilson, Rabbi Estelle Frankel, Joseph Campbell, Mircea Eliade, and George Mosse. Campbell and Eliade wrote extensively on the role and nature of mythology, symbols, and ritual in daily life. Mosse documented the role of racial mythology in shaping the Nazis' final solution. The others wrote of the power of mythic imagery and consciousness in relation to particular historical communities and the experience of racial and gender oppression and exclusion. They wrote from within the ranks of resistance.

What Is Mythology?

In popular use, the term *myth/mythology* suggests a made-up story that is not true—in effect, an untruth, a fable. However, there is another understanding of mythology that is informed by literature, anthropology, psychology, world religions, and philosophy. In this view, mythology is about the deep, powerful stories that inform and animate our lives and the symbols and rituals that invoke and rehearse them. Such stories are collective, multigenerational narratives, not simply the personal stories that mark an individual life. They are the stories that shape collective imaginations and provide interpretative filters for the events of history. They shape our sense of collective identity and are the foundation of historical imagination. In a very real sense, people live out of the deep stories that inform their lives and speak to their experience. While such narratives are typically collective, we experience them personally; they provide a sense of direction and give us a sense of group membership.

The myths that have power for us, collectively, are rehearsed publicly. Such rehearsals can be termed rituals, ceremonies, even liturgies. They involve public activities that call to mind our mythic stories, in effect rehearsing them. These rehearsals involve symbols that are rooted in our collective consciousness and that mediate our relationship to the deep stories. Rites of passage are an example of public rehearsals that invoke deep common stories. Story, ritual, and symbol together constitute what can be termed the symbolic or mythic dimension of life. Mythology, in this sense, is central to identity, especially the collective identities we share with others.

Rituals, of course, can also be personal and not collective. All of us have individual rituals that are part of the way we negotiate the challenges of daily living. They may be activities as simple as the first cup of coffee in the morning or as complex as the repetitive motions that professional baseball players perform as part of their game (baseball players, especially, seem almost obsessed with ritual). Nick Hobson of the University of Toronto, in his doctoral research, found that rituals impact the part of the brain having to do with motivation and control of anxiety. They can help enhance performance. He also noted that social rituals bind people together and can even lead to identifying those who are not part of the "in" group and who, consequently, may be the object of hostility.[20]

Ritual is often associated with religion. Religious liturgies are rituals that rehearse a self-understanding; they tell a story. The story, in turn, contains instructions for living. The word *liturgy* means the *work of the people*. We tend to associate the term with religious ceremony, sometimes narrowly presuming it refers only to the activities of Christian communities. However, its functional meaning is a little broader. There are secular rituals that rehearse deep stories and involve the manipulation of symbols rooted in those stories; that is, they are liturgical. They are in fact the work of the people. Their audience is the people. They are derived from the struggles and stories of the people. They pull people together and create a sense of commonality. They even involve instructions for living, albeit at times indirectly. The singing of "The Star-Spangled Banner" before public events is a secular example of liturgical activity that recalls or rehearses the American story, using a powerful symbol: the flag. Fourth of July celebrations tell the story of our nation's history and its exceptionalism, utilizing the flag and other symbols of our unique history. Similarly, founder's day celebrations that rehearse community history and name the individuals who were instrumental play a liturgical role. The collective reciting of the Pledge of Allegiance is a litany that plays a liturgical role.

There are many other popular celebrations that illustrate the dynamics of ritual, symbol, and myth: Saint Patrick's Day, Cinco de Mayo, Easter parades, even the drama surrounding the Super Bowl. Each rehearses a story that illuminates our sense of national identity, whether in calling to mind the melting pot narrative or the triumphalism of being the best.

What is the social function of mythology? It gives meaning to daily activities. In society in general, it provides a context that rationalizes and connects things as disparate as public policy and community responses to natural disasters. In the words of Michael Pina, "Myth … constitutes a transparent horizon against which … individuals view reality. Every cultural group, nation, or people exist within a particular mythic horizon that corresponds to their particular vision of truth. This is the myth they live."[21] Pina further suggests that myths are lived out; they are a central aspect of everyday experience.

Rudolfo Anaya, author of *Bless Me, Ultima* and editor *of Aztlan: Essays on the Chicano Homeland*, notes that, "For all groups or nations myth offers a core of common meaning and generally accepted values. The element of identity is but a fragment of the totality that permits the experiencing of origins as a comfort zone which enhances ... development."[22] Thus, a nation's foundational myth or narrative binds it together and provides a sense of direction and trajectory.

Anaya's comments provide an intriguing context for understanding United States history, as it's often taught in elementary school, as well as public events celebrating our independence from Great Britain. We are socialized to regard our War for Independence as our origin, our heroic homeland. We remember the Declaration of Independence as a document that rivals the Bible itself. In it we declare our efforts to be free of oppressive domination and proclaim the rights we value for everyone: life, liberty, and the pursuit of happiness. This is surely part of our core narrative, our guiding and integrative myth.

A further word about symbols: a "symbol is a sensory image which represents a concept or an emotion that cannot be expressed in its totality by any other method."[23] Symbols point beyond themselves. They are rooted in experience but are more than a rational explanation of the meaning and significance of experience. The "sensory image, or symbol, is associated with a concept or emotion."[24] The American flag, for example, can call forth powerful emotions, especially when it is used as part of a public ritual or liturgy. Its symbolic power varies, of course, from individual to individual and community to community.

When the flag is combined with the singing of our national anthem, we are called back to mythic time and reminded that our origin was a time of war and struggle (the song, of course, is a reference to the War of 1812, not the War for Independence). The action of standing, placing one's hand over one's heart, and singing hallows the moment. Viewing the flag as we sing and stand respectfully brings all the elements of mythology together: visual symbol (the flag), ritual (standing and placing one's hand over one's heart), and core narrative. It is a liturgy that for many Americans is indicative, even definitive, of patriotism. When professional athletes kneel during the playing of the anthem (calling attention to our failure to live into our national aspirations), it predictably calls forth a strong backlash from those who find the anthem rehearses the fundamentals of American patriotism.

Mircea Eliade noted that myth always has to do with the story of origins and destiny, how a particular group came to be and what their future trajectory is. When one lives a myth, one is replicating the reality it encodes. Eliade further noted that when studying archaic societies, it is crucial to know and understand the mythic foundations that are expressed in daily life.[25] We can say the same for contemporary societies: it's critical to access the deep stories that animate a society if one is to really understand its character. What does this suggest regarding the United States of America? Is there a core narrative that binds us together? Some believe that our core narrative is captured in shorthand by the belief in American exceptionalism. This includes being the land of opportunity and freedom. This is also a clue to the significance of the political slogan "let's make America great again." It evokes the deep story of our exceptionalism and the mythic time when it was our national character. What is not made explicit of course is the belief that white superiority is what made us exceptional (in the core narrative).

Because symbols are powerful and call forth strong emotions, they can have a negative as well as a positive impact. The swastika is an example. It is an ancient symbol, common in many traditions, that was expropriated by the Nazis. For Jews, the swastika has an immediate, powerful, and negative impact. It recalls painful and difficult history, even for Jews who have lived in this nation for generations and whose families may not have experienced the Holocaust directly. The symbology has power for all by virtue of a collective identity. By the same token, many of our public liturgies and related symbols call forth historic episodes that are couched in pain and trauma for communities of color. While all Americans share a nation, we do not all share a common history. American apartheid has given us differing histories. The ongoing power of those disparate histories is rooted in mythology: the stories, symbols, and liturgies that rehearse our differing experience of national life.

Now, a word about language. Symbols are not only visual representations that connect us to deep, powerful realities; words also have symbolic power. They refer us to something else, whether heard or read. When we hear or read the word *chair*, we know what the reference is. We may "see" a mental image of a chair. If the word is used along with adjectives that describe it, our mental image may be quite detailed. When words evoke an emotionally powerful story, their symbolic role becomes mythic; that is, they tap into deep realities that have power in people's lives. Hence, symbols can be heard as well as seen.

The symbolic power of language comes especially clear in racially coded commentary. Ian Haney Lopez, in his book *Dog Whistle Politics*, points out how racially coded language, especially in the political arena, taps into deep biases and the anxiety they invoke. He suggests that racially coded speech operates on two levels: it triggers racial anxiety and, since it does not use explicitly racial language, allows plausible deniability.[26] Some politicians excel in the use of such coded language. When an influential member of Congress recently talked about a "real culture problem" in "our inner cities in particular," he wasn't the first American politician to be slammed for using racially coded language to get a point across.

Mythology and Race: Is There a Racial Myth?

Many scholars have made the case that race is simply a social construct. I have suggested that assignment to a racial group invokes social values that are fundamentally about systemic power. This invocation of values also calls forth a story about racial identities. This means that race is mythic. It connects to a foundational narrative. It is a narrative that defines humanity and primary social value. It clarifies who the superior people are; superiority is conflated with being white. From the perspective of social dominance, this is our nation's core racial myth.

As previously noted, in the first decade of our existence as a nation, we legally connected citizenship with being white. The Naturalization Act of 1790 stipulated that in order to qualify for citizenship in the new nation (if one was born abroad), one had to be white. Citizenship and white identity were legally equivalent, even synonymous. Thus, when Chief Justice Taney noted, some sixty-seven years later, that Dred Scott did not qualify for citizenship due to his race, he was simply reaffirming the original intent of the nation's founders. He was invoking our core narrative, our racial mythology. In the Naturalization Act, we made explicit what the Constitution presumed implicitly. We are a white nation!

George L. Mosse, in his classical exploration of the European origins of the ideology of racial identity, came to believe that the basic structure of the core myth was crystalized in eighteenth-century European thought.[27] The emerging disciplines of anthropology, evolutionary biology, and medical science, as well as a lot of pseudo-science, all contributed to the belief in race as a biological, natural given. Efforts to describe the essence of healthy, exceptional humanity scientifically led to a striking distinction: white Europeans were the civilized norm, and nonwhite people were abnormal. Those who were clearly abnormal included, of course, the Jews. Stereotypical imagery of Jews, Africans, and other nonwhite people were like the rivets holding the mythic fabric in place. The economic needs and political challenges of colonial empires were the source of the energy driving ongoing articulation of the myth. This was also true for the newly independent United States. The myth of race was a constituent part of its emerging national consciousness (and the US was, after all, a European experiment). The myth effectively sanctioned the enslavement of Africans and the eradication of indigenous societies. It established whiteness as the origin of America's exceptionality; it became normative. Nonwhite identities were effectively abnormal.

Social Design and Mythology

A nation's core narrative influences the social form it takes; the fact that social form is complex, dynamic, and constantly changing does not negate the power of the central myth. When the myth is rehearsed, its power and centrality are reinforced. Rehearsal of the myth happens in public holidays, political events, and cultural celebrations. But what if the central myth is also rehearsed subtly, even in the way social dynamics are organized? In that case, social form would express guiding mythology. Social "arrangements" would have mythic significance. This means that community design and dynamics would have symbolic meanings that may be more than the sociological interpretations we normally ascribe. Just as the architecture of a cathedral (or any religious structure) has symbolic meaning, the architecture of a community freights a deeper meaning.

When one enters a cathedral, Roman, Orthodox, or Anglican, it's difficult to escape the sense of awe occasioned by the very architecture of the building. I recall the first time I stepped inside the Cathedral of the Archdiocese of Saint Paul and Minneapolis. This Protestant boy was not prepared for the breathless sense of awe that the interior occasioned. The soaring dome and the experience of immense space were mesmerizing. Then I noted the stained glass windows, each with a different biblical episode portrayed. I remembered someone once telling me that in Medieval Europe, when most people were illiterate, priests used to tell the Christian story by walking people past the stained glass depictions, sequentially. I noted the striking altar, the table, and the huge crucifix. Then I noted that the building itself was shaped like a cross. It hit me that the design of the building—its architecture—told the Christian story. Even before the mass takes place, simply being in the space exposed one to a telling of the story. One is surrounded by symbolic design filled with the symbols of the Christian faith. In a manner of speaking, the building itself is liturgical. The very design of the building tells the Christian story.

Then, when the mass is conducted, it is as though it is a story within a story, a drama within a drama. In addition, there is an objectivity to the story: the telling does not depend on the personal piety or morality of the tellers. Neither does the drama depend on the personal virtue of the attending participants. It is simply a rehearsal of the central story, a narrative. It is mythic in the deepest sense. There is power in the very telling of the story, power for those leading the rehearsal as well as those in attendance. The repetitive telling of the story shapes the imaginations of all involved, whether it invokes strong emotions or not.

In similar fashion, a nation's central mythology, including the symbols and rituals that freight the mythology, all play a role in how society is organized. We mentioned already some of the symbols and public liturgies that rehearse our foundational story. They tend to be devoid of any mention of race that is directly derogatory. But if race is indeed ubiquitous in our society, then it should not surprise us if some of our public liturgies still invoke race, albeit indirectly and even surreptitiously. In order to grasp the ceremonial invocation of race, we need to broaden our understanding of public ritual and symbol. It is important to remember that race is never value-free; racial assignment is fundamentally about the drama of domination, marginalization, subjugation, and disappearance. Given our history, even to invoke race is, in itself, derogatory. It is symbolic abuse of all who are viewed as nonwhite.

If the central myth is also rehearsed subtly in the way society is organized, social "arrangements" have mythic significance. This means that community design and dynamics would have symbolic meanings that may be more than the sociological interpretations we normally ascribe. Just as the architecture of a cathedral (or any religious structure) has symbolic meaning, so the social architecture of a community freights a deeper meaning. It has mythic significance. I use the term *social architecture* to indicate all the dynamics of social design that make up a community: who lives where, who works where, who attends school where, and the repeating patterns of everyday life that can be ascribed to particular groups, especially racial groups. I am suggesting that when we examine the ways communities operate, as well as the basic economic dynamics and political activities of national life, we may well discern the mythic presence of race.

We routinely attribute social realities to economic, demographic, and political factors. This includes the ways neighborhoods and communities develop. We know there are many factors involved in the complex ways that social identities interact and produce inequalities and disparities. Throughout our history, race has been one of these factors. Restrictive housing covenants and other extralegal agreements have been very influential in determining who lives where. Jim Crow laws clearly played a direct role in determining where underfunded schools were located and who attended them. We are clear about many of the legal and economic realities that effectively dictated neighborhood and community design in years past. The fact that many of them continue to play an influential role today, even though much of the supporting legal framework has been removed, suggests that perhaps we need to look deeper. We tend to overlook the mythic significance of these inequalities and disparities and the way they confirm the core narrative: the myth of white superiority.

Ceremonies of Hegemony: Why Does the Power of Race Persist?

I have suggested that a nation's core narrative influences the social forms that constitute it; this means the central myth is rehearsed, albeit subtly, in the way social dynamics are organized and maintained. The visuals in a community (what we see when we move through a community) rehearse a story; they have symbolic power. For example, poor neighborhoods often lack dependable public services and utilities (unlike their wealthier counterparts). They may also become food deserts, where access to affordable, fresh, and abundant food is nonexistent; rather, small convenience stores with higher prices are abundant. Poor neighborhoods often have streets filled with potholes, cracked sidewalks, littered alleys, uncollected garbage, broken streetlights—the list is long. They may be beset by crime, gang violence, and drug trafficking. They are likely to be disproportionately comprised of single-parent families. We also know that, statistically, poor neighborhoods are most likely to be populated by people of color. When we visualize poor communities, we often imagine communities of color. Racial identity is indeed a predictor of how likely one or one's family is to live in a poor community. All of these elements together tell a story; they are, in effect, a liturgical rehearsal.

It is important to ask, "What do such neighborhoods symbolize for those who do not live there? How about for those who do live there?" Do we internalize the visual markers of poverty and associate them with racial stereotypes? Do they invoke beliefs about the residents of poor communities (beliefs that may be more stereotypical than actual)? And, by implication, do they tell us something about those who do not live in poor neighborhoods or communities? Yes, they do! Poor communities and neighborhoods become symbolic. They represent racial and class differences and evoke beliefs about collective identity and capacity. They call forth the deep mythology of white superiority.

When we puzzle about the persistence of poverty and measurable racial disparities, we also need to take into account the story they tell. And we need to ask, "Who benefits from this theatrical telling?" This is more than asking who benefits economically or politically. There is an underlying benefit that is about affirmation or negation of the racial collective one is part of. It is a benefit that denotes social value. Racial disparities and disproportionalities certainly have clear economic, political, and cultural determinants. But I am suggesting that their persistence may well have more to do with their liturgical or ritualistic role in society than with any of the factors normally presumed. They are a powerful ceremony—a ceremony of hegemony! If they do call forth and rehearse the narrative of white superiority, we need at the very least to take this into account in our efforts at social transformation. In Michael Pina's words, they are mythology being lived out. They function as reference points in the underlying myth of American exceptionalism and racial superiority. They are theatrical episodes in the drama of white supremacy.

Hence, when we view ghetto communities through the lens of symbolic activity, we can discern a role that is not immediately obvious. The persistence of poverty, especially among communities of color, is an indirect rehearsal of white superiority and supremacy. It is indirect because it does not immediately call attention to the white collective. But in highlighting the challenges faced by poor communities of color, it also underscores the apparent success of other communities. It is a ceremony of social dominance, not simply an indication of the social forces that cumulatively produce poverty, real as they are. I am suggesting that in a sense, ghetto communities are political theater, from the perspective of their mythic role for the dominant white collective. They are a rehearsal of racially associated deficits: family breakdown, gang violence, decrepit buildings, littered streets—the list of presumed deficits is long.

It is important to consider the subtle as well as explicit forces that create ghettos and maintain them. The very existence of ghettos, communities with some sort of enforced isolation, symbolizes the inability of a particular group of people to deal with the complex demands of our market economy. It represents social inferiority. It stands for the stereotypical features that mark a racialized group. This is not to say that the stereotypes indicate any social reality; rather, from the perspective of dominant society (white society), the ghetto expresses the fundamental inability of racialized groups to do community in a healthy manner. It expresses a belief system that is self-reinforcing. Ghettos reinforce racial ideology. This is why it is important, from the perspective of the myth of white superiority, to maintain ghettos.

However, the mythology that is invoked obscures many of the actual realities of life in poor ghetto communities. The creativity and resilience of impoverished families do not reinforce the core narrative; they are thus overlooked. The narrative blinds us to the actual humanizing dramas that occur on a daily basis in the poorest community. The real exceptionalism of this nation is on exhibit daily; we miss it when we rehearse the mythic greatness of our past and presume it is the doing of white people. It is present in the direst of social circumstances across the nation.

If this is a meaningful assessment, then it also applies to poor rural communities of color, not simply urban ghettos. This includes American Indian reservations, where the multigenerational effects of intentional efforts to disappear people still reverberate, in spite of the emergence of relative islands of prosperity. In the midst of all the brokenness, American Indian communities are a living testament to cultural resilience and creativity. This is not, however, lifted up in much of our public storytelling. It doesn't fit with our core narrative.

Poverty is a necessary feature of our social construct because it rehearses and reinforces the intimate architecture of our society: white supremacy. It is not simply the case that free market capitalism requires poverty to some degree (as many have argued). This may be true. However, the reasons are deeper than economic analyses reveal. They touch on our fundamental sense of social identity and the mythos it is rooted in. Many of us may be uncomfortable with this suggestion. The idea that social arrangements and dynamics play a mythic role may seem a stretch, a stretch that is too difficult to make.

Of course, even the ideology of free market capitalism can be understood in terms of its mythic role. The hidden hand of the marketplace and many other taken-for-granted features of our dominant economic paradigm are simply not in evidence; they are not empirically verifiable. They make sense given a particular philosophical context and ideological bias. They explain the vicissitudes of economic life. It doesn't seem too much of a stretch to suggest their role in our society is mythic. They play a mythological function. They rehearse foundational assumptions about life that tend to guide a great deal of public behavior and commentary.

When logic fails to explain the continued existence of impoverished communities, we must look for a deeper logic. Clearly, society stands to gain when we craft the policy and economic interventions that interrupt the recurring cycles of poverty, broken families, and so on. We really do know how to provide good education, access to good health care, and access to affordable, stable housing. It is easy to quantify society's gains economically: dollars spent on prevention are self-replicating and increase geometrically. Over time, we gain. We become a more productive society.

The ideological disagreements among policy makers do not account for our inaction. What, then, is the deeper logic? I am suggesting that this deeper logic is revealed through the lens of race and the mythic realities it invokes. The continued existence of very poor communities of color exhibiting all the marks of failed communities is a direct testimony to the superiority of others, in particular the white dominant majority. These communities, in effect, are liturgies of superiority and inferiority. We allow poor ghetto communities to continue because they reassure us (white people), at a deep level, of our superiority. We do more than allow. We maintain poor communities in their poverty; we reinforce the dynamics that ensure their existence. How is this done?

It is done through a myriad of public policies—federal, state, and local—that are insufficient interventions in the dynamics that impoverish families and individuals. This includes policies such as sliding-fee childcare, school lunch programs, early childhood development programs, including preschool, health care, and WIC. Such programs benefitting children more than pay for themselves later on. So do such policy efforts as affordable health care for working adults, affordable housing, lead abatement programs, public education, various public assistance programs, child welfare programs, and many more.

Typically, none of these programs is sufficiently funded to be effective. Consequently, we can point to the availability of programs for low-income people, with the caveat that these are not working, the implication being that the issue is the people and not the programs. This is effectively a kind of collective mendacity. Eligibility criteria for many social programs are often framed to limit and even deny access rather than broaden access. An operative presumption is that poor people, especially poor people of color, will take advantage of public largesse and become dependent rather than responsible. Thus, such programs need to be carefully hobbled by insufficient funding and strict eligibility.

Perhaps we should look more carefully at other segments of society that are very successful in obtaining and utilizing public largesse, such as corporately owned farms, financial services institutions, automobile manufacturers, and even tobacco companies. There we are apt to find dimensions of dependence that boggle the imagination!

In addition to insufficient funding for public interventions in poverty, there are several for-profit systems that make money off of the backs of the poor. There are a variety of payday loan companies that make cash available for a very high interest rate, rent-to-own furniture stores that charge exorbitant fees, the secondary mortgage market that offers high-interest home loans, currency exchanges, and so on. Then, there is the prison-industrial complex. Privately owned prisons provide jobs in small rural communities. However, to be profitable, they require prisoners. Inmates are their stock in trade. Is it even conceivable that economics plays a role in the incarceration rates we read about? Absolutely!

The Prison-Industrial Complex as Political Theater

When considering the prison-industrial complex, another aspect of the drama of superiority/inferiority comes clear: the school to prison pipeline. Public education is failing students in poor communities, especially students of color (the case can also be made that public education, in many cases, is not preparing any students for the world we actually live in). There are many complex reasons for this. Our schools tend to be the focal point where many difficult social trends converge, including the effects of homelessness, joblessness or underemployment, poor health, environmental impacts (such as lead poisoning), and the challenges of low-income, single-parent families. This convergence produces social realities that seem intractable. Our schools effectively inherit the results of social programs not really intended to meet the needs of families and communities. Schools become society's disciplinarians rather than the pathways to social success. Young black and brown boys, especially, become the justification for education's failings. This is the conduit that accomplishes mass incarceration of young men of color. The miracle is, of course, that still there are families that negotiate these challenges successfully. They are a testament to the resilience and creativity of communities of color in a society that has an historical investment in their degradation.

Law enforcement and the courts effectively collude in a manner that disproportionately arrests and imprisons young men (and increasingly women) of color. Study after study has made the case that young men of color are especially at risk. We really do know this! It is almost as though law enforcement and related legal processes are predatory in relation to communities of color. Michelle Alexander in *The New Jim Crow* has made a compelling case for dramatic reform of the criminal justice system. Historical context simply underscores the urgency. Young men of color, especially African American and Latino men, have always been disproportionately at risk. Mass incarceration reinforces our core narrative relative to whose life matters and whose activities threaten us. This is not simply a matter of rational assessment or mal intent by the professionals involved. Rather, it is rooted in our core narrative; mass incarceration reinforces its power.

A dramatic case in point is a recent story on National Public Radio.[28] Solitary confinement cells in most prisons are smaller than a king-size mattress. Yet, due to lack of space and too many prisoners, prisons may double prisoners up, even in solitary. Menard Correctional Center in Chester, Illinois, recently added an additional bunk to its solitary confinement cells (euphemistically termed disciplinary confinement). The cells are tiny for one person, a recipe for disaster for two. Two convicted felons, who likely do not know each other, must spend twenty-four hours a day in very close quarters. Recently, at Menard, an inmate in disciplinary confinement killed his cellmate, after warning prison authorities he would do so if placed in a doubled solitary cell. The guards were unaware the men had even fought until the surviving prisoner called them and told them he had killed his cellmate.

The prison administrators complain of a lack of funding, which means they cannot expand to accommodate the flow of prisoners coming in. Overcrowding is cited as the problem. Illinois is among the worst states in terms of this practice, but many states do this. Texas is another state known for this practice.

Finally, what it comes down to is not state budgets and finances, or even overcrowding. It comes down to a matter of value; who are the expendable people in society? That is the real question. It may seem a coincidence that the majority of people placed in solitary and doubled up are people of color. The *Atlantic Monthly* reported on a recent study by Yale Law School and the Association of State Correctional Administrators that revealed dramatic disproportionality. "People of color are overrepresented in solitary confinement compared to the general prison population," said Judith Resnik, a professor at Yale Law School and one of the study's authors. "In theory, if race wasn't a variable, you wouldn't see that kind of variation. You worry. It gives you a cause to worry."[29]

But when we look at the larger picture, its coincidental character fades. Young men of color make up the largest portion of prisoners in county, state, and federal prisons. It is not surprising that they are the majority of men sent to solitary confinement. It is simply a repetition of the story began years before in public school: disciplinary action seems the best option in an institutional setting designed to produce negative behavior.

In effect, they are actors in a very bad play—involuntary participants in a contemporary tragedy, a liturgy of hegemony and superiority. Their primary value lies in playing their parts. Prison life is shaped in such a fashion that there is no clear alternative. This does not mean that these young men are paradigms of virtue. They are hardened men who have had hard lives. They play by rules that make them dangerous to communities. Prison life hardens them, by design. The prison-industrial complex is effectively the progeny of slavery and its aftermath: slave patrols, black codes, vagrancy laws, legal segregation, Jim Crow laws, and so on. These prisoners are actors in the drama of white supremacy.

This tragic drama illuminates and underscores the lie expressed by our prison system. It is not about the business of reforming convicted criminals who are a danger to society. It is not even about removing them from society in order to keep the rest of us safe. It is about conscripting participants in the drama of white supremacy. It is about demonstrating who is expendable in our society and assigning roles that demonstrate why they are expendable. The larger drama is the assigning of social value; this drama is performed by many of our social systems and institutions. The prison system produces and performs one version of the play that justifies the assignment of social value. Arrest rates, the filing of charges, conviction rates, incarceration rates—all are part of the script of this drama of social value and white superiority. They effectively form the pipeline into the criminal justice system and imprisonment. They provide the actors for the drama.

Does this overstate the case? Is it a distortion of reality done by one who is outside such institutional settings? Perhaps. But if I have drawn these illustrative lines too sharply, perhaps it will at least get some attention and introduce difficult questions. Others, more perceptive and skilled than I, have drawn them even more dramatically but are not taken seriously due to their race. They are deemed to have an ax to grind or may even be playing the race card. Of course, we who are white have been playing the race card all our lives without having to own up to it! We do so unreflectively, without reference to history or the experience of others.

When I was a social caseworker many years ago in Maricopa County, Arizona, the majority of my two-hundred-family caseload was black and brown: African American, Mexican American, and American Indian. Most of my clients were families with children. Mid-1960's Arizona was experiencing the same shock waves as the rest of the nation. For nearly three years, social realities educated me, families were patient with me, and I somehow survived the stress of converging expectations, an impossible caseload, and the impact of the public welfare rules of the state of Arizona. The rules were clearly intended to discourage and dissuade applicants for assistance. I slowly began to understand that my job was to establish ineligibility for assistance rather than eligibility. I was a gatekeeper expected to restrict the flow of public money as much as possible. My naiveté did not survive! The experience opened my eyes in ways I was not prepared for (it did, however, sensitize and help prepare me for fifty years of organizing and training leaders in cities and villages around the world).

It remains the case that in the United States, there are more poor white people than people of color, in terms of raw numbers. However, communities of color are disproportionately poor; they constitute a higher percentage of the poor. This becomes clear when we ask, "What percentage of white people live beneath the poverty line?" Then, when we compare this with particular communities of color (i.e., Latinos, African Americans, American Indians, and various Asian communities), the picture is stark. The Henry J. Kaiser Family Foundation notes that in 2016, 9 percent of white Americans lived in poverty; this compares with 22 percent of African Americans, 20 percent of Hispanics, and 13 percent of all others.[30] The state with the highest percentage of impoverished white people is West Virginia (18 percent); this compares with 26 percent of African American West Virginians.

Previously, we mentioned that skin color remains a predictor of how likely one is to live an impoverished life. White poverty, per se, does not reinforce the central story; impoverished people of color do. When we examine poor communities that are primarily white, we are more apt to underscore the role of economics: the collapse of the auto industry, the mining industry, the disappearance of family farms, the impact of automation, and so on. Ghetto communities and reservation communities are seldom interpreted in the light of economic downturns. Rather, the conversation is apt to focus on broken families, absent fathers, missing work ethic, and criminal gangs. Rather than the social context, the focus is the people and their shortcomings. These shortcomings easily become proxies for moral failings.

The issue here, however, is more than what poverty does *to* communities of color; the point is the impact of poverty on our underlying narrative— that is, what it does *for* the white collective. It is a rehearsal of racial superiority. The rehearsal, like a Sunday-morning liturgy, has a certain objectivity. It is not dependent upon the actual capacities of any particular individual or group of white people. It does not require individual mal intent. Its power lies in its imagination-shaping impact (and, consequently, its neural impact). It provides a deep reassurance in the face of rapid change. It is almost like a quiet voice assuring us, "At least you can drink out of the water fountain marked *white only*!"

Conclusion

In this chapter, I have suggested that we must become more sophisticated about the role that myth, ritual, and symbol play in everyday life, especially with regard to race. There has been a great deal of thoughtful commentary and scholarship on the role of symbols and myth in human experience and social processes. But we are not accustomed to applying this scholarship to our efforts at social analysis. Our obsession with quantifiable, measurable stuff tends to produce shallow social analysis. Sometimes, it seems the alternative is to jump into some form of magical thinking that sends us back to Medieval European supernaturalism. We need to use all the tools available to us, however, including asking ourselves, "What is the role of mythology in current affairs? What is the core narrative that is being told and retold, again and again?"

The forcefulness of our consumption-oriented market economy often distracts us from the issues at hand. We are simply not comfortable with conversations about race that take us into realms where simple cause and effect do not apply. Market forces also pressure policy makers to be especially attentive to public policy benefitting the private sector over the common good. When it comes to social policy, intense partisanship is easier than crafting effective policy interventions and providing the funding to make them work.

I have suggested that we need to pay careful attention to the myth of white superiority and the social architecture that repeatedly rehearses the myth. How did we come to our current state of affairs with regard to race? Is there a clear pathway, leading back even prior to our emergence as a nation? Is there a history that makes sense of race and contemporary society? In the next section, we will briefly visit, in summary fashion, these very questions. We will explore the dimensions of our national investment in racial oppression and the historical chemistry that made it seem necessary.

PART II

THE EUROPEAN IMPERIAL-COLONIAL ENTERPRISE

Introduction: Iberia the Crucible

"Crucible: a place or situation in which concentrated forces interact to cause or influence change or development ..." (*Merriam-Webster Online Dictionary* 2017).

The Iberian Peninsula was a veritable crucible in the fifteenth century. Interacting historical forces converged on Iberia in a dramatic fashion, with consequences that still reverberate today. These forces shaped a social context that effectively spewed the Portuguese and Spanish across the world, initiating the age of European imperial-colonialism. We set the stage for part 2 with a brief summary of some of these interacting forces. This is followed by commentary on historical method that contextualizes naming nine motifs that characterize the five-hundred-year history of European imperial-colonialism. As this history unfolded, five crops were especially foundational to the entire enterprise; we will explore how they continue to shape our experience today. This leads to an assessment of the dual character that has marked America from its inception: aspiration and brutality. Finally, we'll note some of the historical outcroppings that dramatically express the nation's investment in racial oppression.

Reconquista and the Crusades

In 711, a Muslim army sailed across the Straits of Gibraltar, then swept across the Iberian Peninsula and into Southern France. At the Battle of Tours-Portiers in 732, the army of Charles Martel, grandfather of Charles the Great, stopped the Muslim advance and forced a retreat back across the Pyrenees Mountains and into Iberia. The peninsula would remain in Muslim hands for the next seven hundred years. The kingdom of Al-Andalus (the Arabic name for the entire peninsula) would become, arguably, Western Europe's most cosmopolitan society. It would be a center of learning and the arts. Jews and Christians were welcomed and protected as long as they submitted to Muslim authority.

In 1064, the papacy endorsed a military effort to regain Iberia and expel the Muslims. The Reconquista (Reconquest) of the entire peninsula was eventually successful, but it would take over four hundred years of struggle and setbacks. The multicentury effort to oust the Muslims and reclaim the Iberian Peninsula for Christendom might be best understood as the initiation of Europe's "Holy Crusades" against the forces of Islam.

In 1095, Pope Urban II launched what is typically understood as the first Crusade in response to pleas of help from the Orthodox Christians of Constantinople. The Seljuk Turks were at the gates, and the city seemed on the verge of collapse. Rather than simply rallying Roman Christians to rescue their eastern sisters and brothers, Urban framed his call as a Holy Crusade to recapture Jerusalem itself. The resulting multicentury effort was instrumental in coalescing and shaping Christendom. It was during the Crusades that Europe, as we know it today, began to emerge. Warring principalities and political intrigue had a new focus: Jerusalem and the Muslim world (even though that included the devastation and pillaging of Constantinople by Christian knights in the seventh Crusade).

Pax Mongolica

During this time, the armies of Genghis Kahn and his sons swept into Europe, threatening the fragile emerging structure of European Christendom and spreading fear that reverberated across the entire continent. The Mongol armies—at the very gates of Vienna—withdrew following the death of Ogodei, son of the Great Kahn, in 1241. What they built, however, was an unusually creative administrative region encompassing the old Silk Road between the Far East and Eastern Europe. This huge free trade zone created new trading relations with the Far East. Rich fabrics, spices, and various goods new to Europe, including gunpowder, were now available. Scholars have termed this period Pax Mongolica. Recent historical research has given us new perspectives on the Mongols and their influence on the shaping of modern Europe.

The Plague

Unfortunately, ideas, technology, and other goods were not the only things to come to the West from the East via the Mongol free trade zone. Bubonic plague, likely originating in southern China, moved with relative speed across Asia to Europe in the early fourteenth century. The plague was a disease of commerce; bacteria-carrying fleas soon traversed the entire Mongol trade zone, eventually reaching Constantinople. From there, it spread to Egypt and then to Sicily. In 1348, it ravaged cities across Italy, and in June 1348, it entered England. It continued to move west and by 1350 had wiped out 60 percent of Iceland's population. Europe lost between one-third and one-half of its total population.

In many parts of Europe, Jews were blamed for the devastation wrought by the plague. Between November 1348 and September 1349, all the Jews between Cologne and Austria were murdered or driven out. Most were burned.[31] Burning Jews at the stake was often seen as a way to halt the plague. In the popular mind, the Jews represented a heresy that was displeasing to God (an attitude encouraged by the Inquisition). The persecutions continued in spite of a papal bull issued by Pope Clement VI protecting the Jews and calling for a halt to persecution.

The Little Ice Age

At roughly the same time that the plague moved from East to West, a climactic period that has come to be known as the Little Ice Age occurred. From around 1300 to 1850, the earth was characterized by regionally cold conditions. There were two clear phases of this time of cooling: the first from around 1290 into the late 1400s. The coldest period was between 1645 and 1715, with a lightly warmer period between the two cold shocks. During the first cold period, winters were bitter, and summers quite cool and wet. In Europe, widespread crop failures and recurring famines resulted. Grain prices increased, grape harvests were minimal (with a resulting shortage of wine), commercial fishing suffered, and in some mountainous areas, advancing glaciers threatened entire towns. Isolated areas in Northern Europe especially were hard hit. Central Europe experienced drought and increased frequency of flooding.

As the fifteenth century began, Europe in general was in a desperate state. The twin scourges of the plague and the Little Ice Age jeopardized society's resilience. In many regions, it was a time of near hysteria and persecution of minorities, including women (under the rubric of stamping out witchcraft, with papal support). For common people, sanitation was nearly nonexistent; water was generally not safe to drink; towns and cities were unsanitary places; a variety of diseases in addition to the plague routinely threatened life and limb. In addition, the well-to-do had gained an appetite for luxury items from the Far East (thanks to Pax Mongolica). However, between Europe and the East—blocking access—were the kingdoms and armies of Islam.

The Doctrine of Discovery

In the context of the Crusades, including the effort to oust the Muslims from Iberia, the papacy issued several bulls that sanctioned the conquest of the Saracens and other infidels, the geographical expansion of Christendom, the conversion and enslavement of non-Christians, and the killing of those who resisted. These bulls collectively have become known as the Doctrine of Discovery. They represented the Roman Church's sanction of European imperial-colonial expansion (and, in particular, the colonizing efforts of Portugal and Spain). This doctrine effectively became part of the fabric of European colonial imagination and provided direct and indirect support for the colonial efforts of the ensuing centuries. It was the mechanism that spewed the Portuguese and Spanish across the world. In turn, their efforts ignited intense competition among several European nations for the riches of the East and the New World. Nigel Cliff, in his book *The Last Crusade*, suggests the authorization of the church "galvanized" the colonial imagination and unleashed a passion for "epic plunder" and conquest in the name of Christ.[32]

In the crucible of Iberia, Europe's multicentury colonial expansion was taking shape. Themes and motifs were being delineated that would be replicated across the entire globe over many generations, prefiguring even the postcolonial nations of the Americas.

5

History, Oppression, and Resistance: Comments on Historical Method

In chapter 1, we noted the centrality of historical narrative in the formation of community. Indeed, the deep impetus for historical scholarship is, in the final analysis, the communal need to tell our story and understand our journey. How did we come to this place, this time? This need is born of the experience of community and the shared consciousness that community shapes, however short-lived. Historical research is existentially necessary. It is more than an academic discipline overseen by the academy. Our lives require it! As human beings, we strive to understand, to interpret our experience. Thus, in the final analysis, "doing" history is the work of the people, in community. Academically trained historians are critical to the people's work. But history is not the academy's property. It belongs to the people.

However we view the discipline of history, it is clearly more than science. It involves discerning the threads that make sense of our lives and weaving them together in a tapestry that illuminates our journey. This is as much an artful enterprise as it is a social science effort. Thus, historical literature and historical scholarship go hand in hand. Artists help us grasp the human dimension of events. For example, Pablo Picasso's dramatic rendition of the devastation of the town of Guernica by the Nazis in 1937 is much more impactful than a trove of scholarly texts. Some have characterized this particular work as "political art." Whatever its political content, its power as an anguished witness to human suffering makes it an important piece of twentieth-century history. As such, it is also an important part of historical scholarship. Virtually every artful medium has been involved in weaving the tapestry of historical narrative.

The Twilight of History

Dietrich Bonhoeffer, the German Lutheran pastor executed by the Nazis, spoke of the twilight of history where innumerable perspectives confuse our judgment and inundate the historical drama with ambiguity.[33] Contrary to much popular opinion, the events and the people that are the stuff of history simply cannot be viewed objectively or from a singular viewpoint. Historical sources, whether primary or secondary, give us a picture distorted by personal bias, ideological frameworks, and worldview. The historical record is not the result of pure science; it is not empirically verifiable. Raw data is not history. Historical facts must be connected and interpreted. Historical events are connected, but the connections sometimes must be inferred; they may not be obvious. Contemporary context and ideological filters influence how we connect the dots. Hence our reading of the record will vary from generation to generation, perhaps even from year to year. We must weigh the testimony of commentators, taking into account their vantage points, and draw conclusions based on the evidence at hand. History, as a recounting of past events, is dynamic and relational. The record is constantly changing, and our perception of its changes depends on our relationship to it.

We cannot change what happened in the past in the sense that what transpired actually transpired. The challenge is gathering the relevant facts and learning what did occur, understanding the historical context it occurred in, discerning the connections that make sense of it, and deciding its significance when it occurred, as well as now, for us. While we can't change what took place, we can, however, rewrite history. We can change our interpretation, our reading of the historical drama. New information and fresh insights can alter our perceptions. We can ferret out connections that perhaps were previously invisible or misunderstood. While there is indeed an objectivity to the events of history, the "facts" we discern are always a function of our biases, no matter how subtle. Thus, interpretative commentary brings an element of subjectivity to the facts.

What we are left with is the latest rendition of the historical record itself and our interpretation of it. Even the record is simply the people, places, and events that others decided were important to remember. It is never an inclusive recounting of all that transpired in any particular place or time.

When we tell the story of European imperial-colonial expansion, a key question concerns the lens we apply, through which we read the historical accounts. What are the assumptions we bring, and how do they color and interpret the telling? If we believe we are telling the story of the glorious expansion of European civilization and the formation of global trade, we will relate events differently than if we believe we are telling the story of the destruction of ancient cultures and the violent subjugation and exploitation of rich and diverse societies. Certainly both of these perspectives are illuminating. Much of the history-telling we are familiar with holds up the glorious dimension of colonial expansion and its contribution to our world today, with perhaps some addenda regarding some of the unfortunate consequences. We are all familiar with history books that celebrate the heroism of the colonizers and relate how their efforts eventually led to the Industrial Revolution and its contribution to today's world.

In general, we are less familiar with the stories and perspectives of the colonized and the terrible price the imperial-colonial enterprise exacted over the centuries. In our moment, we have access to a much more elaborate, inclusive, and nuanced recounting of this drama than previously. There is a plethora of popular history being done, as well as substantial scholarship on the historical episodes and minutiae previously overlooked, ignored, or unknown.

When we examine Europe's efforts at global expansion, two themes that stand out are systemic oppression and resistance. Colonial efforts rode on the crest of waves of systematic domination and exploitation that generated constant, unrelenting resistance; the struggle this dialectic engendered was instrumental in shaping today's world. These themes—oppression and resistance—function as a lens that illuminates several integral motifs that dramatically characterize five hundred-plus years of history.

This perspective tells a more holistic tale than what we may be familiar with. It highlights and illuminates connections that are often overlooked. It takes into account the perspective of those who bore the brunt of Europe's colonial exploitation and underscores the terrible price that has been paid to achieve our twenty-first century. Thus, it helps us grasp the human and ecological cost of imperial expansion without ignoring the technological advances and globalizing economics that colonialism made possible. It does bring an unapologetic ideological bias to the historical record; it values and centers the importance of resistance. Narratives from the perspective of resistance illuminate the oppressive dimensions of Europe's American adventure and deepen and enliven historical scholarship. This lens gives us a place to stand to question many of the taken-for-granted assumptions we frequently encounter in the media and much popular literature about past events and people and their relation to our contemporary world.

In this book, we are talking primarily about the impact of European expansion on the Western Hemisphere, in particular the part that became the United States. We are not even peeking at the devastation Europe visited upon sub-Saharan Africa, the Middle East, South Asia, Southeast Asia, and East Asia. Admittedly, there is an arbitrariness involved with this focus. The impact of the African diaspora on Africa continues even today. We can also make similar observations about the other geographical regions impacted directly during the time of European imperial-colonial expansion. It is necessary, however, to narrow our focus sufficiently to make a compelling case relative to this book's thesis: the intentional investment in racial oppression by the United States and the ways that investment continues to put us in harm's way.

Morality and Historical Evil

"Life belongs to life," noted H. Richard Niebuhr, a Protestant theologian from the last century.[34] We are all bound together; when we break this foundational connection, we are at risk. Perhaps this is the significance of the common religious prohibition against killing. It is an expression of our deepest wiring. It is not necessary to view this as an imperative imposed by some external force somewhere. Rather, it can be understood as a hard-earned learning gained over many generations. It is woven into the fabric of our lives, into the depths of our consciousness. We somehow know that murder puts us all at risk; yet we also are all aware of the terrible history of our species and its willingness to wantonly commit mass murder. What about coercion that stops this side of death in order to force others to do our will? Such coercion has been a constant theme across our world and was certainly a primary mark of European imperial-colonialism. Exploiting the natural resources of the Americas was accomplished by coercing the labor of millions of human beings. Brutal violence was often the means of coercion.

How are we to assess this history? Are we to justify it based on differences in cultural practices, historical expectations, and available technology? Or are we to condemn it as monstrous historical evil that taints the societies it produced? Invoking morality when it comes to historical events and people is always challenging. And yet there is a sense in which we must assess the moral implications of past events in order to discern their significance for our time. Such judgments, however, do not do away with the morass of relativity that always colors the record. They are made in the context of historical relativity. Consequently, moral judgments about historical events cannot be reduced to an assessment of the personal morality of the actors involved—either their virtue or the purity of their motivation. All human beings have to deal with the daily ambiguities of living and making sense of the world we live in. We can allow the actors of history to have lives with dimension and humanity, without reducing them to either pure virtue or manifest evil. Survival is always costly; it is at the expense of others, even when the others are different species.

Previously, we explored the human bias for being in community; we identified empathy as a fundamental driver in forming communal bonds. We used the term *empathic resonance* to indicate the capacity to feel with another, not simply in terms of emotion but also in terms of the subtle cellular responses that activate mirror neurons and create connections among people and communities. Empathic resonance reflects the reality that our lives are bound together. We learn that our individual well-being depends on others. Niebuhr's witness indicates something foundational about the way life is. This manuscript presumes that moral judgments, in the final analysis, are made from the perspective noted by Niebuhr: life belongs to life. Survival itself is at stake—survival of the species and all those that make up the fabric of life. Principles of right and wrong, good and evil are abstractions, save they inform daily decision-making and connect to the choice for life. This is a bit of a different spin on the term *pro-life* than we typically encounter in the public policy battles of our day. It is more expansive than the public debates over abortion. It is an effort to use the term in a manner that is more ecologically oriented and that places the matter of viable human community in the context of the complex web of life itself.

There are times when the vicissitudes of life and the challenge of survival put empathic resonance at risk. It seems to be a luxury we cannot afford. In order to contravene our wiring for empathy, we have to shape and communicate mythologies that dehumanize others and make them less than. Such mythologies enhance personal grievances, fears, anxieties, and anger and frame them in universal terms, identifying an objective cause, irritant, or enemy. The mythology then channels collective energy toward the enemy. The mythos justifies behavior we would otherwise never tolerate in relation to our group.

Some of us may indeed totally lack the capacity for empathy—those termed psychopathic or sociopathic—as a consequence of neurological issues, a difficult upbringing, brain chemistry, or some other yet-to-be-understood determinant. It is our awareness of empathic resonance, however, that enables us to discern that some apparently lack this capacity. It is also our awareness of the centrality of empathy that enables us to see that some powerful mythologies sabotage the foundations of community.

When a social group with power creates and uses stories and sloganeering to excuse and justify brutality toward others, even genocide, what might we name this? From the perspective that "life belongs to life," this is historical evil. Even so, it is evil that we have all known and participated in, even if only on a micro level. Clearly, it breaks the bonds that empathy would fashion. It builds walls around empathic resonance. It creates "in" groups and "out" groups and inculcates the willingness to destroy and brutalize. Making such a judgment is indeed a moral judgment. However, as much as we wish it were so, such judgment does not dispel the twilight of history and its accompanying ambiguity; neither does it invoke divine sanction or moral absolutes that dictate human behavior. Making such judgments requires stepping beyond the pale of pure scholarship, without the certainty of religious fundamentalism. Yet we must make such judgments if our historical method is to provide existential guidance.

The scapegoating of the Jews in Europe during the ravages of the plague is an example of such destructive storytelling and sloganeering. The transatlantic slave trade also relied on such mythos, as did Nazism and the destruction of indigenous cultures and the killing of Native people in colonial America. Interning American citizens of Japanese descent in concentration camps required mythology that tapped into deep prejudices about Asians. Wartime hysteria made it relatively easy to believe that Japanese Americans were not really genuine Americans who could be trusted. We can understand the paranoia behind Executive Order 9066, given the times, without justifying it. The nation was at war with Japan. We were already demonizing the Japanese; it was a short step to demonizing Americans of Japanese descent.

More recently, the presidential campaign of Donald Trump spun out a mythology that drew energy from our white supremacist history. It explicitly and subtly linked people's fears, anxieties, and economic challenges to the administration of Barack Obama, tapping into deep levels of implicit racial bias. The campaign further sought to link Hillary Clinton and the Democratic Party in general with the black president. It rather effectively utilized the intersection of gender biases and racial biases and the irrational fears they both elicit. It demonized Muslims and dark-skinned immigrants on our southern border, casting them as rapists, murderers, and threats to our national security.

When political opponents assert that Mr. Trump lies and then provide what they consider damning evidence, the power of the mythology reasserts itself. Support for Mr. Trump has never been about his personality, his personal integrity, or whether or not he stretches the truth. It is about his sloganeering and the deep stories it invokes; it is about reasserting white supremacy.

Such mythologizing is an example of historical evil as surely as Japanese internment was. It may not rise to the level of *The Final Solution* in Nazi Germany or the hysteria in the US that led to Chinese Exclusion, but it invokes a simpler time when the law protected white access. It invokes a time that clearly centered white identity and made us a white nation, at the expense of people of color, women, and all who did not fit into the value frameworks rooted in white male authority. It was also at the expense of poor and low-income white people, exploited by the system, who may even have drawn some solace, in times past, from the ability to drink from a "white only" fountain.

The Nine Motifs of European Imperial-Colonialism

When we focus our attention on European efforts in the Western Hemisphere and tease out the dynamics of systemic power, several multicentury motifs stand out. Nine, in particular, are integral to understanding the features of our twenty-first-century society. They express the aforementioned themes of systematic oppression and resistance. They fall into two groups. The first six motifs denote the European imperial-colonial enterprise and its efforts to exploit the resources of the New World; the next three indicate persistent resistance to European hegemony. Domination and resistance play out in contrapuntal fashion over these centuries.

These recurring motifs produced the social architecture of our nation. It is a multicentury concrescence of these motifs (a concrescence is a coalescence of disparate parts, over time, into an integrated whole). Previously, I suggested that the term that best captures the substance of the social fabric these motifs produced is *white supremacy*, albeit with contrapuntal resistance built in. This is not to suggest that a cabal of evil men gathered in the mid-fifteenth century in order to design a white supremacist nation. Rather, when we peruse five hundred years of history, we can see these motifs emerging. We can discern opportunistic, desperate, and creative people making assumptions about what was necessary, appropriate, and even moral. We are not privy to their motives and only partially to their beliefs. But we can discern the outcomes of their activities, both in terms of social dominance and resistance.

The Domination Motifs

1) The claiming of territory in the name of church, state, and profit by Europeans; such territorial expansion was a function of ...

2) The authorizing sanction of church and state. This sanction did more than approve the adventures of a few hardy souls; it actively encouraged and even promoted imperial expansion under the aegis of the Doctrine of Discovery, national pride, and economic profit. This sanction led to ...

3) The forceful domination (and even genocide) of indigenous populations and the consequent devastation of indigenous cultures (dominion sanctioned directly by the Doctrine of Discovery and its echoes in Anglican and Protestant thought).

4) The coercion (often violent) of human labor in the service of extractive economic enterprises; this includes chattel slavery, virtual slavery (the Spanish *Encomienda* and the *mita*), and indentured servitude.

5) The disruption and destruction of ancient ecosystems and the unprecedented dispersion of plants and animals across the world (often referred to as the Columbian exchange, or more recently as the Anthropocene).

6) The development of European scholarship, literature, art, and spirituality that further rationalized and even romanticized the imperial-colonial enterprise. One of the products of such scholarship was the ideology of race, given scholastic respectability by the fledgling discipline of anthropology. This was at heart a multicentury exercise that touted the mythic superiority of European Christian civilization.

Some may protest that such language dismisses the courage, creativity, and entrepreneurship that the Europeans brought to their imperial-colonial efforts over the centuries. Perhaps. But those of us of European descent have had our apologists, our storytellers and poets who romanticized our efforts. We've waxed at length about the brave explorers who discovered new lands and made possible the industrialization of America and its contribution to contemporary life. Now the time has come to clarify the significance of our social architecture for the descendants of those oppressed by the European adventure—those whose lifeblood, vitality, and civilizational genius in large part constructed the edifice, albeit unwillingly. This significance is captured in the term *white supremacy*.

Contrapuntal Resistance

The construction of the edifice of white supremacy invoked a veritable torrent of resistance. Its features are as follows:

1) The persistent, enduring resistance of those bearing the brunt of colonization and racial oppression:

- the formation of resistance communities across the Americas and over the centuries (like Quilombo dos Palmares in Brazil, Yanga on the east coast of present day Mexico, and communities within Great Dismal Swamp in the US)
- the creation of subversive networks (like the Underground Railroad in the antebellum United States)
- the subversion and sabotage of production and extraction (by those whose labor was coerced)

2) Ongoing efforts to overturn, deconstruct, and dismantle the official sanction of church and state from within the system:

- challenging the canon of the church, done by some within the ranks of the church itself
- challenging legal support for racial oppression and dominion; for example, the voices for abolition in Great Britain in the last one-third of the eighteenth century (these included John Wesley, the founder of Methodism, who spoke out forcefully against the slave trade)
- advocating enforcement of prohibitions against slave trading, coerced labor, and territorial encroachment

3) The emergence of a spirituality, art, literature, and scholarship of resistance:

- the African diaspora and New World spirituality, enlivening resistance communities from the early fifteenth century to current times, across the hemisphere wherever the daughters and sons of Africa formed communities (this included Africanized Christianity and other African religious traditions, such as Obia, Voudou, Umbandia, Makumba, and Rastafarianism)
- indigenous spirituality: the resurgence and intermingling of traditional motifs that contributed to the persistence of cultural identities; this included the multination Ghost Dance in the western U. S. and a spiritual resurgence among Eastern Woodland nations in the late eighteenth century
- art, literature, and the scholarship of resistance that has given the world talented musicians, poets, writers, dancers, artists, and

scholars who have had and continue to have a powerful impact on contemporary life

These resistance motifs are an aspect of our experience of the architecture of white supremacy (that includes the experience of all of us, wherever we show up in the white-nonwhite binary). This means that cognitive dissonance is woven into the very edifice. Resistance to the system by the oppressed is intimately connected to resistance from within the system. White supremacy contains the seeds of its own destruction. The algorithms of resistance are built in. The entire edifice is threatened by fundamental structural weakness, and no efforts to shore up or patch the cracks will finally stave off its eventual demise. But will its demise result in a viable human community fitted for the challenges of this century?

Further Notes on Resistance

If we believe, as I do, that the multicentury drama of resistance has important clues for efforts to reimagine and rebuild human community, then we need consider this dynamic carefully. In order to do so, there are some challenges we must negotiate that will otherwise frustrate our efforts to plumb the depths of resistance.

First is the absence or demonization of resistance in many of our historical documents. The story is too often told simply from the perspective of European domination and American triumphalism. While we have countless studies of European conquest in the Americas, it is only recently that scholars have focused on the communities of resistance that came into being beginning five hundred years ago. We know of the opposition the Spanish encountered from the Triple Alliance (commonly known as the Aztecs) and among the Incas in South America. It was opposition rooted in huge, complex civilizations. We have attributed the success of the Spanish to superior technology and military genius—implying European superiority. Reality was more complex. We need also to consider the role of indigenous allies of the Spanish and the impact of opportunistic European microbes.

In North America, we remember the assistance provided to European colonists by local indigenous communities; we also remember the stories of the cruel savages and the threat posed to Christian colonies and civilization.

We believed that resistance to European incursions was mounted by uncivilized, cruel, and un-Christian savages or, alternatively, by noble savages who, nonetheless, were doomed by their virtuous innocence. The dramatic story of the "winning of the West" in the United States posited an enemy against whom we had to contend: wild and savage Indians. Hollywood's bread and butter throughout much of the twentieth century consisted of stories of heroic struggle against bloodthirsty Apaches, Comanches, Cheyenne Dog Soldiers, and Sioux warriors.

Another challenge when exploring resistance is the tension between the idealized, romanticized heroines and heroes we remember and the real human beings who populate the historical record, with all the neuroses, weaknesses, emotions, and virtues that adhere to human flesh and blood. This is especially difficult when examining the lives of individuals who are quite removed from us in time. Our collective memory tends to fade. We forget how gritty and basic people's lives were and how far removed they were from the conveniences of daily life that we presume. Sometimes survival required hard decisions that we cannot imagine or appreciate.

When we require ideological purity of the resistors of the past, we may miss significant and impactful examples of resistance. Our insistence that others exemplify our ideological requirements becomes a roadblock. We may suspect questionable motives. Often the resistors had blind spots, were shortsighted, or were not consistently antioppressive. We don't want our heroines or heroes weighted down with the ambiguities of historical decision-making or the messiness of living real lives in morally ambiguous situations.

Bartólome de las Casas, for example, impacted how the Spanish Crown and the Roman Church perceived indigenous Americans. Las Casas was a Dominican priest and bishop in the American colonies. He was shocked by the cruelty of the Spanish toward indigenous people. Many of his contemporaries viewed his tireless advocacy as a bothersome obsession, at best, and as dangerous treason at worst. When pressed regarding the source of necessary labor for the mines and sugarcane fields of the American colonies, he suggested that perhaps Africans were quite suitable. He later regretted this suggestion, as the tragedy of the slave trade unfolded. His voice was crucial in moving the church and the Crown to promulgate the Laws of Burgos, in 1512–13 and the New Law of the Indies in 1542. These sought to curb and correct abuses of the Encomienda system in the Spanish colonies. They were partially successful in mitigating the brutality of the mines and the cane fields.

His advocacy moved the church to view indigenous Americans as human beings, rather than subhuman. It did not, however, call into question the legitimacy of the Doctrine of Discovery. While Las Casas impacted how indigenous Americans were viewed and treated, he did not challenge the right of Christian Spaniards to colonize and Christianize. Nonetheless, in the scope of history, his was an important voice from within the institutionalized systems of oppression. He was in the ranks of resistance. Resistance by some who are part of the systems of oppression is an indication of humanity among the oppressors. It is rooted in conscience. It indicates the presence of empathic resonance and the stealthy, treasonous experience of compassion. It may well be the result of witnessing suffering or seeing resistance among the oppressed. Such resistance threatens the systems of oppression and puts those who dare to voice resistance at risk. It also links the voices of resistance within the domination system to those outside the system who refuse to passively comply. However, the voices on the margins of those effectively outside the system are the key to the future. It is their lived experience that documents and testifies to the failure of the system.

Sometimes, little-known players have made the decisions and done the deeds that produce dramatic change. Mildred and Richard Loving, an ordinary couple whose marriage violated the antimiscegenation statutes of Virginia, apparently never saw themselves as civil rights activists. They thought of themselves as ordinary working folks who simply wanted to be together and have a family. Nevertheless, their decision to be a couple, as an African American-American Indian woman and a white man, led to the Supreme Court decision in 1967 that struck down the Virginia law as unconstitutional. It was a significant legal victory against American apartheid. It moved us toward a more just and equitable society. Without it, it is doubtful that marriage equality would be the law of the land in our day.

How do we know when resistance is historically necessary and not simply a part of competition between adversaries seeking power, wealth, influence, and empire? If we understand historic necessity as a matter of choosing the course of action that is most pro-life (as in "life belongs to life"), then there is a bit of guiding clarity amidst the twilight of history. When the social canon (the dominant social mode that is generally presumed legitimate) justifies brutality and oppression, resistance is natural, legitimate, and necessary. Once again, the voice of H. Richard Niebuhr gives us a compelling clue: innocent suffering.[35] Innocent suffering necessitates resistance. The term "innocent" does not suggest that the oppressed are either morally pure or individually virtuous. They are, after all, real human beings with real lives. Innocent suffering is suffering inflicted that is undeserved and unnecessary, and that sabotages the foundations of community, thereby jeopardizing the fabric of life itself. Innocent suffering legitimates resistance as a moral response.

In summary, this chapter on historical method and moral judgment provides the context for naming characteristic motifs of European imperial-colonialism and some elaboration on the dynamics of resistance. When we consider the drama of the past five hundred years, we can do so in a manner that invites the actors in the drama into our commentary in all their humanity, whatever their location in the unfolding story. This gives our historical narratives substance, depth, and a bit of reality. The voices of the past can then address us in ways that illuminate current dilemmas and inform our collective decision-making. Now, we turn to consider the impact of the European imperial-colonial enterprise in the shaping of twenty-first-century America.

The Foundational Crops: a Timely Investment

6

The Past Lives: A Personal Witness

"The past is never dead. It's not even past. All of us labor in webs spun long before we were born, webs of heredity and environment, of desire and consequence, of history and eternity" (William Faulkner, *Requiem for a Nun*).

I've always been addressed by this quote from Faulkner. It expresses an insight that is incredibly important, easily overlooked, yet crucial if we are to understand our present moment. Faulkner's words suggest that not only are we organically linked to past events but the past lives today. The historical "web" that brought us to be still touches us and holds us tightly. Faulkner's poetic sensibilities give us a way to be present to some of the historic episodes that still shape our social reality.

The multicentury history of the European enterprise in the Western Hemisphere arguably witnessed the birth of production agriculture, the predecessor of today's agribusiness giants. The Western Hemisphere enriched Europe in countless ways. Certainly, silver and gold from the Spanish colonies impacted the emerging global economy of the sixteenth and seventeenth centuries. However, agricultural produce from the Americas even more dramatically impacted Europe and the postcolonial nations of the Americas. While there were and are a variety of crops and natural resources that flowed from the Americas to Europe, there are a handful of crops that especially enriched the economies of the imperial-colonial nations and that also powerfully impacted the United States in its infancy. While these were certainly not the only noteworthy agricultural products, there were five that were foundational to the entire enterprise.

Five Crops and Their Roles

Sugar and Coffee

A while back, as I stirred a spoonful of sugar into my first morning cup of coffee, I began to reflect on historical linkages. I remembered the brutal history of sugar in the Western Hemisphere and how instrumental it was in developing Europe. Historian Eric Williams, the former prime minister of Trinidad and Tobago, suggested that the production and consumption of sugar effectively subsidized Europe's Industrial Revolution.[36] Some may consider his conclusion controversial and may suggest that the history of industrialization is much more complex and multifaceted. Be that as it may, it is nonetheless quite clear that over some four hundred years, the cultivation of sugar cane and the production of refined sugar, molasses, and rum had a major economic impact on the colonial powers involved and Europe in general.

This is a brutal history because thousands upon thousands of enslaved Africans, likely millions, were the primary labor force that made the production of sugar possible. Life on sugar plantations and in the sugar mills was hard. Sugar cane wore out the land where it was grown and took an awful toll on those whose coerced labor was used in its cultivation, harvesting, milling, packaging, and loading.

It then occurred to me that each crystal of sugar I stirred into my coffee was like a drop of crystalized sweat—or perhaps even blood. As the earth turns coal into diamonds over many years, so this history has turned blood and sweat into the sweet crystals I stirred into my coffee. Then I remembered that coffee had a similar history, although not quite as long. It was also grown, harvested, washed, dried, packaged, and transported using slave labor. Even after slavery finally ended across the hemisphere, debt peonage was often used to create a virtual slave labor force on large coffee plantations in Brazil, the Caribbean, Central America, and Mexico.

Each sip of coffee seemed to link me to this past. You may think I'm speaking metaphorically. I am. But I experience these metaphors linking me to the past in a powerful manner. Sometimes, in a flash, I feel this past enveloping me. I really enjoy coffee, especially early in the morning. I'm not suggesting that such shocking realizations should lead me to stop drinking coffee and using sugar. I am suggesting that when I am self-conscious, the simple act of drinking coffee with sugar discloses to me that the past is alive. It is invoked in the products I use. It holds me firmly, whether I want it to or not. Even when I am unreflective, it lives. It travels through my body with each sip of warm, sweetened coffee.

The United States was not a major producer of sugar in the early days. Cultivation of sugar cane was limited to a few regions in the Deep South—and later in Hawaii (this was prior to the advent of the sugar beet in US agribusiness). However, even before independence from Britain, the New England colonies were intimately involved in sugar production and the transatlantic slave trade. Molasses from the sugar-producing colonies in the Caribbean was distilled into rum in New England distilleries. Ships built in Rhode Island carried captured Africans across the Atlantic as well as necessary products to the sugar plantations: barrel staves, clothing for enslaved Africans, machinery, and so on. Some wealthy New Englanders owned plantations in the Caribbean.

Coffee was not produced on US territory prior to our obtaining Puerto Rico, the Virgin Islands, and Hawaii. But as the pace of industrialization quickened, our taste for coffee encouraged increasing production in Brazil, Central America, the Caribbean, and Mexico. Trading relationships bound us ever more tightly to the coffee producers in our hemisphere. Our consumption made us complicit in the labor and land practices that converted an African bean into the quintessential American drink.

Cotton

A little later, as I chose a shirt for the day from among several hanging in my closet, I happened to glance at the label sewn into the inside of the collar. The shirt, a simple long-sleeved pullover, was 60 percent cotton and 40 percent polyester; it was made in Bangladesh. My curiosity tweaked, I examined the rest of the shirts hanging in the closet. All but one were a cotton blend (usually with polyester; one a blend with linen) ranging from 35 percent to 60 percent cotton (the lone exception was 100 percent cotton). The shirts were manufactured in ten different nations—none in the US. The nation producing the largest number was Bangladesh (six); next was Vietnam (five). Several nations had provided only one.

As I reflected on this, I remembered how critical cotton was to our nation's history. Between 1793, when Eli Whitney invented a new type of cotton gin, and the beginning of the Civil War, cotton was the central pillar of the new nation's economy. (Note that we give Whitney the credit; some believe his lady-friend suggested the idea and that she received it from an enslaved African). The United States, over a period of just a few short years, became the world's largest producer of cotton. Cotton from the American South was so crucial to the textile mills of Great Britain that when the American Civil War broke out, British industrialists were thrown into a panic. Apparently, there was even talk in some quarters of intervening in our Civil War—on the side of the South—in order to protect British access to US cotton. Instead, British efforts focused on ramping up cotton production in one of its colonies: India. Unfortunately, Indian farmers couldn't compare favorably with American cotton plantations. They lacked one crucial ingredient: a large and growing pool of slave labor.

Enslaved Africans were responsible for our nation's prodigious cotton output. There were virtually no technical innovations after Whitney's gin that accounted for the incredible growth in production. What changed was the number of enslaved Africans dispatched to work the cotton fields—that and the expanding number of acres devoted to cotton production.

Thus began perhaps the most onerous chapter in the history of chattel slavery. In the Deep South, cotton became king, requiring thousands of slaves to produce the mill-ready bales that were sent north to textile factories in New England and to the mills in Great Britain. Picking cotton was incredibly labor-intensive. Working in the cotton fields was difficult and exhausting. The productive life span of Southern slaves on the cotton plantations was short and especially onerous. Being "sold down the river" meant being sentenced to hard labor and a short life.

We have learned that monocropping is very hard on the land. It becomes necessary, after a time, to expand to new acreage—not simply to increase production but even to maintain production as the soil is drained of nutrients. Cotton, like tobacco and sugar cane, is particularly hard on the land. The pressure to put more and more land under production was one of the central economic pressures that drove the politics behind the Indian Removal Act. Indigenous Americans occupied prime cotton-growing land in Mississippi, Alabama, and Georgia. The synchronicity between Native disappearance and involuntary servitude was never clearer in our history than during the time when cotton became king and the United States cornered the world cotton market.

I was reflecting on these matters as I pulled on the chosen shirt and felt its cool fabric touch my skin. At that moment, I recalled—in a flash—an old photo I had recently seen of enslaved Africans working a cotton field. Even though very old, it was clear enough to see men, women, and children stooped over and plucking the white bolls, each dragging a bag behind.

Once again, I felt the past reach out to grasp me. Even though I knew that technology had changed everything and that machines were used now to harvest cotton, it was as though I could feel others' hands pulling my shirt down across my torso. I knew that even changes in technology and labor practices did not remove us from this history. One thing does lead to another. Even though the shirt I chose to wear was made in Bangladesh, I suspected it had an historical connection to our pre–Civil War economy. Bangladesh is part of what was the British colony of India. Although farmers on the subcontinent have grown cotton for hundreds of years, today's large-scale production is more closely linked to British efforts during our Civil War.

Curiously, none of my shirts was manufactured in the United States, even though the National Cotton Council of America reports that in 2012, the US was the world's third largest producer of cotton (behind China and India). It further notes that in that year, 65 percent of the US crop was exported and that the industry generated some $27 billion in revenue and had a total economic impact of some $100 billion.[37] Nothing to be sneezed at! One can trace this success back, step-by-step, to the time when slave labor, not automation, was the crucial factor. One can also discern cotton's broader links to the new nation's entire economy in the period leading up to the Civil War. Beckert's assessment of what was required to assure cotton's centrality is striking. "The coercion and violence required to mobilize slave labor was matched only by the demands of an expansionist war against indigenous people."[38]

I was gripped yet again by the realization that many of the products I have come to presume in my daily life link me in a direct fashion to the five-hundred-year history of large-scale agriculture and coerced labor. I realized that, metaphorically speaking, much of my social existence is subsidized by centuries of slave labor—and other forms of coerced labor.

The power of metaphors, of course, is that they reveal aspects and dimensions of reality that may not be obvious in everyday experience. Hence, to speak metaphorically is not to speak abstractly; it is to speak in a manner that holds us directly against reality, a manner that reveals what may have been hidden but is nonetheless real and powerful.

Tobacco

As I pondered these matters, my thoughts went to another of the crops that was integral to our being as a nation: tobacco. I recalled filling out a health questionnaire during a recent physician visit. I noted on the form that I was a former smoker but that I had quit in 1974 (I neglected to add that I still enjoy a rare cigar). Tobacco has had a major impact on our nation, both economic and health-wise. The Centers for Disease Control and Prevention reports that some sixteen million Americans are living with a disease caused by smoking. We all remember the tobacco industry's steadfast and rigorous denial of the health risks of smoking in years past. In the 1960s, it seemed that everyone was smoking; at least many of my friends did. We all knew about the studies, even then, that suggested a strong statistical link between smoking and lung cancer.

Today, the health risks of tobacco use are well documented and generally presumed. However, notwithstanding its tarnished reputation, tobacco has had a significant historical impact on the nation's economy, political life, and culture. Tobacco production played and plays a major role in the economic development of several states. It continues as a major contributor to the nation's economic strength. The Economic Research Service of the US Department of Agriculture has documented tobacco's continuing importance to the nation in reports as recent as 2000 and 2011.[39]

The founding of Jamestown in what is now the state of Virginia marked the beginning of the commercial production of tobacco in the United States. Over the next three hundred years, tobacco cultivation would be central to the economic vitality of several states, including Virginia, North Carolina, and Kentucky. Tobacco made the Commonwealth of Virginia the crown jewel among the colonies during the last half of the eighteenth century.

John Rolfe thought that Virginia might be an outstanding site for tobacco growth. Early attempts to sell Virginian tobacco had fallen short of expectations. Consumers favored the flavor of tobacco grown in the Caribbean; it was smoother and less harsh than the native variety in Virginia. Rolfe reacted to consumer demand by importing seed from the West Indies and cultivating the plant in the Jamestown colony. Those tobacco seeds became the seeds of a huge economic empire.

By 1630, over a million and a half pounds of tobacco were being exported from Jamestown every year. The tobacco economy rapidly began to shape the society and development of the colony. Growing tobacco takes its toll on the soil. Because tobacco drained the soil of its nutrients, only about three successful growing seasons could occur on a plot of land. Then the land had to lie fallow for three years before the soil could be used again. This created a huge drive for new farmland.

Virginia planters had a disproportionate voice in the debates that shaped the colonies' resistance to British authority and that led to the decision to fight for independence. It's not a coincidence that many of those we recognize as founding fathers were Virginians. Nor was it a coincidence that several of our early presidents were from the Commonwealth. We often forget that most of them owned enslaved Africans.

When we assess the role of tobacco, it becomes clear that it was at the center of our struggle for independence and that it continues to wield significant influence, even in a time when antitobacco voices seem louder than its supporters. Years after a federal judge ruled that tobacco companies had misled the public about the health impacts of tobacco use, the industry has been forced to publicly detail the deadly effects. Industry lawyers successfully fought against such disclosure for eleven years. According to an Associated Press report, advertisements paid for by the industry began appearing in late November 2017. The spots bluntly disclose, "More people die every year from smoking than from murder, AIDS, suicide, drugs, car crashes and alcohol, combined." The ads continue, "Cigarette companies intentionally designed cigarettes with enough nicotine to create and sustain addiction." According to the federal government, in 2016 the percentage of adults who smoked had dropped to a low of 15 percent. Nonetheless, tobacco use still accounted for more than 480,000 deaths. In spite of the ads acknowledging the harmful effects of tobacco and the role of tobacco companies in promoting addiction, the industry still spends "more than eight billion annually on marketing."[40]

On those rare occasions when I indulge in an after-dinner cigar, I remember these things as I puff away. Tobacco continues to link us to the saga of coerced labor, expropriation of land, and disappearance. These historical linkages continue to impact us and contribute to our efforts to deconstruct and disempower race. Tobacco takes its place as one of the foundational crops that continue to shape our nation and define its character.

Rice

When I lived in the Philippines, I learned how to cook rice. I learned to measure the water-rice proportion with my finger and how much uncooked rice per person to put in the pot. My Filipina colleagues taught me how to consistently cook fluffy rice, not too wet and not scorched. A Japanese friend offered additional advice, suggesting presoaking.

Recently, as I was preparing some curry-fried rice, I reflected on my tutelage with gratitude. I still remember the lessons. I also remembered that rice is still a commercially important crop in some regions of our nation. Some areas have begun to specialize in particular types of rice: basmati, jasmine, black rice, Arborio, and so on. I remembered that rice is incredibly labor-intensive, when grown in the traditional manner. A Philippine folk song begins, "Planting rice is never fun, work from morn to set of sun; cannot stand and cannot sit; cannot stop for little bit!"

From the early eighteenth century up to the Civil War, rice was the primary crop cultivated in the colony and then state of South Carolina. It subsidized the development of a plantation-based economy and an accompanying culture that arguably shaped the character of the entire Deep South. Rice was cultivated from Wilmington in southern North Carolina south to the Savannah River area and into northern Florida. Rice plantations were prevalent in the moist coastal and inland areas but not the drier piedmont region. Rice, like the other foundational crops, was labor-intensive. Rice production was especially hard on those involved. Laborers in the rice paddies tended to have shorter lives than their counterparts farther north who worked in tobacco production. The southeast was hot and humid; venomous snakes were common, as were alligators. Swarms of mosquitos and other insects spread disease in addition to incredible discomfort. These discomforts were on top of the coercive demands of overseers charged with maximizing production.

Rice cultivation and harvesting also required a skill set that was unique. Consequently, rice plantations developed a labor force that was more similar to sugar production than to tobacco, coffee, or cotton. Indentured servitude did not provide a labor force sufficiently skilled or consistently able to withstand the back-breaking labor. The transatlantic slave trade did. Carolina planters, consequently, were especially interested in enslaved Africans who were experienced in rice production. This meant procuring men and women from the rice-producing areas of West Africa (including current-day Sierra Leon and The Gambia). It also meant organizing the labor force along the lines of task-groupings rather than work-gangs.[41]

South Carolina developed, initially, around 1670 as a private venture, rather than a crown colony. Settlement was organized on purely economic terms; original efforts at settlement were initiated from Barbados. The Caribbean-South Carolina connection persisted over the years and likely gave the colony its unique cultural flavor. The plantation culture of South Carolina reflected the colony's roots in the Caribbean. Some families even maintained connections with relatives and business associates in the British sugar colonies.

Before rice became the key to wealth and power, income was generated from a variety of food crops, wood products, cattle, deerskins, and other pelts from trading with Indian nations—and a brisk trade in human beings. In the early years (roughly 1670–1717) a little-known, tragic chapter in our history unfolded. English traders encouraged what historians have termed the *Indian Slave Trade*. Slave traders purchased captives from the more powerful Indian nations and sold them into slavery. Most were sent to sugar plantations in the Caribbean; some were sent north to New England to be household servants and farmhands.

During these early years, the colony was in a vulnerable position. Nearby Indian nations were much stronger militarily. Both the Spanish and the French were ongoing threats. The Southeastern Indian confederacies found it made strategic sense to ally with one or more of the competing European powers, at times even playing them against each other. They also found European products very useful and consequently developed brisk trading relationships. When it became clear that English traders would provide premium goods for human beings, opportunistic raiding parties would prey on outlying groups and families living on the margins of large settlements.

The historian Alan Gallay, in his book *The Indian Slave Trade*, suggests that "the trade in Indian slaves was the most important factor affecting the South in the period 1670–1715."[42] During this period, more enslaved Indians were exported through the port of Charles Town than enslaved Africans were imported. Based on his research, Gallay concludes that between thirty thousand and fifty thousand indigenous Americans were captured and sold into slavery during this time. Indians were captured and sold into slavery by both the larger Indian confederacies (principally the Cherokee, Creek, and Chickasaw) and by British slavers who scoured the countryside far inland for isolated groups who were easy prey. According to Gallay, most of the Indians enslaved were women and children.

Thus, beginning at least in 1670, the economic and social practices that over time shaped the life style of South Carolina rested upon the trade in and commodification of human beings. When rice became central to the colony's (and later the state's) economy, the importance of this trade intensified. Rice production and slavery were so intensely intertwined that any attempt to analyze and understand the emerging colonial culture must take this into account. In this, rice is similar to cotton; we cannot grasp their economic import—and therefore their central role in our history—apart from the trade in human flesh and the coercion of human labor.

By the same token, as mentioned previously, the character of South Carolina was intimately connected to the sugar plantation culture of the Caribbean. Some have suggested that this connection produced a very tradition-oriented society that was intensely averse to change. South Carolina's decision to be the first Southern state to withdraw from the Union may well have been, in part, an expression of this intense sense of tradition and connection to the past.

The Foundational Crops and the United States

These five crops were foundational to the European imperial-colonial enterprise. Consequently, they are also intimately intertwined with the history of the United States. They have, in no small way, shaped our character, making us who we are as a nation. Even those that were not grown within the boundaries of our nation still powerfully impacted us.

They have as much to do with our national identity as the mythic revolt against taxation without representation. They are all examples of what might be called large-scale production agriculture. As such, they are the antecedents of today's agribusiness giants. In all five, there is a history of efforts to maximize production in order to enhance profitability, even at the expense of ecological and worker health. These crops illuminate the role that the brutal coercion of human labor played in colonial societies and our development as a nation.

Many of us may remember the grade school lessons about Cyrus McCormick and his reaper, and the revolution in agricultural production it sparked. This revolution made the United States the breadbasket of the world. American wheat, corn, soy, other crops, and animal products traverse the globe, enriching our agribusiness enterprises. However, we often forget the links between our agricultural revolution and the five foundational crops.

It's easy to lose sight of our connection to the colonial past and its impact on contemporary practices and relationships. Today's agricultural productivity rests on the foundation of the practical knowledge gained and market dynamics engendered by the five foundational crops. Their history represents a multicentury investment in coerced labor, expropriation of land, and violent subjugation. Millions of lives were broken and spent in the process. These crops enriched Europe and facilitated the rapid development of the United States, as well as the other American nations. This history illuminates an economic paradigm that birthed a mythic-ideological idea: race. These five foundational crops substantiated this paradigm and shaped our emerging national character in the early decades of our life as a nation. This paradigm continues to impact all our lives through today's globalizing economy.

7

America: Aspiration and Brutality

In this chapter, we will explore the economic paradigm that emerged over some five hundred years of European imperial-colonialism and note its relation to the dual investment that marked our nation's development. This will be a brief description of the character of the economic paradigm birthed by European imperial-colonialism, rather than an in-depth exposition of the economics of colonialism. It was an economic paradigm that prioritized extraction over regeneration. To the Europeans, the bounty of the New World seemed endless. Limitations to the extraction model were unimaginable; hunger for the wealth of the Americas was ravenous. The extraction of resources from the Americas initiated and stimulated vigorous worldwide trading relationships. Today's globalizing economies with their complex trading relationships and agreements are rooted in large part in five hundred years of European imperial-colonialism.

We'll highlight three examples of the extraction paradigm that are rooted in colonial economics: mining, large-scale production agriculture, and the associated labor practices. This will contextualize the story of our development as a nation simultaneously marked by soaring aspiration and callous brutality. We'll note how the founding fathers carefully protected slavery and how echoes of the Doctrine of Discovery legitimized the decimation and removal of Indian nations.

The Extraction Paradigm

The European imperial-colonial enterprise was driven by the profit motive, the desire for national/imperial influence, and the hunger for territory. The resulting economic model disrupted ecosystems and contravened the earth's regenerative capacities. It had, and continues to have, a clear bias for increasing productivity over sustainability. Nature seemed to provide an inexhaustible supply of resources; when productivity began to decline in one region, our European ancestors simply moved to new areas. Colonial economics depended on coercive labor practices, using brutal violence as necessary (violent coercion seems almost to be a default setting, a preferential option). This included the multicentury transatlantic slave trade as well as the virtual enslavement of indigenous Americans and widespread use of indentured servitude.

Sven Beckert, in his groundbreaking study of the role of cotton in the world's economy over the past two hundred years, termed this paradigm war capitalism. It involved "new ways of organizing production, trade, and consumption. Slavery, the expropriation of indigenous peoples, imperial expansion, armed trade, and the assertion of sovereignty over people and land" were fundamental in Beckert's view.[43] Granted, we are straining to move beyond this paradigm as we work to incorporate values promoting sustainability, regeneration, and humane, just labor practices. However, we are dealing with the momentum of centuries—momentum that still favors extraction over regeneration. It is very much like attempting to turn a large container ship; there may not be sufficient time before we crash on the shoals. Turning the ship requires envisioning new core values that are transformative. This means changing the fundamental rules of economic life—in effect, changing our paradigm.

Today's global economy is incredibly complex and multilayered. It expresses many values and commitments; some are clear and easy to grasp, while others are hidden, less obvious, and mind-boggling. One of the features that links us clearly with the past is the overall extractive character of market-oriented economics. This has been our approach for over five hundred years. In broad terms, the economic ventures of imperial-colonialism sought to extract wealth and power from natural and human resources. Extraction continues as the thrust and character of economics, utilizing human resources to extract the maximum possible from natural resources, for the sake of survival and profit.

This is not to suggest that economics is intrinsically bad or evil. Economics is foundational to community. We are economic beings (that is not all we are, however). Using human ingenuity and energy to coax the necessities of survival from nature is as old as the species. When we figure out how to generate more than is immediately necessary—create surplus, so to speak—we can plan for tomorrow, create trading relations with others, and enhance the likelihood our community will survive. However, a bias for extraction over other values—for example, ecological regeneration, sustainable production, and communal well-being—seems especially characteristic of what Beckert termed European war capitalism.

When we step back and take stock, it is clear the issue is not whether we are economic beings but how we go about it. What is the fundamental template or model of economic relations that makes sense and is effective? And, especially, what are the rules that guide how this template is implemented? Rules are fundamental in any paradigm, even when implicit and unarticulated. The rules of the European imperial-colonial economic paradigm express a clear bias: extraction and maximized profit over other economic and community values.

Three Illustrations

Large-scale production agriculture (agribusiness), mining, and the associated labor practices are clear illustrations of the fundamental paradigm we have inherited. Following is a brief exploration of agribusiness, mining, and the labor practices that have characterized both.

Production Agriculture

Much has been written about the use of slave labor and indentured servitude in the production of sugar, tobacco, cotton, coffee, and rice. Many of the practices developed in the mass production of these crops continue to influence large-scale agricultural production. Agribusiness enterprises continue to feature monocropping, growing only one crop in an area and using the chemical inputs, labor, and irrigation necessary to maximize production. The intent is to extract the maximum output from the soil. In turn, soil is often viewed as simply a container; chemical inputs deal with weeds, pests, and provide nourishment. In the United States, the federal government has promoted this approach for generations. "Fencerow to fencerow" and "get big or get out" are slogans that, in recent years, conveyed the government's message to farmers. Millions of acres of fertile land were plowed with scant attention to guarding and enhancing the soil's natural fertility. One consequence of this approach was the dust bowl (many factors coincided to produce this ecological disaster; federal agricultural policies were central). It's only in recent years that policy makers and government technocrats have been interested in the notion of regenerative agricultural practices. Many farmers have been clear about the importance of conservation practices for years. But without the support of agricultural policy, including federal subsidies, it was not an approach that was economically viable.

Today's farm operators utilize computer technology to determine the precise amounts of water and inputs necessary, tailoring their approach to the needs of particular crops and even individual plants. Production is much more efficient than previously; yields are higher. But the vagaries of climate and the pressures of the market still make farming very challenging. Federal subsidies tend to favor larger producers; small operators are often at a disadvantage, even with the advantages of computer technology and associated efficiencies.

The extraction paradigm has frequently encouraged labor abuses in agribusiness. In the United States, migrant labor (primarily from Mexico and Central America) has been critical to large growers across the nation in the cultivation and harvesting of lettuce, grapes, potatoes, blueberries, oranges, grapefruit, green bean, sweet corn, sugar beets, and other crops. In recent years, the Department of Labor has routinely brought charges against some large producers for their labor practices. Migrant farm workers have been denied salaries, forced to live in run-down housing (sometimes in dormitories, even, in a recent case, in dilapidated school buses), forced to work long hours, denied bathroom breaks, exposed to harmful farm chemicals, and even kept as virtual prisoners. The formation of the United Farm Workers Union in the 1960s under the leadership of Dolores Huerta and Cesar Chavez is one well-known example of organizing among farm workers. Huerta and Chavez organized grape and lettuce harvesters in the far west. Similar organizing has been done across the Midwest, the Southeast, Southwest, Northwest, and Pacific coast among workers laboring on large, corporately owned farms.

This is not to suggest that all farming enterprises that have used migrant labor have been abusive. There are many that have gone to extremes to protect and provide adequate amenities for farm workers and their families. I am acquainted with farm families that look forward to the annual return of migrant families they have known for years. Such attentiveness tends to be especially characteristic of smaller, family operated farms. However, market pressures in combination with climatic conditions make it challenging to pay farm laborers a living wage. Profit margins suffer when labor costs rise. Small producers especially feel the pinch. Year-to-year survival is often a challenge. Economic viability is precarious and often depends on factors beyond farmers' control. The cyclical mass exodus of small producers from farming illustrates this fundamental fragility.

Dependence on migrant labor is simply a fact of life in American agriculture. Some of the migrant labor that farmers have come to depend on is undocumented. When the federal government attempts to halt illegal immigration, it often means serious labor shortages for America's farmers. Crops go unpicked, and livestock uncared for. Actions initially framed as immigration crackdowns effectively become federal agricultural policy.

Generations of labor practices in large-scale production agriculture express a centuries-old model: extract as much productivity as possible at the least cost. These practices harken back to the time of slavery and indentured servitude. Slavery was clearly superior to indenture relative to maximizing production while minimizing labor costs. It was lifelong (unless an owner emancipated his enslaved people) rather than of predetermined length, as in the case of indenture. Hence it was not necessary to provide land, clothing, or currency upon the completion of a labor contract. A slave labor force was easily replenished. Enslaved people who labored in sugar, rice, and cotton had a markedly higher mortality rate than those who labored in the tobacco fields and coffee groves. It was often viewed as more cost-effective to simply replace enslaved people who died in the fields rather than provide the support systems that would ensure health and safety. Indentured servants were not necessarily treated better than enslaved persons. However, once their contract was fulfilled, they were free. In fact, historical records suggest that in many settings, indentured laborers were treated as harshly as enslaved laborers. Mortality rates were equivalent and, in some cases, even higher.[44]

This rule, maximize production while minimizing labor costs, is fundamental in the extraction bias of the market paradigm we have inherited. Over the years, it has encouraged abusive and coercive labor practices. These practices have run the gamut from outright enslavement, and the associated commodification of human beings, to more subtle forms of coercion, including constantly changing work quotas, debt-peonage, and subminimum wage compensation. When we hear examples of such labor practices in our time, we are shocked and tend to dismiss them as the exception rather than the rule. The most egregious examples may indeed be the exception, but the biases of the market continue to legitimate (even if subtly) labor practices rooted in five hundred years of history.

Mining

Mining has been foundational to our development as a nation. Virtually every product we use in our daily lives is either directly or indirectly the result of mining, including the cars we drive, the fuel they use, the power that lights our homes and keeps us warm, the clothes we wear, the food we eat, the appliances and utensils we cook with, and the laptop I am using to write this book. The objective of mining, whatever the material mined, is maximized extraction. Traditionally, a mining enterprise was pursued to the point of exhaustion; the process continued until the substance being mined ran out, regardless of the impact on land and water. This was necessary and reasonable from the perspective of maximized profit. The industry did not prioritize the reparation of the land following the closure of a mine—or, for that matter, mining in a manner that minimized negative environmental impacts. When the government began to press mining enterprises about mountaintop recovery and cleaning up mining sites, resistance was immediate and reluctance persistent. Maximized production meant maximized profits. Mining enterprises became huge, multinational conglomerates with major political influence, from copper mining firms to petroleum companies.

Today's mining companies have produced sophisticated media presentations demonstrating their commitment to reclamation and ecological responsibility. Be that as it may, mining remains one of the most dangerous occupations and one of the most ecologically impactful. I grew up in a small mining town in eastern Arizona. I remember vividly the scarred hillsides resulting from open-pit mining and the abandoned mine shafts that peppered the hills around our town, as well as the polluted streams. Smoke from the smelters would occasionally blanket our town, making outdoor activities almost impossible. Once I was running in a track meet when the wind shifted, and thick, sulfurous smoke wafted across the field. Runners were momentarily blanketed; I remember an intense burning sensation in my lungs as I ran. Once started, races typically aren't stopped, so we ran our mile run to completion, notwithstanding the noxious fumes.

Some argue that mining companies today are more ecologically responsive. But their fundamental commitment is still maximized extraction; environmental practices result from public pressure and government regulations. This is not to say that mining enterprises are essentially evil; they are central to the world we live in. It is simply to point out that mining is linked to the past and expresses the fundamental extractive character of our economic paradigm. Companies invest in and incorporate regenerative practices in direct proportion to what the public and governments require. When governments can be corrupted, or oversight is minimal, mining enterprises tend to overlook ecological consequences, community impacts, and, in some cases, even safety concerns.

Mining has frequently been the focus of intense labor struggles. Maximizing profit meant minimizing labor costs. Increased productivity often meant direct as well as subtle coercion. The intent was to extract as much from the labor force as possible, while minimizing the cost of doing so. Prior to and during the Civil War, slave labor was used in the iron mines in the South; after the collapse of Reconstruction, prison labor, primarily African American men imprisoned under vagrancy laws, was used in the mines.

Some of our nation's most difficult and violent labor struggles involved miners and mining companies. The Battle of Blair Mountain in West Virginia in 1921 is perhaps among the better known. Some ten thousand coal miners fought a pitched gun battle lasting several days with the security forces of nearby coal mines. The battle was ended only by the intervention of federal troops. It is notable that many of the miners involved were African American. Labor has not always breached the walls of race in its organizing efforts. The labor action at Blair Mountain was an exception. It was the culmination of years of organizing against the abuse of miners and their families by mining companies. The struggle of West Virginia coal miners is further dramatized in the movie *Matewan*, based on actual events in the mining town of Matewan, West Virginia, in 1920.[45]

In the Southwest, Mexican American miners working in copper, zinc, lead, tin, and manganese mines were frequently involved in labor actions in an effort to improve working conditions in the mines. One well-known example was the organizing done at a zinc mine near Silver City, New Mexico, in the early 1950s. This effort was dramatized in a feature-length movie titled *Salt of the Earth*.[46] The film was co-produced by the International Union of Mine, Mill and Smelter Workers and the Independent Productions Corporation. At the time, it was roundly criticized as being Communist propaganda. Some union organizers may well have been Communists or had Communist sympathies; nonetheless, the film accurately dramatized working conditions and the organizing efforts of the miners and their wives and families. The film also powerfully illuminated the intersection of race, class, and gender. It was shown in union halls and a few local theatres across the Southwest. It was so controversial at the time that the careers of some of the actors involved were ruined as a consequence of the anti-Communist hysteria of the day (in particular, the Mexican actress who played the female lead).

Factory workers have been organized in much of the nation for decades—especially in the Northeast, upper Midwest, and far west. Labor unions have been responsible for assuring a living wage and good working conditions in most industries. Corporations that move operations to regions with cheaper labor costs typically resist union organizing intensely. The prospect of a unionized workforce suggests higher production costs, thus undermining, in the view of many corporations, the viability of new factories. The difficult history of labor relations in our nation makes the prospect of a collaborative working relationship between organized labor and management often seems unimaginable.

Traditional labor practices tend to mirror the extractive character of the imperial-colonial economic paradigm. The workplace extracts the maximum output at the lowest cost possible. In our day, many companies are sensitive to the need for the workplace to be more humane. Supportive services such as childcare, workout rooms, and even clinics are typical of some large corporations. These corporations have learned that employee longevity and satisfaction enhance the bottom line. Others, however, continue to follow the rules of the extractive paradigm, thereby making workplace organizing necessary as well as challenging. Even in a time of strong antiunion sentiment, the labor movement in our nation continues to play a crucial role in workplace safety, livable wages, and meaningful employee engagement. Labor unions have not always been at the forefront in the struggle for racial and gender justice, but their commitment to fairness and worker empowerment continues to prod them into working for inclusive economic and social justice. They have been a crucial factor in shaping today's society with all of its gifts and challenges.

In summary, we can conclude that the imperial-colonial enterprise developed an extractive economic paradigm driven by the profit motive, the desire for national/imperial influence, and the belief that natural and human resources were expendable and inexhaustible. For much of the past five hundred years, military might and violence have been part and parcel of global economics. Even as we strive to imagine and shape economic activities that are regenerative, sustainable, and enhance the common good, this past history continues to influence us. But not only is it our past; it is alive in today's globalizing economies. The past lives. And it lives in ways that continue to pay interest and dividends on our original national investment in race and the associated oppression systems.

The New Nation

Our national history is like a richly colored, multilayered tapestry. However, when many of us tell our story, we tend to simplify the telling and focus on the struggle for independence from Great Britain and the irrepressible courage of the settlers who enfleshed the nation's Manifest Destiny. We do not tell the story from the perspective of communities of color. We also tell our story as if we are the Americans, even though we are only one nation of several in the Americas. We have claimed American as our nationality; the name refers to us, not to Brazilians, Argentinians, Chileans, Mexicans, or Canadians. And over time, we taught the rest of the world that this is our identity.

When we severed colonial ties with Great Britain, we ceased to see ourselves as British. We might have termed them our "cousins" when feeling magnanimous. Over time, we even ceased to see ourselves as European. The Europeans lived "over there." Our European roots were our past. While we did indeed remember them and could name our ethnic backgrounds, we had moved beyond them. What were we? Who, indeed, did the term American refer to? It did not refer to enslaved or freed Africans; it would take a civil war and intense political struggle before the sons and daughters of Africa could claim citizenship. Neither did it refer to American Indians; it would be 1924 before all Indian people within the United States were recognized as citizens. This was more than thirty-five years after the General Allotment Act and the sanctioned theft of millions of acres of tribal land. It did not refer to people termed mulatto, Melungeon, Redbone, Yellow Hammers, or Caramel Indians. American referred to white people. Who were the white people? For a time in our history, the "white camp" did not include the Irish, Italians, Jews, Greeks, or Eastern Europeans. European immigrants had to earn their way into the terrain of white identity; this meant spending time in a sort of sociological purgatory, neither this nor that. Neither did the term white refer to Asians: Chinese, "Hindus," Japanese, Filipinos, or Middle Easterners.

We developed as a nation with an apartheid vision at its core. We legally sanctioned the separation of communities based on race. From the beginning, we internalized values that justified commodification of human beings and efforts to wipe others from the face of the earth. Thus, 241 years after the Declaration of Independence, we have yet to live into our professed vision of nationhood. We are at the same time a nation of aspiration and a nation with stealthy commitments to callous brutality. We are the land of the free and the home of the brave; we believe in freedom and justice for all. We are also the land of Indian Removal, boarding schools for Indian children, and Wounded Knee; the land of Jim Crow, segregation, and lynching. We are the land of exclusion, internment, and restrictive covenants. We are so sensitive about our identity that those among us who point out the stealthy brutality of our national character are viewed as unpatriotic troublemakers or perhaps bleeding-heart liberals. (Of course, our brutality is only stealthy to white people. It has always been obvious to others.) Thus, we have developed as a nation with two faces, a dual identity. This dual identity—aspirational and brutal—was, in a manner of speaking, juxtaposed with our intentional dual investment in slave labor and Indian disappearance.

The architecture of our society includes power dynamics that still stack the deck and unlevel the playing field. This stacking even cuts across the fundamental dynamics among class, gender, and race. The "deal" that was made in colonial times that bound wealthy planters and poor and working-class whites together still holds. Many low-income white

Americans continue to believe that their best interests are served by the wealthy and those who control the functions of systemic power. When push comes to shove, race trumps class and gender; the belief that we can trust wealthy white men to have our backs is about race. Put in other words, it is about the way class and gender intersect in race.

How did this come to be? How did this dialectic of aspiration and brutality become our national character? These questions require us to review some of the events, motifs, and people that were present at the birth of the nation. Many scholars have written in great detail about the historical context, the social dynamics, and the individuals involved in our War for Independence and its aftermath. What follows is a brief examination of some of the connections and events that illuminate our dual identity.

Postindependence: The New Nation Takes Shape

Ruth G. and Alfred W. Blumrosen, in their careful examination of the politics involved in the Declaration of Independence, the work of the Continental Congress, and the framing of the Constitution suggest that we, as a nation, were prepared to build an economy based on slave labor from the very beginning.[47] The colonial economies fueled by slave labor were crucial to the struggle for independence from Britain. Virginia, especially, was an economic powerhouse that the Northern colonies could not afford to alienate if resistance to Britain was to be successful. As noted previously, it's more than coincidence that four of the first five US presidents were Virginians and that the voices of Southerners were quite influential in the councils and debates that shaped our emerging national character.

Even the Northern colonies, however, were deeply complicit in the slave trade and in providing practical support to slave-holding planters. We previously noted that Northern shipyards built the ships used in the transatlantic slave trade; Northern sailors sailed the vessels; Northern factories produced the clothing, tools, and foodstuffs Southern planters depended on. This complicity was, after all, good business. It turned a profit. Some wealthy New England families even owned sugar plantations in the Caribbean.

The compromises that guaranteed slavery would be protected began with the Committees of Correspondence that bound the colonies together in common cause against Britain. Initiated by Virginia, a committee was organized in each of the original colonies. These served to link the colonies together in their common struggle with Great Britain. The committees formed the Continental Congress and were instrumental in selecting representatives to the Constitutional Convention. The Blumrosens suggest that the impotence of the federal government as well as the weakness of state governments created a postwar crisis.[48] Virginia called for a convention in Philadelphia to amend the Articles of Confederation, with the hope of creating a stronger federal government. Eventually, twelve states agreed, and the Constitutional Convention began in Philadelphia in May 1787, even as the Continental Congress was meeting in New York.

The compromises about slavery were crafted by men we remember as the fathers of the nation and as exemplars of wisdom, bravery, and commitment. They were also complicit from the beginning in ensuring the centrality of slavery to the nation. They were men of their times who simply presumed the legitimacy of some social realities; slavery was one of these realities. Some of these men found slavery distasteful; some, like Franklin, had become abolitionists. Others, like Jefferson, were deeply involved in the slave system yet were troubled by its impact on the new nation and its future. However, they all knew it generated the wealth necessary for a successful struggle for independence. They were effectively bound by commitments others before them made. It would have taken unusual imagination, nerve, and political skill for things to be different. Perhaps the weight of history and the needs of the moment seemed too great.

Antislavery delegates from Northern states at these two monumental gatherings, the Continental Congress and the Constitutional Convention, were not simply expressing moral outrage and abolitionist sympathies. They were also working from recognition of economic interests. Representatives of the Northern states sought to protect settlers in the Northwest from having to compete with slave labor, which many assumed would devalue the labor of "free men." The Blumrosens make a compelling case for the commitment to protect Northern settlers in the Northwest Territories from "unfair" competition with slave-owning land developers.

By the same token, delegates from the Southern states presumed that the southwest was the direction that the new nation would expand. James

Monroe (also a Virginian) had visited the Northwest and concluded it was not prime agricultural land. It was taken for granted that the task of clearing and planting new territory required slave labor.

The passage of the Northwest Ordinance by the Continental Congress in the summer of 1787 enabled the resolution of the stalemate that had developed at the Constitutional Convention regarding the makeup of the two houses of Congress. The ordinance was a compromise designed to protect the interests of both the Northern states and the Southern states. It specified that slavery would not be allowed in the territories north of the Ohio but explicitly stated nothing about slavery south of the Ohio. In effect, the ordinance protected slavery in existing states and opened the way for the expansion of slavery into new states to the west and south. Once it was clear that slavery in the Southern states would be protected and that slavery would not be permitted in new states in the Northwest Territory, then the constitutional delegates were free to support a Senate based on equal representation and a House based on proportional representation. This proportional representation would be arrived at by totaling all free people and three-fifths of all others (excepting Indians). This gave the Southern states, with their large enslaved population, the largest delegations to the House of Representatives.

The historian Don Fehrenbacher concluded that the Constitution was essentially neutral on the matter of slavery. It neither prohibited nor required slavery in any of the states. The reference to slavery was indirect with the infamous three-fifths clause. By saying nothing explicitly regarding slavery, the document tacitly allowed slavery. Slavery, after all, was a fact of life in Southern states. Due to its economic importance, it was presumed to be simply a fact of life in the new nation—a necessary, albeit distasteful fact. Fehrenbacher further concluded that since the Constitution strengthened the power of the federal government, it had both proslavery and antislavery potential. For the first seventy years of our national life, the power of the federal government seemed to favor a proslavery position.[49]

In 1787, the new nation was thus intimately bound to slave labor; those who were struggling to shape its legal contours entered into compromises that effectively protected slavery. Many could not imagine a nation without slave labor. Just as unity was necessary to successfully sever the colonial relation with Britain, delegates believed that union was fundamental to survival as a nation. The Blumrosens suggest that the Northwest Ordinance was "an extraordinary act of statesmanship" that preserved the union;

however, it also effectively extended the life of slavery another seventy-eight years.[50] It expressed the young nation's decision to invest in human degradation as the price of unity, a price to be paid by generations of Africans in America. It might be said that this price was a down payment on today's society—a down payment whose terms were written in blood.

Echoes of the Doctrine of Discovery

The language of the Northwest Ordinance also presumed the right to expand the new United States north and west of the Ohio River. The postwar Treaty of Paris in 1783 ceded this area to the United States. Clearly both Great Britain and the new United States assumed the right to give, take, and occupy this region. It never occurred to either the new Americans or the British that those living in this area might have other thoughts. The operating presumption apparently was that the Indian people inhabiting these lands were occupiers but not legitimate owners. They need not be consulted. They would have to be dealt with, but the cession was not their business. This presumption was effectively a three-hundred-year-old echo, a reverberation of the Doctrine of Discovery that previously initiated the European invasion of the Americas.

Some of the states formed from the original British colonies (Massachusetts, Connecticut, Virginia, the Carolinas, and Georgia) claimed vast areas of land beyond their western borders. The other states would not sign the Articles of Confederation until these states agreed to cede their claims to the new Congress. Consequently, the Articles were not signed by all the states until 1781, following the cession of land claims by the aforementioned states to the Congress. These cessions effectively meant that the Northwest would eventually become new states rather than simply an expansion of some existing states. Again, the presumption was that the future status of this area was a matter for the Continental Congress to decide on behalf of the new nation. The indigenous residents of the area had no say in the matter.

Indigenous resistance to the westward expansion of the new United States was persistent and creative. While the Northwest Ordinance was being shaped, the Shawnees and their allies were assiduously working to keep white settlers south of the Ohio and from expanding into the regions between the new states and the Mississippi River. Their organizing efforts extended as far south as the current states of Alabama, Mississippi, and Georgia. In May 1787, a gathering at the Creek town of Little Tallassee (in current-day Alabama) included representatives of the Iroquois, Huron, Mohawk, Oneida, and Shawnee nations. Gregory Dowd suggests that this was probably the time of greatest unity among the Eastern Woodland tribes, as they sought to impede the western expansion of the Americans.[51] In September 1792, representatives of some fifteen Indian nations met in council on a plain known as the Glaize near present-day Defiance, Ohio. Previously, in 1791, an Indian force comprised of nine different nations defeated an American force of 1,400 commanded by General Arthur St. Claire. The battle took place near Fort Jefferson, north of present-day Cincinnati. This loss was the most lethal suffered by American troops against Indian forces. Some 630 US soldiers were killed or missing (and presumed captured).

In subsequent negotiations with the Americans, Indian nations continued to insist on the Ohio River as the northern boundary of American expansion. The language of the Northwest Ordinance made it clear that the settlement of the Ohio Valley and environs by Americans was a foregone conclusion, with or without the compliance of the Shawnee and other Indian nations. American negotiators simply would not accept the Indian position. The result was continued warfare; the Americans were resolved to open up lands north and west of the Ohio to settlement.

In August 1794, a three-thousand-man force commanded by Anthony Wayne successfully broke Indian resistance. In the aftermath of victory, the Americans built a series of forts from Cincinnati to present-day Fort Wayne, Indiana. From these posts, forays into the countryside destroyed villages, burned fields, and effectively reduced Indian settlements to ruins and their inhabitants to starvation. In the Treaty of Greenville in the summer of 1795, Indian people came to terms with the Americans. The treaty gave the Americans virtually all of what is now southern, central, and eastern Ohio. The Shawnees and their allies were left with the northwestern corner of today's state. It would be another ten years before militant leadership among Indian nations would once again rise to thwart the northern and westward expansion of the new nation.

Ironically, the third article of the Northwest Ordinance stated, "The utmost good faith shall always be observed towards the Indians; their lands and property shall never be taken from them without their consent; and in their property, rights and liberty, they never shall be invaded or disturbed, unless in just and lawful wars authorised by Congress; but laws found in justice and humanity shall from time to time be made, for preventing wrongs being done to them, and for preserving peace and friendship with them."[52] However, it was force of arms that opened the Northwest Territory to settlement, in spite of language in the ordinance calling for justice and respect for Indians.

In a cynical vein, one might even suspect that this language was intended to provide moral cover for subsequent events. Some scholars suggest it was added to the ordinance in order to gain the support of delegates who were advocates of Native rights. Whatever the case might have been, settlement of the new Northwest Territories required difficult and bloody warfare over many years. There seems little, if any, evidence that the language of the third article had any impact on events north of the Ohio River. Rather, the ghostly presence of the Doctrine of Discovery was a constant in the violent conquest of the Northwest.

In the South, civil war within the Creek Confederacy pitted the Red Stick of the Upper Creek Confederacy against the various groups known as the Lower Creek. The Red Sticks had heeded Tecumseh's call to take up arms against the Americans; however, most of the confederacy chose to remain neutral or even sided with the Americans. In the Battle of Horseshoe Bend on March 27, 1814, an American and Indian force under the command of Colonel Andrew Jackson of the Tennessee Militia defeated the Red Sticks and killed the majority of the defenders of the Red Stick fortress. Many of the remaining Red Sticks made their way to Florida and joined with the Seminoles in continuing resistance to the Americans. The Battle of Horseshoe Bend marked the virtual end of armed resistance to the Americans in the Southeast north of Florida.

The experience of armed resistance by indigenous nations and the costly struggles that followed were instrumental in crystalizing American resolve toward indigenous people. All the indigenous groups that had made the lands east of the Mississippi home for centuries had to go. Removal seemed the only sensible solution to the tensions arising from a burgeoning white population and the many tribal groups they encountered. Some sixteen years after the Battle of Horseshoe Bend, President Andrew Jackson's administration successfully shepherded the Indian Removal Act through Congress. This legislative achievement gave a singular focus to American Indian policy and contextualized federal efforts toward Indian people for decades to come.[53]

The Removal Act authorized the federal government to enter into treaties with Indian nations residing east of the Mississippi River in order to *remove* them westward to what was termed *Indian Country* (present-day Oklahoma). Removal treaties split tribes and generated intense intratribal conflicts. Some nations were removed without treaties; some, like the Cherokees, resisted and were forcibly removed. The Choctaws in Mississippi were the first to be removed. Their removal gave birth to the term "Trail of Tears." The term is most often associated with Cherokee removal; however, it aptly describes the experience of virtually every Indian community that was removed. The death rate on the journey to Indian Territory from disease, exposure, starvation, and exhaustion was appalling. Removal meant that *disappearance* had, indeed, become the nation's primary intent regarding indigenous nations. Even though the nation continued to enter into treaties with Indian nations for another forty-one years, the Removal Act signaled the use of force, violent when necessary, as the preferential option for dealing with Indian people. It presaged the congressional action ending treaty making in 1871.

The Two Faces of America

Thus, the new nation was simultaneously a land of soaring aspiration and almost wanton brutality. We sought to embody a new vision of nationhood, even as our national enterprise continued the brutal coercion of labor, the commodification of human beings, and the violent expropriation of land and natural resources. In a letter to his friend, John Holmes in 1820, the aging Thomas Jefferson noted, "We have the wolf by the ear, and can neither hold him, nor safely let him go."[54] Jefferson felt that our investment in slavery effectively jeopardized the nation's future. The aspirational language of the Declaration of Independence notwithstanding, the careful wordsmithing in the Constitution masked our national commitment to slavery. In similar fashion, the Northwest Ordinance and the Indian Removal Act were neither straightforward nor transparent regarding our intent to uproot, remove, and *disappear* Indian nations. Both of the new nation's faces expressed foundational commitments. Our dual identity was rooted in a fundamental contradiction at the deepest levels of national life. This contradiction is cast in bold relief by our willing investment in racial oppression.

The Peaks of a Submarine Range

8

Our Investment: Continuing Dividends

In this chapter, we will further explore our nation's original and continuing investment in racial oppression—and the interest and dividends paid over the years up to our present day. This investment freights the wrenching pathos of our history. It places our dual character—aspiration and brutality—in sharp relief. We'll summarize a few of the federal government's actions that effectively represent and express the dividends our investment paid over the years. The chapter concludes with commentary regarding present-day interest and dividends: the *perks* of white supremacy.

A Submarine Range and Its Peaks

If we imagine our national history as an ocean, then race would be a submarine mountain range traversing the entire ocean. Its peaks would jut above the surface like mountainous islands, seemingly separate and isolated but in reality simply part of the hidden range. The peaks, to continue the metaphor, would be those momentous events that catch our attention and dramatically express what lies beneath. We begin this chapter with a brief recounting of a few of those peaks that jut out of our historical sea. These events are especially noteworthy because they express actions of the federal government, indicating our official appropriation of race. They express our ongoing investment in race and, hence, in racial oppression.

Clearly, there are many dramatic events in our history that involve movements of people, individual actors, major struggles, episodes of stark brutality and suppression, as well as moments of exhilaration and victorious struggles. Many of these events may be unfamiliar to most of us. The work of bringing them to light is crucial and ongoing. However, I've chosen to highlight events that underscore the role of law and the federal government in the dynamics of racial oppression. This brings a crucial perspective to our effort to understand and respond to our multigenerational investment in race.

Part of our national narrative is that we are a nation of laws—that we believe in the rule of law. This narrative suggests that the law is neutral and objective, perhaps even color-blind. It may be misused but is not, in itself, problematic. However, there are persuasive voices that suggest this perspective is not entirely accurate. There is more to say. Ian Haney Lopez, in his influential book *White by Law: The Legal Construction of Race*, suggests there is a great deal more to say. Lopez documents the role of legislative action and judicial decision-making in constructing and centering race in our society. He notes, "Through law, race becomes real becomes law becomes race in a self-perpetuating pattern ..."[64] His research illuminates the ways that racial ideology has been impactful from the early days until current times in shaping our legal framework. Lopez further notes that law, consequently, not only enforces racial ideology but creates racial ideology and reinforces common belief in it. While many other social factors play a part of the formation of racial identity, law plays a critical role in shaping and spelling out the social significance of racial identity, thereby embedding it even more deeply in the social fabric.

The following illustrations are a few examples of the role of law in the history of racial oppression in our nation. These illustrations single out actions by our federal government—congressional, presidential, or judicial—that express our ongoing investment in the politics, economics, and culture of race. I will summarize each very briefly. These are but a few illustrations; it would take several volumes to thoroughly explore the participation of the federal government in shaping and promoting racial oppression.

The federal government has also played a role in ferreting out and nullifying the power of race in response to social movements and local organizing. Each of these illustrations of our historical investment stimulated vigorous resistance. Each stimulated a flurry of counter organizing and antiracist activity. Some of this resistance resulted in legislative, judicial, or presidential action that dramatically or partially deconstructed the legal codification of race. Many of these actions are well-known (such as the SCOTUS decision *Brown v. the Topeka, Kansas, Board of Education,* the Civil Rights Act of 1964; the Voting Rights Act of 1965). Many others are less known or even forgotten. My primary intent in this chapter is to note federal participation in legalizing race and racial oppression as part of the process of sanctioning our investment. Each of these illustrations is an outcropping of the same submarine range; upon examination, each provides access to the same deep, molten Geist: the Geist of racialization. They disclose the contours of white supremacy.

Indian Removal Act of 1830

This act was the legislative jewel of Andrew Jackson's first term. It was the central plank of his campaign in the election of 1828. This act gave the federal government authority to enter into treaties with tribes located east of the Mississippi in order to remove them to Indian Country (present-day Oklahoma and Kansas).[65] The act was the pivotal piece of legislation regarding Indian nations until the Dawes Act of 1887 (General Allotment Act). It signaled the nation's intent to remove, confine, and disappear Indian nations. It also contextualized and effected all subsequent policy decisions regarding Indian people. It opened up land for settlement and agriculture—land that was previously occupied by Indian nations. It was an indication that the federal government did not view Indian nations as truly sovereign. Treaty making was expeditious. Our government would continue entering into treaties with Indian nations for several years. But the Removal treaties were a bit of a sham; tribal groups that resisted entering into Removal treaties were simply forcibly removed. There were those who simply refused—some groups of Seminoles in Florida, for example. The policy objective, however, was consistent: removal, by whatever mean necessary.

The Annexation of Texas and War with Mexico

When Congress annexed the Republic of Texas, it set the stage for the Mexican War. Following Texas's fight for independence, there was widespread popular support, and congressional support, for annexation. Mexico, of course, could not sit by and allow this. Annexation left the Mexican government with no choice; it had to be war.

Mexico had originally invited immigration from the southern US to Texas. The territory of Texas was huge and severely underpopulated. It was also far removed from Ciudad Mexico, the administrative capital of the new Mexican nation. Mexico had outlawed slavery. Many of the new southern immigrants brought enslaved Africans with them to Texas, intending to grow cotton. Thus, Mexican law placed their property at risk. The central government of Mexico struggled with political instability, a weak economy, and resistance to central authority in several of its far-flung regions. When Texans opted for independence, the Mexican government simply could not muster sufficient resources to block their efforts, notwithstanding the success of General Santa Anna at the Alamo.

Annexation of newly independent Texas by the United States gave Mexico the option of war or acquiescence. The struggle was unequal from the beginning—the end result a foregone conclusion (although General Santa Ana stated that if he had one more division of San Patricios—US soldiers who were Catholic immigrants of Irish and German descent who deserted to fight with the Mexicans—things might have turned out differently). From the beginning, the US assumed that mixed-race Mexicans were no match for white American soldiers. It was commonly assumed that racial hybridization produced racial mongrels who were essentially inferior to white, racially pure people.

The Treaty of Guadalupe Hidalgo

The Treaty of Guadalupe Hidalgo in 1848 dramatically expanded the territory of the United States. We gained virtually all of the current-day Southwest: Texas, New Mexico, Colorado, Utah, Nevada, Arizona, as well as California. We paid Mexico the sum of $15 million for nearly 55 percent of her territory. The treaty guaranteed Mexican citizens living in the conquered territories that their culture and their possessions would be respected and that they had a year to decide whether to become Americans or remain Mexican and relocate to Mexican territory. Of course, these agreements were not honored, and Mexican citizens very quickly became second-class citizens in the new US territories and states.

Indian Appropriations Act of 1851 (The Reservation Act)

This was the first of two innocuous bills appropriating federal money to implement policy. The Act of 1851 (also known as the Reservation Act) appropriated funds to settle western tribes on clearly defined reservations, in order to effectively control their activities, thus assuring they would not impede western movement and settlement. It was apparently presumed that whatever resistance tribes might have to being confined could be overcome, by military force if necessary. Some of the rhetoric employed to pass this act suggested that reservationizing Indian people was for their own protection and, in the final analysis, in their own best interest.

Dred Scott Decision of the US Supreme Court (1857)

Scott was an enslaved man of African descent who had brought suit alleging his emancipation because one of his owners had taken him to states prohibiting slavery. The court determined that Dred Scott, by virtue of his race, was not eligible for citizenship. Chief Justice Taney, in his summary of the majority opinion, wrote that people of African descent, *whether enslaved or free*, "had no rights which the white man was bound to respect; and that the Negro might justly and lawfully be reduced to slavery for his benefit. He was bought and sold and treated as an ordinary article of merchandise and traffic, whenever profit could be made by it."[66] The decision sent a very clear message to Africans in the nation, whether free or enslaved: *There is no future for you in this nation. You do not and will never qualify for citizenship.*

The court also declared the Missouri Compromise of 1820 unconstitutional. The compromise presumed and continued the thinking written into the Northwest Ordinance that prohibited slavery in new states north and west of the Ohio River. It simply altered the boundary of slavery's northward spread; Missouri was admitted to the Union as a slave state, and Maine was admitted as a free state. In stating that Congress did not have the authority to craft such a compromise, the court effectively opened up the nation to slavery. Thus, even though Scott's owners had indeed taken him to states where slavery was not practiced, this did not free him. He was private property, and this ownership had to be respected regardless of where his owners might take him in the United States. In the *Dred Scott* decision, SCOTUS made the national rupture of 1861 nearly inevitable.

The court's judgment was not about the constitutionality of slavery, as such, but rather about race and citizenship. Thus, the decision reinforced and strengthened a manufactured social identity, a racial identity. It was a racial identity that had been under construction for many generations, a construction process intimately connected with the economic, political, and cultural development of the nation. This decision linked slavery to racial identity and, at the same time, distinguished the two. It seems to support Don Fehrenbacher's conclusion that the Civil War was about race, not slavery. The two are distinct.

As a nation, we learned to associate enslavement and racial identity: black people were essentially fit for slavery. Hence, even when slavery was dismantled by the Thirteenth Amendment, former slaves were still viewed by many as subhuman and inferior to whites. Slavery was the appropriate status for Africans; they were not deserving of freedom and not eligible for citizenship. Thus, when a constitutional amendment following the Civil War made them citizens, it seemed appropriate to pass additional state legislation that maintained them in their appropriate social setting: subservience. This was the role of the Black Codes enacted in many Southern states following the collapse of Reconstruction. It is also a clue regarding contemporary dynamics that continue to disadvantage African Americans.

Indian Appropriations Act of 1871: The End of Treaty Making

In 1871, the US Congress passed legislation ending treaty making with Indian nations and communities.[67] This act was the second innocuous piece of legislation that tends to be lost in conversations about our history. The act was a clear message that, in the eyes of the federal government, Indian nations were not actually independent and sovereign. They were not to be considered equals with the United States. Relations with tribes would henceforth be shaped by congressional action, presidential decisions, and Supreme Court judgments. This legislation made it clear that Congress considered the future of Indian nations to be the federal government's business, with or without the participation of Indian people. It is noteworthy that from Removal times onward, policy decisions regarding Indian nations were frequently framed as an action in the best interest of Indian people. Previously, we pointed out that the Removal Act itself prefigured this legislation. Once Congress decided it could remove tribes in order to make room for white settlement, the die was cast. Treaty making would end as soon as politically feasible.

Chinese Exclusion Act of 1882

The Chinese Exclusion Act of 1882 prohibited further immigration to the United States by Chinese people. The act was re-upped several times by Congress. Originally, a ten-year expiration was written into the act; it was not finally repealed until 1943.[68] The act expressed the suspicion and distaste felt by many Americans for Asian people in general, and Chinese people in particular. Many Chinese had immigrated to the US during the gold frenzy of the 1849–50s; when gold petered out, they migrated up and down the West Coast and encountered a great deal of hostility from the white population, as well as anxiety about the economic threat Chinese people supposedly posed. The Exclusion Act began a process of racialization that stereotyped Asians of all ethnicities as perpetual foreigners.

The General Allotment Act of 1887 (The Dawes Act)

The General Allotment Act of 1887 (the Dawes Act) required Indian tribes to enroll their members in order that each family be allotted a parcel of land. The public relations for the act noted that this was to aid in the assimilation of Indian people into the mainstream (for their own good, of course). Allotment was to help Indians become property-owning Americans and leave behind the common practice of communal ownership of land. Policy makers had long assumed that the practice of communal ownership was the primary roadblock to assimilation of Indian people.

The process of allotment was to be overseen by a federally appointed commission chaired by Senator Dawes, the author of the act.[69] Allotment left millions of acres of surplus land, which the federal government then sold to homesteaders and others, thereby reducing dramatically the land owned by Indian nations. Effectively, it was sanctioned theft of Indian land. Understandably, Indian nations resisted. The federal government used a variety of means, including the threat of military action, to pressure tribes to undergo allotment. In 1934, after tribal lands had been decimated, allotment was rescinded.

Plessy v. Ferguson, 1896

When the court sided with Ferguson in this famous case, it made segregation effectively the law of the land. Not only did the majority decide that segregated facilities are not inherently unequal; it also affirmed that, in the court's view, states have the legal authority to define race and to impose segregation in public facilities. This authority was not limited to Southern states only; hence, the decision provided the highest legal sanction for segregation, nationwide.[70] While many states did not impose segregation in public facilities, forms of subtle, de facto exclusion and segregations became increasingly common across the nation.

The Curtis Act of 1898

The Curtis Act of 1898 withdrew federal sanction of Indian governments in Indian Territory, thereby terminating Indian republics as legal entities in the eyes of the United States. The act mandated allotment and gave tribes two years to negotiate suitable processes for undergoing the allotment process. The federal government, responding to pressure from corporations—most notably the railroads and mining companies—and land-hungry settlers, was able to bring a great deal of pressure on tribes to undergo enrollment and allotment. The Dawes Commission began to issue allotments to the Choctaws, for example, in 1903 (they had previously been awarded US citizenship in 1901).[71]

The Spanish American War, 1898

A contrived war with Spain in 1898 delivered several Spanish colonial territories to the US. It marked a new phase in US expansionism; we began to look beyond our continental shores. The treaty marking the end of the war gave Cuba, Puerto Rico, Guam, and the Philippines to the United States for the sum of $20 million. In 1899, we invaded the Philippines and began an occupation that cost two hundred thousand Filipino lives compared with four thousand US soldiers dead. In 1902, President Roosevelt announced victory in the Philippines. However, resistance to US occupation continued. The invasion of the Philippines marked the extension of US colonial efforts into the western Pacific and Asia.[72]

The Asiatic Barred Zone

The Immigration Act of 1917 prohibited immigration from several classes of undesirable people; it also prohibited virtually all immigration from most of Asia, with the exception of those parts that had been claimed by the US.[73] It represented, in effect, an expansion of the Chinese Exclusion Act of 1882 and reflected popular American sentiment regarding a wide range of Asian ethnic groups. The act set the stage for immigration quotas in the next decade. Its reverberations can be felt in recent efforts by the Trump administration to restrict travel to the United States from several majority Muslim nations.

Japanese Internment

Two months after the Japanese bombing of Pearl Harbor, President Roosevelt issued Executive Order 9066. The order authorized the secretary of war to designate areas within the United States from which designated groups may be excluded for military and security reasons.[74] While the order did not explicitly target any particular ethnic group, it became the basis for the internment of Americans of Japanese ancestry residing on the West Coast, both citizens and legal residents. In March 1942, Lieutenant General John DeWitt (head of the US Army Western Defense Command) declared an exclusion zone along the West Coast and ordered all persons of Japanese descent to report to assembly areas. Some 120,000 people were forced to abandon homes, farms, and businesses and were relocated to ten internment camps across the nation. Some noncitizens were repatriated to Japan.

No comparable order was issued in Hawaii (where roughly 30 percent of the population was of Japanese ancestry); nor was such an order issued against Americans of German or Italian ancestry. The right of the government to intern its citizens was challenged in the US Supreme Court in October 1944. The court decided in December 1944 in *Korematsu v. the United States* that the government acted within its constitutional authority.[75] This controversial decision has been compared to *Plessy v. Ferguson* in terms of its negative impacts. It's also important to remember that many young men and women from the internment camps enlisted in the US military and served with distinction in the European theater.

Citizens in the internment camps were allowed to return to the West Coast beginning in 1945. The last of the camps was closed in 1946. In 1988, the US Congress awarded restitution to survivors of the camps and their families. Each survivor of the camps was to receive $20,000 (a small sum given the scope of the losses families experienced). This concluded one of the most shameful episodes in our history; it was a clear and callous violation of civil liberties and an example of public policy driven by intense racial prejudice reinforced by the anxieties of wartime.

Indian Termination and Relocation

In 1949, a federal commission recommended intensifying efforts to integrate Indian people into American society. It suggested that assimilation was in the best interests of tribal people and that it would save substantial federal funds. Federal programs for Indian people could be cut, as they would no longer be necessary. The Eisenhower administration endorsed this approach to Indian policy. In 1953, Congress adopted House Concurrent Resolution No. 108; the resolution declared that federal benefits and services to Indian tribes be terminated as quickly as possible. Between 1953 and 1966, federal recognition was withdrawn from 109 tribes. The government ended its trust relationship with each, eliminated reservations, and delivered jurisdiction over former Indian lands and people to the respective states. In 1953, Public Law 280 gave criminal jurisdiction over reservations to six states that had large Indian populations. While these efforts were framed as actions in the best interest of Indian people, they effectively accomplished a singular multigenerational policy objective: disappearance. (As noted elsewhere, however, the perseverance of Indian communities and the resilience of tribal cultures are not functions of the permission of the federal government.)

Interest and Dividends

These *peaks*, as it were, pushing through the waters of our history help us discern the underlying mountain range that is simply a ubiquitous aspect of our nation. They represent our underlying investment in racial oppression. Do these historic investments continue to accrue interest and pay dividends in our society? If so, what are they? What is meant by interest and dividends? Dividends are earnings on an investment; they are paid to those who invest in a particular fund. Such earnings may be a function of market value of an investment or of interest accrued on the investment.

In this sense, each of these illustrations of federal action that sanctioned racial oppression is also an example of interest accrued and dividends paid. Each stands on decisions and actions previously taken. Each is an accrual effect, a compounding of previous decisions that strengthened dominant power dynamics of the nation. These outcroppings reveal dividends paid to the white collective; they are a reiteration of and reinforcement of white superiority and therefore white supremacy. Each of these federal actions specified a particular group for whom access was to be denied or restricted—access to the institutions and systems of American life. As we discussed in Part 1, this is racism: the misuse of systemic power.

In Part 1, I suggested that systemic power is fundamentally about access to and control of the institutions of society and their resources. It is also about who has the power to articulate and embroider the underlying social mythos that permeates society's social systems and institutions. Previously, I suggested that because systemic power invokes the aura of legality, it also invokes the presumption of legitimacy. This is especially important and authoritative in a nation that views itself as a nation of laws. This way of viewing ourselves suggests that the law is primary and that the law is neutral and does not favor one group over another, providing, of course, that the groups under consideration obey and follow the law.

A conversation about the dividends our investment has paid and is paying needs to examine the metrics indicating who benefits from our institutions, who has advantageous access, not individually but as a group. This means examining disparities and disproportionalities associated with all the systems of our society and the institutions that comprise them. Many studies have documented these disparities and disproportionalities; they illuminate the role race plays in accessing institutions and the resources they provide. While there clearly are individual differences within and among racial groups, it is demonstrably the case that, in general, those of us who are white enjoy advantageous access. The results of such advantageous access are that we tend to live longer, accumulate more wealth, and have higher educational levels, higher employment rates, fewer dangerous encounters with law enforcement, and access to affordable housing.

Indeed, some systems are, in effect, predatory. Like heat-seeking missiles, they *seek out* individuals and families whose racial identity makes them most vulnerable. Previously, in Part 1, I suggested that payday loan companies, used car companies that charge very high interest rates, and rent-to-own furniture companies are examples of this predatory bent. While these companies suggest they are providing a service that no one else will provide, in fact, they are taking advantage of social realities in ways that are profitable to them. This illustrates the intersection and collusion of race and class. Since it is the case that higher percentages of communities of color live in poverty, this means that a higher percentage of families caught in the snares of high interest rates are in communities of color.

Some systems are, in effect, systems of control. They have inherited a historical role that is about controlling some in order that others are safe. The original purpose of the reservation system, for example, was control. It was about confining Indian nations to defined chunks of geography in order to control their comings and goings. This was to ensure the safety of white Americans, as well as removing Indian people from land desirable to others. When groups of Indian people left the reservation, it was an occasion to call out the US Army or state militia to capture and escort them back. Leaving the reservation was seen as a breakout, in effect an escape from prison. Since Indian people were not yet citizens, it fell to our military system to control them. Protecting the relative safety of white settlers and townspeople was, in effect, a dividend of our original and continuing investments.

The police and the criminal justice system are also an example of this dividend. They are instruments of public safety from the perspective of dominant society. Children are taught that the policeman is their friend (Officer Friendly). From the perspective of many communities of color, however, there is another side that must be understood. Police and the criminal justice system have often been experienced as an instrument of control, often by violent means. When people of color break out of their assigned place (as in a ghetto neighborhood), they are apt to experience harassment, arrest, even violence. Historically, of course, this was due to some communities of color being viewed as a threat to public safety, unless they occupied their accustomed place and role in society.

This is not a question of the integrity of individual officers or even entire departments or officials in the court system. It is a matter of the weight of history and subtle expectations that are built in. It is a matter of the cumulative impact of self-replicating systemic practices. Individually, particular rules, statutes, and practices may not explicitly be about race; but when intersecting with other dynamics, they produce racial disparities. For example, previous sentencing guidelines regarding possession of powdered cocaine versus crack cocaine seemed to make sense, initially. But when implemented, they had a clear disproportionate impact on communities of color. Crack cocaine was usually cheaper, which meant it was more prevalent in poor communities. Poor communities were often made up primarily of people of color. Powdered cocaine was, for some time, a drug of affluent white communities.

While the rhetoric of policing suggests the work is protecting the community from the mischief of criminals, statistics regarding stop and search rates, arrest rates, incarceration rates, and who tends to be most at risk of being shot by the police all raise difficult questions about policing and racial identity. The fact that white parents don't have to worry about giving *the talk* to their children is further evidence of the realities about race and the police (the talk concerns how to behave when stopped by the police. Parents of color, especially African American, Latino, and American Indian, understand this is a matter of life and death).

John Gall's insights about systemic change are helpful in understanding the challenges present in law enforcement with regard to race. The problem does not lie at the level of the actors; rather, the problem lies in the script, which includes instructions about the system's role and rules regarding implementation.[76] Here lies the issue. Further, the script may not be explicit; rather it is present in the accumulated practices over several generations. These practices are multigenerational and effectively maintain deep values regarding whose lives are most valuable. The cumulative weight of history, even in the practices of past actors, has to be explicitly addressed. This means explicitly and directly intervening in the culture of policing in order to embed new values. To reiterate, the issue is not, in the final analysis, individual law enforcement officers; it is the system and, more specifically, the script. When we discuss the role of implicit bias (and even its existence) in an individual officer's actions, we are discussing the internalized script.

Race and Stress

Measurable racial disparities and disproportionalities also reveal a deeper dividend. They occasion stress. The challenges that disadvantageous access creates mean that people of color, as a whole, have more day-to-day stress to deal with. We live in a very stressful and complex society. We all experience the impact of stress. Race simply adds a layer of stress on top of the stress we all experience. When you look at the intersections of oppressions, stress is simply intensified. For example, the intersection of race, class, and gender is especially challenging. Low-income single parents of color find the daily challenges of access especially difficult and incredibly stressful.

As we all know, chronic stress comes with certain costs. It is physiologically harmful. It has predictable health outcomes: high blood pressure, diabetes, learning difficulties, even obesity. Previously, we noted the continuous high levels of cortisol that are associated with race and poverty. High levels of cortisol are especially damaging for young children. Cortisol affects the areas of the brain responsible for memory and appropriating new information.[77]

Let's return, for a moment, to our discussion of policing and the criminal justice system. Police officers are effectively on the front line. Functionally, they are both the protectors of white supremacy and the engineers of a more just society. The weight of history brings baked-in expectations regarding the system's role; community organizers and civil rights activists press concerns for social justice. Consequently, police officers are the recipients of multidirectional expectations that are humanly impossible to deal with. Stress is one consequence. Policing is an incredibly stressful occupation and one that entails significant health risks (not simply from the personal danger involved). It is not difficult to understand that many police officers feel scapegoated and that they are being required to account for something they may not be personally invested in. This is part and parcel of what it means to suggest that the issue is systemic.

The Dividends of Race for White People

The dividends of race accrue to those of us who are white and consequently experience advantageous access. This is true across the board in spite of all the disparate ways we experience our racial place. These dividends continue to accrue, even though we are generations removed from the original investment. However, they are not accruing at a constant rate. Like compound interest, they mount up. They are cumulative over time. These are the dividends that together are grouped under the terminology of white privilege.

These dividends are important. They make a difference. They are not inconsequential or incidental. They amount to a lifetime of micro affirmations. They are a consistent counterpoint to the daily microaggressions experienced by people of color and others whose social identity marginalizes them. The experience of microaggressions is directly related to the misuse of systemic power, as is the experience of micro affirmations.

Those of us who are white can all think of exceptions to the previous comments. We may have family members who don't seem to receive the benefits of being white; we may know entire families, even communities, that seem beyond the pale of white privilege. The impact of class is real. Certainly the opioid crisis of our moment is apparently most damaging in rural white communities, especially those experiencing economic stress. That is why it is crucial to be clear about the historic, multigenerational advantages of white identity, and why it is important that we speak about the white collective as a whole. As the old saying goes, "if you're white, you're right"—at least relatively speaking (when compared with communities of color, in general).

There are many scholars, social commentators, writers, and artists who have been educating us for years about the experience and scope of white privilege. The list is quite long: Peggy McIntosh, Tim Wise, Toni Morrison, Robin DiAngelo, and more. It is a conversation we have been having for at least thirty years. Nonetheless, the daily barrage of data and images from various media continue to reinforce images of white identity as normative, even when these images are subtly adjusted to account for generalized changes in perception—having gay neighbors or seeing women in leadership roles.

Perhaps, the core dividend that accrues to white people is the experience of being normal. We inhabit a terrain whose parameters are sketched out by social norms. We experience these norms, in effect, living in us. These include standards of beauty, definition of family, acceptable sexual expression and preference, gender roles, and gender characteristics. We have been *normed*. Social norms birth expectations. They make life familiar and predictable.

One of the roles of media is to shape visual representations of this terrain. The result is that we live in echo chambers that constantly bombard us with images shaped by social norms. These images, in turn, indicate acceptable behavior and attitudes. Even the echo chambers that dramatize changing norms still tend to be racially framed. They still make clear who is at home in the terrain. These echo chambers are in effect racial theater. They are long-running productions. We view snatches of them whenever we watch television programs, including commercials. We will explore the echo chamber phenomenon more thoroughly in chapter 10.

Some of the social stress that expresses itself politically is the result of many of these norms undergoing fundamental change. Many of us experience changing norms as a personal assault. It feels like we are under attack. When norms are changing, those whose lives are most tightly shaped by these norms experience angst and insecurity. Thus, even while we live in the terrain of normalcy, we experience a rumbling underneath and deterioration at the edges. We may even remember the way things used to be with nostalgia. When a political candidate comes along who skillfully capitalizes on our angst, reassuring us that he (or she) can make things as they were—great again, so to speak—there will be a powerful pull to gamble on him.

However, this desire to bring back the past is not a desire for the America of our aspirations; it is a desire to return to the nostalgic comfort (for some) of white supremacy. It is an endorsement of the troubling side of our national persona, the side of callous brutality (even if we refuse to see this aspect of our character). What does this temptation to opt for the familiar, with all its racial trappings, tell us about who we are and where we live? What, especially, does it tell us about the white collective—the centered, normalized social identity whose edges are indistinct, fuzzy, and sometimes concealed? These are crucial questions we shall have to unpack.

Therefore, What Are We to Do?

We cannot undo what was done in the name of God, Christ, national glory, profit, and even independence. But we can transform its significance and the shape of its continuing impact on future generations. Some may indeed decide that our history was filled with such evil and injustice that they want nothing to do with it. There is a great temptation to simply view the past through the lens of rigid ideology and dismiss the deeds done as not worthy of our time. Others may choose amnesia over lucidity. However, we are where we are, and where we are is the result of the past, all of it. Where do we go from here? That is the question. We can move from no other place than this time and this space, even if we buy into the ideologies that glorify, excuse, or demonize the past.

Answering this question requires some additional work; it requires a visit to the interior recesses of white consciousness. Perhaps such a visit will enable us to discern the impact of our historical investment in racial oppression on white people. We can quantify what it continues to do to people of color; many have written about its impact on self-image and the price of survival it exacts. Some have written persuasively about white privilege and its impact on white people's expectations and sense of value. Now, let's see if we can get underneath the rhetoric and explore its deathly impact on those of us who are white.

PART III

THE COST OF WHITE SUPREMACY

In part 3, we will examine the impact of this nation's historical investment in racial oppression on white people. Clearly this investment has hurt people of color. It is not as clear that this investment also hurts white people. I will make the case that its impact on white people has been especially pernicious and hidden. Further, because it is hidden, it works a good bit of mischief. We will explore the architecture of white supremacy, the way this architecture is experienced by white people, the collective identity this architecture fashions, and the pathology it engenders that jeopardizes the nation's future.

It is my intent to speak as forthrightly and honestly as possible. Since this subject matter is rarely discussed in most circles and tends to be hidden, some commentary about method is important. My approach to social analysis in this section can be termed phenomenological: writing about us through the filter and litmus of my own experience. Some might term this as an existential approach. This approach requires a mixture of humility and boldness. I do not wish to project my baggage upon others; nor do I presume that others' experience is the same as mine, or that it means the same. Neither, however, do I want this work to be abstract. My intent is to talk about us in a manner that connects to others' experience. This does presume that the particularities of my experience connect to and touch some deep commonalities that will resonate with others. Thus, I speak about us from my space as a straight (cisgender), white, aging male with a graduate degree, solidly middle income, of a progressive political bent, functionally bilingual, with Choctaw and African strands in my genetic heritage (I mention these as they would have made me nonwhite had I lived at a different time in our history).

Racialization creates racial collectives by assigning individuals a racial identity. In turn, racial collectives weave a shared consciousness, born out of shared experiences and common mythology that interprets these experiences. This is the context that validates a phenomenological approach: my interpretations of my experience also reflect a shared consciousness, a common water table, so to speak. I am not just me; I am a microcosm of us.

Existential analysis is at times more helpful than traditional scholastic exposition and social analysis when examining complex social realities. It enables us to do analysis from the inside out. At times, this requires favoring analogy over pure analysis and the indicative over prescriptive. We previously mentioned the value of analogy and analogical thinking. Analogical commentary enables us to consider matters that may not easily be quantified or viewed directly. When we use analogy, we are saying, "This is to this as that is to that." Analogical thinking uses poetic metaphor and visual imagery. It operates in the linguistic mode of "it is like …" When anthropologists suggest that culture is like an iceberg or a tree, they are using analogical thinking. When our commentary is indicative, it is simply pointing out "what is" before we entertain what "ought to be." It indicates before it prescribes. Thus, it is my intent to describe what the terrain of white identity is like and how it operates.

I have drawn from a number of sources. I am especially grateful to others who have been courageous enough to speak from their own experience and in doing so have owned their place in the processes of racialization. It is my intent to be transparent regarding my use of the insights and research of others.

9

The Architecture of White Supremacy

When I was two years into my college journey, my parents moved from Globe, Arizona, to Las Vegas, Nevada, where my father took a job in an automobile dealership in Las Vegas. The summer between my second and third years, I joined them in Las Vegas, hoping to find summer employment. It was clear to me that financial prospects for the coming academic year were not good. I needed significant income in a relatively short time if I was going to register for classes that September.

It turned out that one of the member families of the Methodist Church my parents attended owned a local construction firm. One Sunday, my father spoke with Kent Jones regarding my need for work. In response, Kent offered me a job as a construction laborer. Nevada is a union shop state. If your workplace is unionized, you are involved with a union. This meant higher salaries than in many states for all skill levels in construction. It also meant union dues. However, unions made allowances for college students working to earn money for school. So, there were two of us working for the same construction firm for good money with no union membership or dues required.

This job was the first time I had worked closely with African Americans. Almost all of the laborers were African American men in their thirties, forties, or fifties. All the supervisors were white; in addition, white men held down most of the skilled positions. I was grateful for the opportunity to form friendships and respectful relationships across racial lines. I had deep respect for men and women who worked with their hands for a living.

Most of my extended family and the families of friends did so. And this was hard work. Summertime on the Mohave Desert is frequently above 110 degrees Fahrenheit. Construction labor is hard work in any climate; it's especially challenging in the desert Southwest.

One of the men I frequently worked with was a former professional boxer (heavyweight). He was also African American. Howard was several years older than me yet was very willing for me to work beside him. At the time, I was really into boxing (had I not been very nearsighted, I might even have tried my hand at the sweet science). Consequently, I was fascinated by his experience and found him easy to talk to and work with. He had dropped out of the professional ranks after being knocked out. As someone who had been winnowed out of the fight game, construction labor was the available employment option.

I was clear, however, that construction labor was not my occupational track. I did not see myself doing construction labor in my thirties, forties, and fifties. But I also knew that this was the occupational track that most of the men I worked with were stuck in. It was clear to me that race was playing out before my eyes. My father's social currency had opened the door for me to find a job that paid well (for a college student). I was able to earn enough money to register for classes, with enough left for room and board, at least long enough for me to line up a work-study job. The job that opened up put me in close relationship with men for whom construction labor was a lifelong occupation. History and the resulting social realities of the 1950s assured this.

I did not realize it at the time, but I was experiencing the realities of white supremacy. The impact of class made it necessary for me to work my way through college. I could not count on family resources to assure a college education for me. The intersection of class and race opened up before my eyes when I temporarily became a construction laborer and earned the money needed to take the next step in my educational journey. However, my prospects were not the same as those of the men with whom I worked. Race, even more than class, shaped our prospects.

How was I experiencing white supremacy? Often, the term invokes memories of the Ku Klux Klan and conversation about Neo Nazis or the Aryan Brotherhood. However, as mentioned previously, here the term simply refers to the fundamental social architecture of American society. This same architecture effectively conspired to grant me a hard-earned college education. I had access to a job that provided the income needed for college. This architecture expresses the foundational mythology of our nation: the superiority of white people. This is the social context we live in. It is longer lived and more powerful than the Klan or the current manifestations of racial terrorism.

In complex systems some operating procedures tend to become default settings; they are standardized and self-replicating. In effect, "this is the way we do things." Even when the rules change, these defaults continue to shape organizational reality. In our society, organizational procedures that privilege and value white identity are examples of such default settings. In effect, *the white way is the right way*. The superiority of white people effectively becomes an organizational assumption. When it comes to social identity, the superiority of white people and their ways of being is a primary systemic default in our society. This default assures that the prospects for white people, especially white cisgender males, tend to be better than those of people of color (as well as others who don't quite fit the white male form).

White supremacy is social formation that is a coalescence of multiple generations of social fabrication. In chapter 5, we noted nine motifs that especially marked European imperial-colonialism. These motifs, woven together and playing out over six centuries, have produced an integrated social architecture, an edifice that expresses the presumed superiority of white people.

I am especially interested in exploring the interior of this architecture as it functions in the United States. These motifs produced similar architecture throughout the Americas, albeit with differing features prominent in today's Western Hemisphere nations. Having lived for a time in Jamaica, Venezuela, and Mexico, it is clear to me that race played and plays a major role in each. The unique history of each nation has produced an architecture that is distinct. However, every nation in this hemisphere has been partially shaped by the white supremacist character of the United States (some more than others).

Many years ago, I was part of a team of organizer–trainers that was doing a research trip through Latin America. We were visiting with scholars, community organizers, pastors, and others who were socially active; we were also conducting occasional workshops and seminars. One afternoon I was visiting with a young Brazilian pastor in Sao Paulo, Brazil. It was several months prior to an upcoming presidential election in the US. Pastor Paraiba startled me with the comment that they (Brazilians) should be allowed to vote in the US presidential election, "because whoever is elected will have an immediate impact on us and will influence our life as a nation."

Some of my Canadian friends put it this way: "It's like sleeping next to an elephant. Even when it is asleep and not intending anything in particular, it still can roll over and mash you!" We are a major presence in the affairs of virtually every American nation, albeit some more than others. Of course, that is also true of our role in international affairs, in general. Our history has positioned us to be a player on the world scene.

Cognitive/Existential Dissonance

The nine motifs we previously explored have given us the social architecture of white supremacy, including the discomfiting sense of dissonance in how we experience this architecture. This is more than cognitive. It is also profoundly existential. It is always present, even if only as a background motif or troubling irritant, like a sliver in your big toe. It is rooted in our deepest sense of identity. When we allow it free run, it reverberates throughout our being. It seems much safer to entomb it, bury it out of sight, hearing, and mind. Unbidden, it occasionally rushes to the fore and demands attention. From the far remote areas where we have assigned it, it keeps calling to us, saying our name, refusing to be silent. Let me reiterate: I am talking about the white collective, about our shared experience. This dissonance, of course, is rooted in the resistance to white supremacy, resistance nourished and nurtured in communities of color.

As a nation, we have been unapologetically heterosexist for most of our history. We have also been unapologetically sexist and patriarchal. Effectively, these have become features of white supremacy. Consequently, it is increasingly clear that we cannot work on race in isolation. Working to deconstruct white supremacy means working to interrupt all the symbiotic cycles of systemic oppression. They form interconnected default settings. The work is not easy, and the outcomes are not a foregone conclusion. The presidential election of 2016 reminds us that all we have gained can be taken away. We may be redefining marriage and, consequently, what it means to be family. Women have gained more access to historically male preserves, providing leadership in political, economic, and cultural institutions and communities. There is, however, much more to do. The

"Me Too" phenomenon has cast in bold relief the power of patriarchy and the risk involved in challenging traditional male territory. The gains achieved are costly, and the current electoral backlash places all at risk.

The filter of resistance, especially, helps us grasp that our sense of nationhood has been substantiated in the midst of cognitive-existential dissonance. We know there is a fundamental social contradiction expressed in the measurable racial disparities that highlight social inequities. This dissonance reverberates across all the oppression systems that impact access to the necessities of life. It is the fertile seedbed that incubates and grows organizing initiatives that challenge the status quo and envision an alternative society. This gives us a society marked by constant struggle, stress, and strain.

White Supremacy: A Persisting Legacy

Previously, we noted that the Naturalization Act of 1790 clarified who was eligible for citizenship in the new United States: "any alien, being a free white person … of good character."[69] The act couched a definition of citizen in our legal framework that continues to reverberate today. Until the Fourteenth Amendment, citizenship and white were equivalent terms. What it meant to be a citizen was to be white. Additionally, since women did not yet have the franchise, it also meant that citizen and white male were equivalent terms. One of the legacy reverberations of this equivalency is that if you ask someone to close their eyes and imagine the all-American boy, it is unlikely that they will imagine (in their mind's eye) a dark-skinned person. Instead, the first image that flashes on the mental screen is likely to be a light-skinned (white) boy with blond hair and blue eyes. The inner auditor does have very fast reflexes; it can very quickly require an alternative image. Which image comes first? We have learned, over many generations, to equate citizen and white identity. Cognitively, we know this is not accurate or real. However, in a very deep manner, the association continues. To quote a very old bit of popular doggerel: white is right! White men still dominate social life, even though the explicit rules and legal mechanisms involved have changed. November 2016 was the first time one of our two dominant political parties championed a female presidential candidate. Several nations have had female heads of state. They did not sink into an abyss of social chaos! Our nation is slow when it comes to moving beyond the old rules. And the old rules prioritize the dominance of white men, especially wealthy white men.

So, what more can be said about white supremacy in this context? The phrase refers to the legal framework that shapes public life; it also refers to the multitude of social systems that provide the locus of public experience—including the individual institutions that comprise these systems. All of these thousands of institutions adhere to rules that are promulgated by the state (some more closely than others, certainly) and that apply to the particular system they are part of. Health care institutions, for example, follow a set of rules promulgated by federal, state, and local governing authorities that set forth what can be done and cannot be done in fulfilling their mission.

In a deeper sense, white supremacy refers to the generalized culture that generations of systemic dynamics have produced. This includes the dominant language, the worldview, social expectations, daily community activities, and family practices. The term white supremacy suggests that the doggerel "white is right" is pervasive and enculturated. We still understand that the white way is the right way!

Social Defaults and the Challenge of Change

Social default settings are similar to the default settings in computer software. They are comprised of a set of fundamental values, principles, and the rules that govern how they play out in society. When we take a systemic view of society, we can see that social default settings are exactly that—the mode of operation the system automatically returns to. Default settings can be changed. In computer software, the way to change defaults is clearly outlined. But one must explicitly change the settings.

Social defaults are a bit trickier to change. They represent common taken-for-grantedness when initially shaped. They express values that society in general endorsed and bought into. Hence, responses to efforts to change the settings may not be positive. Unless the efforts to change the settings express widely held values, they are apt to encounter resistance.

When the Naturalization Act of 1790 specified that being white was a requirement of citizenship, it was echoing generations of power dynamics in the American colonies. The language of the act resonated with people, in particular the white men who wrote and passed the act. It fulfilled expectations about who exercised power and authority in society. This piece of early legislation, in effect, articulated a fundamental default setting. It set in motion the dynamic processes that equated citizen with white. SCOTUS reinforced this default in 1857 when it announced that Dred Scott, by virtue of his race, did not and could not qualify for citizenship.

In order to change social defaults, there has to be widespread buy-in among the populace. The new setting must express value and principles that have the weight of general approval behind them. Otherwise, they will be resisted. Certainly, unpopular settings can be enforced if those in authority are prepared to do what is necessary to assure obedience. We have seen unpopular regimes around the world stay in power through the willingness to use brutal violence and the threat of violence. In our imperfect democracy, unpopular change is messy and generally unsuccessful. Even the weight of majority opinion does not guarantee easy changes in our social defaults.

The Thirteenth and Fourteenth Amendments to the US Constitution are a case in point. The Thirteenth Amendment abolished slavery and involuntary servitude (except in the case of a convicted felon); the Fourteenth granted citizenship to "all persons born or naturalized in the United States."[70] It was especially intended to extend citizenship to formerly enslaved Africans. Both of these amendments were endorsed by a majority of states (primarily Northern and border states that had not joined the Confederacy). This meant that eligible voters in the states voting "yes" endorsed the changes. This did not mean that the majority of the populace in these states endorsed the amendments. In addition, there were states voting "no." The states that did not support these amendments launched serious and vigorous resistance. The vagrancy laws enacted in Southern states following the end of Reconstruction were one expression of this vigorous resistance. The constitutional amendments were an effort to change fundamental default settings in American society. We are still engaged in the struggle to change these fundamental settings.

The Supremacy of Whiteness

The consequence of this persisting legacy of self-replicating default settings is that white identity is normalized. This normalization produces a society in which economic processes, political matters, and cultural life are dominated by the white collective. This dominance is not, finally, about demographics. It is not simply a matter of how the majority of Americans identify, racially. It is not about numbers. It is about the dynamics of systemic power and the fabric of society itself. This society has been and continues to be constituted by race. It is racially constructed. This is effectively what it means to say that race is ubiquitous.

Clearly, there are things going on that challenge our racialized society. For example, the election of Barack Obama to the presidency in 2008 was a sea change. A black man occupied the nation's highest office. A black family occupied the White House. This was a prospect never envisioned by the founding fathers! Even forty years earlier, it was almost impossible to imagine. However, the election of Barack Obama did not mean that the way we do politics also changed. The fundamental rules remained. But in spite of this, things will never again be the same. There are new prospects in national life that Barack Obama's election signaled.

Even television commercials today signal that some defaults are degrading and losing their sharply defined edges. Visual messages are powerful, even when their primary role is marketing products. Marketers are going where none would have dared go just a generation ago. Nonetheless, the visuals we are exposed to still tend to prioritize white identity and to tread carefully in relation to other intimately related identity issues: sexuality, gender, body image, and so on. There are clear signs that fundamental change is needed. In order to examine the prospects for fundamental change, we need to look a little more carefully and deeply at the dynamics that normalize white identity and then explore the impact of these dynamics in the experience of being white.

10

The Echo Chamber Effect

White supremacy derives its power from the deep stories of our past that still undergird our society. Its power is mythic; it comes from the mythic underpinnings of American society. In chapter 4, we explored the significance of mythology in the fabrication of society. A society's deep mythology is not like a suit of clothing that can be taken off at any moment and exchanged for something new. In effect, it is soldered to our collective psyche. This applies especially to the white collective. For us, the undergirding mythology of white supremacy is everywhere. We breathe it. We eat it. We think it. We dream it. Our language reflects it. It is more than an external social architecture; it also shapes an interior terrain that is the common landscape of the white collective. It is white racial consciousness.

Previously, we explored how the dynamics of racial assignment create and shape racial collectives. For those of us who are assigned white identity, it is clear that nonwhite people are organized into such collectives. It makes sense to us to talk about African American people, Hispanic/Latino people, Asian Americans, American Indians, and Arab Americans. It even makes sense to ask an individual, "What do black people think of...?" Our shared stereotypes of other racial groups further reinforce the sense that there are racial collectives, but they don't include us. We typically don't experience ourselves as part of a racial collective. I am just "me, James." I experience myself only as an individual. One of the marks, especially, of the white collective is hyperindividualism. Our racialization teaches us that we are just individuals. In turn, every aspect of our lives is mediated by hyperindividualism that teaches us that what we have accumulated is a result of our individual effort. When we miss the mark, it is simply a result of our own shortcomings. We tend to believe in meritocracy. "If you simply roll up your sleeves and work hard, you'll succeed!" We admonish those who struggle economically to simply get it together and work hard, with the implication that their success or failure in this society is no more than a function of individual effort. Certainly, there is truth in such statements. But they do not take into account systemic dynamics that are shaped to favor the individuals in one group over others.

One consequence is that when we (white people) think or talk about race and racism, it turns out to be difficult to go beyond the boundaries of individual attitude and action. We individualize racial matters, thus obscuring the underlying systemic realities that actually maintain racialization. The chimera of individualism effectively becomes one of the central pillars that maintains the architecture we have termed *white supremacy*.

Underneath our hyperindividualism, however, is an awareness of our collective identity. We experience ourselves as white in response to the *otherness* of nonwhite collectives. While we may try to appropriate aspects of other racial groups, we know we are not "them." We are white. This awareness may not always be front and center (our individuality is), but it is always there in the background.

John Gall, in his book *Dancing With Elves*, suggest that socialization teaches us to pay attention to our mental programs rather than reality. Consequently, they effectively become default settings.[71] I am suggesting that hyperindividualism is such a program. It is one of several interlocking programs that comprise white supremacy. It is a central program. Further, it is a collective program. We create social echo chambers and pay attention to the program the echoes create, rather than what's happening outside the chamber in the real world. In chapter 8, we did an initial exploration of the echo chamber of white identity. It is our home. Let's return to the metaphor and unpack it a bit.

The Echo Chamber and Its Impact

One of the ironies in our ideology of individualism is that we as a population are becoming increasingly wired together. Our digital communication systems, including all the social media, wrap us round in a fashion that actually binds us collectively. We live in the midst of the deluge of images and sounds in the chamber. The binding is not so much in what or even how we think but rather is a matter of the medium. Our conscious lives are lived in a common place—cyberspace. Connectedness is ubiquitous. We are wired together and are inundated with one another's thoughts and commentaries. We experience our lives in the constant babble of social media. This babble is a feature of our collectivization. Being disconnected is experienced as a threat, as being deprived of something necessary. Consequently, even as we cling to the ideology of individual self and individual achievement, we are becoming more and more collective.

"If you're white, you're right!" This old ditty is actually an expression of what I've termed the "echo chamber effect." This refers to all the socializing messages that, in effect, normalize white identity. This effect is substantiated by the subtle feedback dynamics that bounce back at us reflecting our image, our racial identity, and that tell us, in effect, white is right. This effect is most prominent in all the forms of media: television, movies, magazines, and news reports that centralize and normalize white identity. This even includes the comics in the daily and Sunday newspapers (for those who still read the printed newspaper).

What more can be said about the echo chamber effect? We see *us*. Images of white people bounce back to us. Everything seems to be about us. Even when our narratives seem to highlight people of color, it's still about us. We are the center of the story. Narratives hinge on us or highlight us.

This effect gives credibility to the political commentaries that echo themes like "let's make America great, again!" Something seems to be slipping away! There are disturbing voices that now and again intrude into our program, echoes that seem dissonant, don't quite fit. Something is not quite right; let's make it right again!

The echo chamber effect makes white privilege / systemic advantage virtually invisible to many of us, thereby making it necessary for progressives to continue calling for the tough conversation about race and white privilege. It is indeed noteworthy that many have been calling for this conversation for many years. Yet it still seems difficult to have. It's the echo chamber effect at work and the subtle and hidden ways it reinforces white supremacy. It reinforces our unconsciousness about racial realities and our difficulty with critical thinking.

The echo chamber effect insulates us from reality. It prevents images of the real world from intruding upon us. The messages that do penetrate create uncomfortable dissonance. This, in turn, stimulates defensiveness and encourages us to latch onto simplistic ideological positions that further insulate us. Or we hatch narratives that highlight our responsiveness to others' plight, or how we were the source of clearheaded stability in challenging moments. The story, however, is still about us.

Case in point is the old film *Dances with Wolves*.[72] When it hit the theaters, it received a good bit of critical acclaim. It actually portrayed Indian people as human beings. Much of the narrative was in Lakota, with English subtitles. It was a captivating story with wrenching episodes. The title refers to the Lakota name given to the main character. His friendship with an aging wolf that hung around his camp provided a poignant motif in the story. However, in spite of the sensitive treatment of the difficult history of the Lakota, it was not about Indian people. Nor was it told from the perspective of Indian people. It was about the white guy (Kevin Costner's character) and his personal journey from disaffection and despair into humanity. His humanization resulted from his growing intimacy with Lakota people and a white woman who had grown up Lakota. Their return to white society (in order to tell the truth about Indian people) was the final episode of the film. In the end, it romanticized Lakota people and was about the white guy's journey. It was about us. It was about us being awakened and courageous with the support of our faithful Indian friends.

The echo chamber does not portray us, necessarily, as violent racists. It often provides a nuanced exploration of the range of human emotions, behaviors, vices, and virtues. It is, however, still about us. Humanity is universalized through us, through our experience. We are normalized. The echo chamber effect rehearses racial narratives; it infers that humanity is racially defined. Its locus is the terrain of white identity; white people are the *real* human beings.

Randall Robinson, in his book *The Debt,* speaks of the inability of white America to see—to really see. Our inability to see, he suggests, is linked to consistent, rigorous denial. We are in denial regarding the moral outrage of slavery and its fundamental role in the development of this nation. We are in denial about what is owed to black Americans as a consequence of downplaying both the role of slavery and its continuing legacy. For white people, denial is one of the defense mechanisms dissonance evokes. When the dissonance is social and collective, our denial becomes an aspect of our collective consciousness. It also tends to become multigenerational and multilayered. It becomes enculturated. This is precisely what has happened in relation to race. Denial is embedded in the white collective. It has become, functionally speaking, part of what it means to be white. It is a primary feature of the terrain.

Robinson suggests there is not a statute of limitations on fundamental issues of social justice, especially those of the magnitude of slavery and the accompanying devastation of Africa.[73] Robinson clearly spoke from his perspective as an African American man. Similar analyses of the experience of all communities of color and the role played in the development of the nation could be made.

Robinson also points out some illustrations in recent times of societies making restitution for crimes committed against a group of people. Germany's restitution for the genocide committed against the Jews under the Nazis is one of his illustrations. Germany made financial restitution to Israel and to individual Jewish families. Similarly, the United States made financial restitution to the families of Japanese Americans interned during World War II.

The inability of white America to see is perhaps a fundamental impetus of the previously mentioned Black Lives Matter movement. While focusing on the injustices of the criminal justice system, especially police violence against young people of color, it is bringing all of us to the point of discernment, of seeing what is happening. If we are to slip from the pathological grasp of white supremacy, seeing is necessary. We must see what is being done to maintain our echo chamber—to others and, finally, to us. We must see the terrible price white people are paying.

The metaphor "seeing," admittedly, is an example of ableist language. However, in a society that tends to subscribe to the importance of color blindness, its use here seems especially relevant. Our society is constructed in a manner that presumes sight. It was people whose sight was compromised that developed the tools and systems, like Braille, that provided access to a sight-biased society. Our challenge is to develop the tools that enable us to see through the façade of color blindness and in order to grasp the damage it has done.

Discerning the Damage Done

Crossroads Antiracism Organizing and Training has developed a useful template for exploring the impact of racialization upon people of color and white people. It is a tool that facilitates conversation about the internalization of white superiority and the internalization of racial oppression. The template has four aspects: the deep impact of racialization on the sense of self; the way that relationships are constructed within racial collectives; relations with other racial collectives; and behavior within white institutions.[74] A brief examination of each of these categories will set the stage for a "trip" to the terrain of white identity.

Sense of Self

White racialization teaches us to experience ourselves as separate units that manifest the norms of the larger society. We inhabit normative land. The articulation of social norms effectively shapes our identity (and our individualism enables us to see how we inhabit an acceptable range of abnormality). This is a consequence of our decision that white is the normative identity: white people are normal. One of the consequences is that much medical research has been traditionally based on white men. They have been perceived as the norm. Fortunately, that is beginning to change. As previously mentioned, hyperindividualism is one of the marks of our collective identity. We are intellectually, emotionally, physically, and morally superior; this superiority is manifest in the economic, political, and cultural life of our society. While we may not necessarily own up to our sense of individual superiority (many of us are socialized to be rather modest, if not self-depreciating), we nonetheless know it. Former US Senator Jim Webb, in his book *Born Fighting*, points out that one thing a poor white man living in the Deep South during the time of Jim Crow knew was that when he came to town, he could drink out of the fountain labeled "white only."[75] The fountain helped him experience his relative superiority. In the moment he drank, he was special! He was white. Individually, many of us may well struggle with the impact of self-depreciation; we may well have been socialized to see ourselves as victims. But our individual sense of self notwithstanding, we know we are part of a collective that is racially superior!

We construct our social lives to function as an echo chamber that constantly normalizes white identity. While we may not think of ourselves as part of a collective, our superiority is collective, not individual. We know this. Herein lies an interesting internal contradiction: we believe we are just individuals, yet we experience ourselves, also, as part of a racial collective.

Intragroup Relations

In our white terrain, we live in the midst of difficult intersections constructed by other oppression systems. The intersections among these are stealthy with regard to race. Race provides solidarity across the hierarchies society constructs. It is like the gravitational force field maintaining the difficult tensions among other socially constructed identities. The hierarchies themselves generate intensely competitive struggles. This means we are not just one undifferentiated mass of whiteness. We construct boundaries that delineate subgroupings. These boundaries create and reinforce the experience of intersecting social identities: gender, sexuality, class, age, ability, and so on. These boundaries are maintained by rigorous power dynamics. At the center of these power dynamics are wealthy white heterosexual cisgender males. Being at the center generates the basis for limited solidarity among those occupying the center. This is the social reality that some have appropriately dubbed white patriarchy. Intragroup relations tend to be fraught with struggle, stress, and pain—as long as the focus is within our racial group, the white collective.

The hierarchies constructed by oppression systems survive and thrive. We scratch and claw each other all the while we know who is "in" and not "in" the club! This, after all, is a club designed to control the institutions and systems of society. It has strict membership rules. There may indeed be different layers of membership, and the innermost layers clearly are reserved for those with resources and connections, most particularly those who are cisgender male.

Intergroup Relations

White identity contextualizes our relationships with nonwhite groups, being white is the basis for solidarity that cuts across the stress-filled interior hierarchies and binds us together in relation to the threats that nonwhite groups bring to white supremacy. Our solidarity may be expressed politically, economically, and culturally. It may be relativized by intragroup hierarchies and struggles, but it is strong in relation to other racialized groups—that is, all who are nonwhite. Thus, the phrase "don't ask, don't tell" is a tacit recognition of the binding power of white supremacy. "If you don't tell us you are different (i.e., homosexual and therefore abnormal), we will pretend you are just one of us (i.e., white and therefore normal)." This is why we can say that "don't ask, don't tell" strengthens white supremacy.

Although we may play with anyone, including those not in our club, we know that being in the club is our home. We are even prepared to open the door to membership to others, provided they pass muster. Passing muster has fundamentally to do with maintaining the racial rules and roles. We'll make you white—or at least an honorary white—if you don't rock the boat. We'll exceptionalize you! We may even declare your community a "model minority." If you're an honorary white, you'll lose this honor if you do rock the boat. If you've become a real part of the collective, we'll still claim you and expect loyalty even if you roil the waters, provided you do so in ways we can excuse.

Behavior within White Institutions

The rules of institutional life protect us. Effectively, they are white identity writ large. The rules, written and unwritten, of institutional life presume the primacy of white identity. We are quick to resort to accusations of reverse discrimination when our place in institutional life is threatened by people of color. We will tolerate people of color as long as they play by our rules, one of which is, "Thou shalt not make white people uncomfortable!" Legal remedies framed as historical interventions that open access to institutional life, such as affirmative action, threaten our sense of the natural order in institutional life! Hence, they must be attacked and every venue (overt and covert) used to challenge and delegitimize them.

"I know someone who was passed over for a promotion that went to a less qualified person of color!" "I have a friend who was not hired for a position he/she was qualified for in order that the company could meet a racial quota!" All of us have likely heard some version of these accusations. When I hear such comments, I press for details and documentation. I have yet to see or hear any. Still the stories continue to reverberate throughout our collective. Affirmative action / equal opportunity policy, after all, does not require hiring unqualified people; nor does it set out racial quotas.

We know there are dynamics of control that are racially defined. These have to do with who makes, sanctions, enforces, and has the authority to change the rules of institutional life. These govern who has access to institutions. They also include the authority to structure and activate accountability. Our anxiety is triggered when we experience or fear that our access is threatened. It is easy to project the blame on people of color. Scapegoating is a time-honored tactic.

This fourfold template is a helpful tool when we engage in conversations about the deeper dimensions of racialization. It helps us discern the damaging impacts of the racial echo chamber we inhabit. In a sense, it is like a portal to the terrain of white identity. The template discloses that white identity is not a static entity but rather a bundle of socializing dynamics that together shape an interior terrain: our terrain, the landscape of white consciousness. This landscape is the locus of white identity.

explicit racial
animus
& bigotry

carefully cultivated
public innocence

the continuum of hidden complicity

White Racial Consciousness: a Wrenching Polarity

11

The Terrain of White Identity

In this chapter, we will explore the terrain of white identity. Why use the metaphor "terrain"? Landscape is fundamental to our experience of being human and living in community. We identify with place. Even in our digital age when we converse daily with others around the world, being in a place is still fundamental. White racial consciousness is almost palpable; it is like a place, a landscape upon which we live. While this place is critical in our sense of identity, there is more to each of us than this place. Our identity is finally not contained by this place. We have the capacity to be more. The terrain of white identity is our collective racial identity, but we are more than the terrain. We may have the capacity to transform the terrain.

We will use this metaphorical way of speaking to identify and examine some of the primary features of white racial consciousness. This will set the stage for examining the pathologies of white identity and, consequently, how white supremacy threatens our future as a nation. It is not my intent to be glib, cynical, or moralizing in this exploration. I am clear that my own humanity is at stake as well as the integrity of my nation.

The social architecture we termed white supremacy is actually quite visible. However, the interiority (the terrain of white identity) of this visible architecture tends to be hidden and not a part of ordinary discourse. Frankly, it is a frightening terrain to us. It contradicts some of the mythic characteristics of the American persona: freedom loving, hardworking, passionate for justice and fairness. This terrain is synergistically connected to the visible architecture. Each reinforces the other and draws energy from the other. This terrain is the common home of all of us assigned white identity. Individual white people are aware of this terrain in varying degree. Many of us simply do not reflect on these matters. This is not a personal failing; it is a feature of our socialization. Nonetheless, the synergistic connections between the external architecture and the interior terrain are rooted in our psyches. They comprise our effective captivity.

Racial Assignment

Being white has been done to us. We don't start out as racial bigots. None of us is born white. We are assigned a racial identity at birth. This means we are assigned to a racial collective. There was a time when all newborns were given a racial identity on a hospital birth record, and this info was then transferred to a state form that was the basis for an official birth certificate. Historically, the fundamental background constant of racial assignment is white–nonwhite. The assignment slots on the nonwhite side of the binary have varied throughout our history: Negro, Hindu, American Indian, and others. Previously, we mentioned that this means the boundary between white and nonwhite has sometimes shifted and is often ambiguous. Common knowledge regarding our parents' racial identities and the rules couched in law provide the context within which our racial assignment occurs. The identity categories commonly used on government forms provide the slots for racial assignment. This process is lifelong, and its impact is cumulative. It takes place every time we (or someone else on our behalf) fill out a government form and check off an identity category. It happens when we watch TV and discern racial categorization in action. It happens as we play with our friends, attend school, shop, drive—participate in all the daily minutiae of our lives.

Those of us who are white are assigned a racial identity that is functionally dominant, with all its rights and privileges. We are socialized into a collective racial identity termed white that is socially dominant by design and oppressive by function. Our daily life experiences, interpreted through the filter of racialization, reinforce, naturalize, and normalize our racial dominance. This dominance is the functional significance of being white. It defines our racial identity. European heritage, especially British, and light skin are certainly considerations when it comes to being white.

However, it is collective social dominance that indicates our racial identity, even more than ethnic heritage.

As previously noted, I experience myself as simply James. Not, in the first instance, as older, straight, white male James. But even before James, with all his uniqueness and particular gifts, comes on the scene, his older, straight, white maleness makes an impact and creates socio-psycho space. This space allows James's individuality to come into play. This space is collectively generated; my individuality does not shape it.

My racial collective creates this space for me. It then allows James to make his statement, to be a unique individual in society. In most circumstances, I do not have to deal with a negative racial stereotype in order to make my real presence known. I just go about being me. My assigned racial identity may indeed have stereotypical impact, but it is positive; it creates space for me. It lightens the load. In my experience, this space is the norm. Thus, my experience of self is normalized, racially speaking. Even if there are other aspects of me that tighten and restrict my space—if I am female, gay, transgendered, physically challenged, old, poor, and so on—my racial collective still works for me, intervenes socially on my behalf.

Captivity

Reverend Joseph Barndt, in his classic work *Dismantling Racism: The Continuing Challenge to White America*, points out that the significance of racial assignment is *we are not free!*[76] We do not choose our racial assignment, and we are not free to be unraced! Racial assignment is not a sociobiological equivalent of the food court. We don't select from several options, willy-nilly. When we become aware of our race and its significance, we may indeed be quite uncomfortable. Our discomfort notwithstanding, we don't get to choose. As long as the systems and institutions in our society shape identity around race, we cannot avoid being affected. It is also true that as white people, we cannot avoid the benefits of our racial identity. "I am the master of my fate, the captain of my soul."[77] Not in relation to race! This does not mean that we consciously choose racial bigotry or that we are even aware of prejudice against people of color. Nonetheless, we do make decisions in the context of racial assignment. When we become aware of our assignment, we make decisions about it. We have to decide how to relate to our racial assignment. This is the arena where a conversation about freedom is especially relevant: how we relate to our assignment.

Clearly, our life experiences can call into question our naturalized, normalized dominance. This space, the space of critical reflection, is key to the recovery of our humanity and to our ability to resist racialization. Later, we'll explore this further. First, more on the identity that racialization shapes. This is not intended as commentary on the essential nature of our humanity. It is not part of the debate about free will. Rather, it is a witness made from the inside. It is commentary about the experience of being white in a racialized society. It is testimony revealing the phenomena of white identity. It is descriptive of the experience of walking this terrain.

White Identity: A Difficult Polarity

Our racial identity, as the white collective, is experienced as a wrenching polarity that plays out along a continuum. We even learn to medicate ourselves to mitigate the impact of the experience. It is as though we experience ourselves moving betwixt the two polar opposites of the continuum: overt (or in some cases, covert) and intentional racial bigotry, on the one hand, and hidden, albeit well-intentioned, complicity disguised as public innocence on the other. We may even assert our nonracist character with such fervor that our racial biases are hidden even from ourselves. Both of these poles, overt racial bigotry and public innocence, are an aspect of our experience of racialization. (Remember I am describing *us,* not necessarily any individual.) We often experience bouncing back and forth along the continuum between these two poles.

All of us recognize racial bigotry and prejudice. We have seen it in the social behavior of others, perhaps even family members and friends. However, I am suggesting something more pernicious than the knowing that comes from observation. I am suggesting that all of us know it at the most personal level; we experience it. Of course, some of us know it and experience it more intimately and intensely than others. This is a consequence of our reflexive relationship with negative stereotypes. They impact our decision-making and influence our behavior. As they influence us, our thinking and behavior reinforce them, and they grow more powerful. This is what has been termed implicit bias. Implicit bias is a consequence of living in a racialized society.

These days, most of us experience counter messages that teach us to become aware of, undo, overcome, and discipline our deep prejudices. Racial prejudice and bigotry lack their previous legitimacy. They are not politically correct. Unfortunately, we also experience a daily barrage of messages that promote and reinforce negative stereotypes. Many of these are so subtle that they elude or stealthily pass through our defenses. Then, from the inner recesses, they ambush us when we least expect. A short anecdote will illustrate.

A few summers ago, I was walking through the riverside parkway along the Mississippi River in downtown St. Paul, Minnesota. This was early in the morning, first light. The sun was just illuminating the park. The air was fresh and cool on my arms. As I walked, I came upon a young black man sitting on a park bench with a wallet in his hand. He was casually dressed. As I passed, he perused the contents of the wallet. He glanced up at me as I passed, nervously it seemed to me. The immediate thought that flashed through my mind was, *He has stolen that wallet and is looking for items of value. Who did he take it from?* The next thought (as I experienced a bit of discomfort with the stereotype) was, *Maybe he just found the wallet.*

As I reflected (we do learn to audit our default conclusions almost immediately), I realized that if he had been a young white man, similarly dressed, I likely would not have paid any attention. I might have wondered, but I would not have assumed first that he had stolen the wallet. I have no idea whether that was his wallet or not. That is not the point. The point is the immediate conclusion that flashed through my mind. I experienced this conclusion as an ambush!

Now, I have to say that I do not think of myself as a stereotypical racial bigot. I have worked on my prejudices as long as I can remember being aware of race. I even conduct antiracism workshops, training events, and consultations. My family is multiracial. I have children on both sides of the white-nonwhite divide. The young man on the park bench was about the same age as my youngest son (who is also black). The conclusion I drew flashed in my mind without my permission. If you press me, I have to say that I do not know where it came from. I certainly did not allow it in! In fact, I felt as though I had been ambushed! Nevertheless, it was there. I have to confess that I have had frequent experiences of a similar sort, so frequently that I am not comfortable owning up to them! Sometimes the subtle associations that emerge from my mind shock me. When I reflect on them, I believe they teach me something about the terrain of white racial identity and therefore something about the impact of racialization on my own sense of self.

As soon as I become aware of these disturbing associations and conclusions, I am heading toward the other end of the continuum pell-mell, as fast as I can—that is, toward the pole of innocence and carefully hidden complicity. Now this movement takes place in my imagination. It involves the way I see myself and want to be seen. I want to be seen as innocent of racist behavior—as being, in effect, nonracist. I may be willing to admit to having had racial prejudices, but I have overcome them. This is the self I desire to cultivate and, especially, the self I want others to see.

This requires me to carefully hide the deeply embedded racial stuff that unexpectedly ambushes me—the stuff I do not self-consciously allow, the stuff that is counter to my professed (and very real) values and commitments. How can such associations be part of who I am? They contradict the image of self I fashion for others to see. Having to hide them, however, means that I know, in a deep manner, of my own most personal complicity in the very processes that racialize. This is complicity, when I move to the pole of innocence, that I dare not own or claim. Hence, this movement is along the continuum of hidden complicity.

When we gravitate toward the overt bigotry pole, we tend to focus our energy and efforts toward defending and shoring up the walls of racial advantage, even if we don't name it as such. So it may be easy for us to proclaim, in the heat of political rhetoric, that we must "take back our country!" Or perhaps "make American great again!" When Barack Obama was president, these frequently heard slogans took on an especially disturbing edge. President Obama occupied a place that was not designed, originally, for him. It is a place that historically has been reserved for white men of means. This historical intent is clearly fulfilled in the election of Donald Trump.

When we move toward the pole of innocence, we may focus our efforts and energy on the social disempowerment of people of color and the brutal disparities that are a social marker of race. Our efforts may, in effect, be aimed at rescuing or (in the words of Joseph Barndt) fixing individuals and communities that bear the brunt of America's racial apartheid. Our focus itself then becomes a witness to our personal innocence. It may even be a testimony to our moral superiority!

In summary, the terrain of white racial identity has three prominent features: the common experience of racial assignment, effective captivity (we are not free to be nonraced or to choose a racial identity of our liking), and a collective identity shaped by the frantic movement between the two poles of intentional racial bigotry and public innocence. When we look more closely at the terrain, its creek beds, hills, and bushy plains, we can discern the places where the pathologies of white identity hide and germinate.

This metaphorical examination of the terrain of white identity is the context that prepares us to explore the pathologies of white identity. In medical science, the term pathology indicates "anatomic and physiological deviations from the normal that constitute disease" and is also the "study of the essential nature of diseases and especially of the structural and functional changes produced by them."[78] I use the term pathology to suggest that white identity is dehumanizing and destructive. It tears the fabric of community and undermines efforts to restore and repair it. A behavior is pathological when it becomes a self-replicating default that prevents relevant and creative engagement and responses to the real situation. It insulates us from reality and is therefore dehumanizing—to others, clearly, but also to us who are white. Perhaps, especially to us!

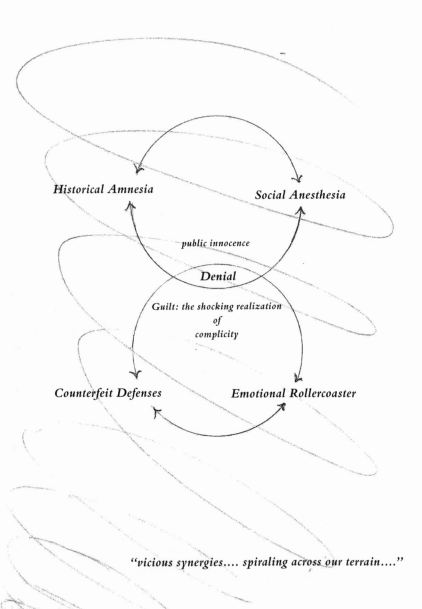

Historical Amnesia

Social Anesthesia

public innocence

Denial

Guilt: the shocking realization
of
complicity

Counterfeit Defenses

Emotional Rollercoaster

"vicious synergies.... spiraling across our terrain...."

12

The Pathologies of White Identity

What, then, are the pathologies of white identity? I have appreciated the use of the term "toxic whiteness" by Everyday Feminism. Their workshop series termed *Healing from Toxic Whiteness* is one of several efforts to help white people understand and heal from the wounds of white identity.[79] What are the interior dynamics of collective consciousness that germinate and propel destructive behaviors—however well intentioned? How do we understand and speak of the toxicity of white identity? In this chapter, we will attempt to address these questions.

First, we'll explore the threefold interior dynamics associated with the assertion of innocence that is characteristic of white identity. Then we'll look a little deeper and explore the dynamics associated with the revelation of guilt and its fellow travelers: imprisonment and inattention. Third, we'll examine the notion of historical loss and trauma and investigate its relevance for the terrain of white identity. Lastly, we'll introduce the idea of historical accountability and sketch out a framework that connects it to historical trauma and sets the stage for our work in Part 4.

The Face of Innocence

Denial is the toxic, pathological center; it is the generative force beneath our assertion of innocence. Denial of our complicity in racial oppression is almost a default response, publicly and privately. "I/we didn't enslave you!

My family never even owned slaves in those days! We didn't take your land! After all, a lot of white people died at the hands of Indians … etc. I/we am/are not accountable for deeds done by others before our time or in other places; they were not our doing! After all, I was involved in the civil rights movement!" Denial takes these and other forms even before the conversation turns to accountability and responsibility. It expresses the assumption that talking about race entails an assignment of fault or blame. It is a desperate exclamation, "This is not my/our fault!" It is an indication of endemic toxicity!

Second, denial is fed and strengthened by historical amnesia. As a nation, we are socialized to forget—and even not to know most of our history. In his book *Lies My Teacher Told Me*, James Loewen walks us through the selective and even distorted versions of American history that we are exposed to in our educational system—public and private—in this country.[80] In his book *Lies Across America*, he continues to explore the ubiquitous presence of distorted versions of our history.[81] The versions that we all learn are built around the triumphal story of American democracy. We learn of American exceptionalism, how we became the greatest nation in the world. We do not learn of the consistent, ubiquitous role race has played in making us who we are as a nation. We learn of the glory of Manifest Destiny; we do not teach our children of the brutality and savagery that were its substance. We learn of the courage of the pioneers journeying to the west in covered wagons; we do not learn of the courage and imagination of Africans in this land or of the suffering, endurance, and creative resilience of tribal people in the face of white intrusion.

As a consequence of our amnesia, we cannot see the racial realities that people of color routinely point out to us. It is as though we are blind to obvious social realities. Because we cannot see these realities, we tend to dismiss the voices of people of color and even psychologize their witness. "You see race in everything! This is not about race! You're playing the race card again!" Such dismissal makes us seem hard of hearing; it is as though we cannot hear what we are being told.

Such apparent blindness and deafness are, of course, mendacious. They are an expression of our collective denial. They are not physiological realities that genetics, accident, or disease have given us. They are not simply a function of comprehension. It is not simply that personal experience contributes to a lack of understanding. It's not just that we have not walked in another's shoes. Something is covered up! This is denial in action. This is pathological behavior.

A third toxic component is social anesthesia. We learn to numb and desensitize ourselves. In so doing, we lose the capacity for empathic resonance. Sympathy comes easily with respect to the hardships and suffering occasioned by race; empathy is in short supply. We cannot feel the violence and pain wrought by race. Thus we are not bound to others by a sense of solidarity born of common humanity. This numbing effect is sometimes the result of pharmaceuticals: legal and illegal. But it is also the result of our daily experience of the micro affirmations provided by systemic access: white privilege. We live out our lives in an echo chamber in which images of ourselves are constantly fed back to us via the media, thus normalizing our experience of our collective identity. Effectively, our privilege insulates us. A related source of the numbing is the constant bombardment of messages urging us to buy products and experiences. We learn to define ourselves functionally as consumers and in so doing further insulate ourselves from the impact of others' suffering. We calculate our personal value in relation to the goods and experiences we can purchase and consume. We are told we deserve this and learn to calculate the cost of our consumption in personal and family terms—but not social and ecological.

These three—collective denial, historical amnesia, and social anesthesia—whirl about in a synergistic dance across our terrain. They drive an almost desperate attempt to proclaim our innocence! "We are not to blame! After all, enslaved Africans had better lives in America than they would have had in Africa! We made America productive! Indians weren't making good use of resources! Stop guilt-tripping me!" And on, and on, and on ...

The Revelation of Guilt

When our denial is challenged, it sends us to a very difficult place. It triggers a difficult emotional roller coaster: we often experience an array of emotions, often in rapid succession. Anger, remorse, shame, regret, anguish, and ambiguity all may be part of our cascading experience. We may even act out these intense emotions in our social lives, perhaps without even disclosing their origin. Our position as the white collective means access to systemic power. Thus, our acting out may be done in ways that express our power, such as public policies that hurt and further marginalize communities of color, media campaigns that distort social realities—stoked by talk show hosts who opportunistically search out the sound bites that have traction. Our acting out is fraught with danger for communities of color.

Individually, we may be overwhelmed by such difficult emotions; we may feel powerless. This sense of powerlessness may even lead to individual acts of violence. Unfortunately, we are all too familiar with seemingly senseless and random acts of violence that devastate families and communities. Some of these random acts appear to target people of color. Many of them (certainly not all) are episodes of mass murder perpetrated by white people, frequently young white people. Whatever the personal circumstances may be that occasion these outbursts, the terrain of white identity is often a common contextual reality! It is the background constant that connects these seemingly senseless acts.

This is to suggest that the common context of white identity fuels and interprets these difficult emotions. This does not mean that being white causes these emotions. Rather, white identity is the fertile seedbed that cultivates and gives texture to them. It produces an emotional fragility that is sometimes marked by volatility. It is never as clear as simple cause and effect. This common context is the cumulative result of manufacturing and assigning stereotypical identities to others; we have stereotyped ourselves in the process. Racialization has rebounded upon us!

Our public expressions of these difficult emotions often take the form of manufactured defenses that are counterfeit rationalizations that at bottom are mendacious; their role is to protect us, not to reveal social reality. They are intended to protect a collective sense of self that cannot bear the shocking light of reality. Diatribes about American exceptionalism come easily, as do attacks on those threatening the racial status quo: "We need to see this guy's birth certificate and verify its authenticity! We may also need to examine his academic record!"

Robin DiAngelo writes of the phenomenon of white fragility. "We have very little tolerance for racial discomfort and respond poorly."[82] Her book, *What Does It Mean to Be White? Developing White Racial Literacy*, is one of the growing number of helpful commentaries on the phenomenon of whiteness and the work that we have to do, if we are to join others in the work of deconstructing white supremacy.

One of the interesting aspects of white fragility is that it can become generalized. That is, a sense of emotional fragility begins to dominate us, and we have a great deal of difficulty dealing with people and events that challenge our sense of stability, whether of a racial nature or not. This is especially true, of course, in relation to race. While this experience of fragility is very real, there may well be a deeper and pernicious reality. Our emotional fragility may well be a charade, a clever and rather sophisticated defense mechanism. It feels very real, but it may mask a deeper awareness.

The consequence of such emotional drama is intensified denial marked by an accelerating sense of desperation. We sense something fundamental is at stake, and it seems palpably fragile. Our denial is driven by a deep unease; we know at a fundamental level that there is more to the story than personal and collective innocence. Deep in the crevasses of our consciousness lurks the reality of guilt! This is more than a difficult emotion; it is the shocking realization of personal and collective complicity.

If we imagine a courtroom drama—perhaps a popular television series—we begin to grasp the significance of our sense of guilt. We can imagine the jury filing back into the courtroom following deliberation. The judge asks, "Madam foreperson, has the jury reached a decision in the matter of so and so versus the state?" "Yes, Your Honor, we have," responds the foreperson. "How, then, do you find the defendant?" queries the judge. "Well, Your Honor, we find the defendant is feeling guilty!" she responds.

Of course, this makes no sense. In a courtroom scene, the determination of guilt or innocence is not a commentary on the defendant's emotional state; rather, it is a judgment that interprets the pertinent facts at hand and announces their significance. Similarly, our deep unease and troubling sense of guilt, despite all our pernicious efforts to avoid it, is simply the revelation of reality: our actual complicity in the dynamics of racial oppression. History, we know, has found us guilty, and our efforts to appear innocent are revealed as a sham! Guilt, as shocking awareness, is our state of being!

Guilt and shame are often associated. It is important, however, to be clear they are not the same. The realization of guilt as complicity may indeed trigger a sense of shame. Brené Brown has posted some very thoughtful comments about shame on her Facebook page. "Based on my research and the research of other shame researchers, I believe that there is a profound difference between shame and guilt. I believe that guilt is

157

adaptive and helpful—it's holding something we've done or failed to do up against our values and feeling psychological discomfort. I define shame as the intensely painful feeling or experience of believing that we are flawed and therefore unworthy of love and belonging—something we've experienced, done, or failed to do makes us unworthy of connection."[83]

The vicious synergies flowing from these points wrap us in a cycle from which there is no release: denial, historical amnesia, social anesthesia; cascading emotions, counterfeit defenses, and, again, intensified denial. Spiraling across our terrain tornado-like, they leave a swath of personal and collective destruction. When we speak of the racial nightmare of this nation, we initially focus on the experience of people of color, typically African Americans. The multigenerational brutality of racism's impact on communities of color is clear and must never slip from our sight. However, when we peruse the terrain of white identity, it is also very clear that racialization has captured us and has done, and is doing, a kind of deep violence to the spirit that leaves us feeling powerless to end our involvement in the nightmare.

The Reggae poet and singer Bob Marley continues to capture the imagination of young and old alike, more than thirty years after his death. One of the tunes he made famous was a poetic rendition of Psalm 137 from the Hebrew scriptures: *By the Rivers of Babylon*.[84] The psalm gives voice to the grief of the Hebrew people as they experience very difficult captivity at the hands of the Babylonians. Marley's reggae rendition suggests the psalm also echoes the experience of enslaved Africans in the Americas.

It has always seemed to me that, on second reflection, the psalm and its musical version speak powerfully to the deep experience of those of us who are white, as well. Racialization has, in effect, stolen our humanity. It imprisons us perhaps even more rigidly and intensely than others. Clearly, there are also perks. My colleague Joseph Barndt suggests that white people are also imprisoned by racism but that we experience some desirable perks, prison amenities that play out in the daily experiences we have termed white privilege.[85]

The power of our experience of imprisonment stems from our multigenerational investment in racial domination, degradation, and dispossession. The cumulative power of this investment persuades us that we benefit from this history. We experience, in ways we cannot honestly articulate, our identity defined by this history. Our influence has shaped a society committed to a belief in scarcity and marked by hyperindividualism.

Economic stability is a constant struggle for most of us; we experience stability as a fragile ephemeral place. We sense that fundamental change places us at risk; we stand to lose the relative advantage our history has provided. The vast majority of us favor racial justice in principle, yet our sense of well-being is welded to the very historical dynamics that have created the racial nightmare.

A deep consequence of the dynamics that comprise our collective pathology is that we have great difficulty, as a collective, focusing our attention in a sustained manner on the primary issues that confront our society. Our attention span is fleeting. Politically, intense partisanship and ideological warfare is easier. Economically, we are wedded to short-term measures of growth that cannot take into account long-term costs. Culturally, the story of American exceptionalism continues to fuel our global presence and drive our educational system. It is as though we are in the grip of a sort of collective distraction. Something prevents us from being attentive to what is actually transpiring around us. This is the pathological character of white identity.

White People and Historical Trauma

What is trauma? How is the word used clinically? What does it indicate, and is it useful when we examine the damage done by race/racism?

Trauma[86]

1. a: an injury (as a wound) to living tissue caused by an extrinsic agent
   b: a disordered psychic or behavioral state resulting from severe mental or emotional stress or physical injury
   c: an emotional upset

Antiracist therapists and scholars, using the language of *historical loss and trauma*, provide some of the most compelling commentary about the impacts of racialization on communities of color. Their work suggests that the impacts of race are multigenerational and that historical trauma rooted in the past continues to work mischief in people's everyday lives. These impacts may even be cellular. "Native healers, medicine people and elders have always known this and it is common knowledge in Native oral traditions,"[87] according to LeManuel "Lee" Bitsoi, Navajo, PhD research associate in genetics at Harvard University during his presentation at the Gateway to Discovery Conference in 2013. Bitsoi notes that epigenetics is beginning to uncover scientific proof that intergenerational trauma is real. So, an obvious question is, "Has racialization traumatized white people?" I believe it has. If so, it is important to carefully explore how this is so and how it is manifest in the white collective.

Names are powerful. The name we give to a process interprets the process and has emotional impact. When we use the word trauma in our conversation about white identity, what does the term indicate? In the medical sense, trauma indicates severe stress and injury—emotional and physiological. How have we who are white experienced injury as a consequence of racialization? It should come as no surprise that many people of color resist and even resent white people using this term to indicate the impact of race on the white collective.

"Give me a break!" This would not be a surprising comment from someone who has experienced and witnessed the damage done by racialization to people of color. It might seem that once again white people are trying to find a way to excuse our history or elicit a bit of pity. Is this yet another example of theft, even if it only seems to be linguistic theft? We must take these sensibilities into account and walk carefully as we do our work. When we use the language of historical loss and trauma to indicate the experience of white people, we need to clarify how our trauma differs from that of others.

So then, how does the language of trauma illuminate the experience of white people? First, it helps us understand the stubborn persistence of denial and the complex layers of white racialization. Second, it locates us historically and illuminates the multigenerational power of white racialization. Third, and perhaps most to the point, it clarifies the stake that white people have in deconstructing race and ending the racial nightmare. To speak in a colloquial manner, it is about us realizing that we have skin in the game and that we have as much skin in the game as anyone, albeit in a different fashion. We will be dependable coconspirators in the struggle when it is clear that our lives are also at stake. Then we will be more than allies in others' struggle. After all, allies can change allegiance! As long as we are clear that our lives are at stake, we will be present in the struggle.

How are our lives at stake? Racialization has been like carbon monoxide in the development of the white collective. Its negative impact can be neither smelled nor seen. Yet, it's deadly. It is, in fact, toxic. It takes major effort on the part of white people to be aware of and present to the daily deluge of micro affirmations that constitute the white experience. To look beyond the deluge and discern something deeper that is working deadly mischief is challenging and nonsensical to many of us.

We must wonder about the apparent paralysis of spirit that silenced well-meaning white people during the time of legal segregation. This was perhaps most dramatically evident in lynching across the nation (not only in the South). Such silence and evident numbness indicate what some have termed "moral injury." Racialization has sabotaged our moral sensibilities and our capacity for personal and collective responsibility.

We must also wonder about the idealized narratives about American Indian people that seem unaware of or unconcerned about the vicissitudes of life on most reservations. Many white people hunger to participate in sweat lodge ceremonies and purchase Native goods yet seem unconcerned about daily realities for Indian people or the myriad ways the nation has ignored its trust commitments. I believe this hunger testifies to a profound vacuum at the center of white identity—in effect, a spiritual vacuum. Racialization is making us two-dimensional, diminishing our humanity in the process. It is cultivating insensitivity and indifference.

Social norming and the normalizing of white identity are at the heart of our experience. The phenomenon some have termed white fragility is, perhaps, an expression of a normalized social identity that is all about race, albeit in subtle ways. It is an expression of the echo chamber effect. The traumatization of white people happens in the experience of being normed. Our normalized collective identity is based on the mythic inferiority of nonwhite identity and the social subjugation of people of color. We learn to hide those aspects of our identity that do not appropriately reflect social norms. Since hyperindividualism is part of our socialization, we may even hold tightly to those aspects of our personalities that make us unique, different from others. We learn to pretend our abnormalities don't exist. Our pretensions become a kind of self-inflicted psychic violence.

We know in a very deep way what our identity costs others. However, selective blindness and deafness gives us permission to believe otherwise. In order to bear this belief system, we must deaden empathic resonance. We must not feel the price that is being paid by others and by ourselves. We

161

experience this constructed identity as tenuously attached to the centers of power and authority in society. This tenuous attachment feels fragile to us. We are one step removed from a place of uncertainty, ambiguity, disruption, and terror. Even as we fashion social dramas that express our superiority and that normalize us, we can feel our exposure and our vulnerability. Perhaps the election of 2016 most poignantly expressed the deep anxiety of the white collective.

Friends who do family therapy tell me that family abuse touches all the members of the family, including those who witness but do not perpetrate the abuse. Perhaps, in a similar fashion, even well-meaning white people who would never choose self-consciously to be a part of racial violence are nonetheless hurt by the violence they know is done in their name. This is a deep hurt that indicates an awareness that life belongs to life; we know intuitively that we are all linked together. When we also know that we are complicit in the harm visited on others, this knowing becomes a deep injury that remains tender even when scar tissue covers it. It is not only people of color who bear the multigenerational wounds of racial violence (that is, violence done to the family). It is also we who are assigned to the white collective, even when we can't relate our pain and sense of injury to race, except in a manner that compounds the damage done to others (as when we believe that people of color use government programs to gain an advantage over us).

When we say that race is ubiquitous in our society, it means that white identity extends to other aspects of social experience that are not explicitly racial. The normalized identity we inhabit does not exist only in "racial" situations (even though it is in racial situations that we are most aware of our white identity). Hence, the behaviors that are rooted in our racial trauma may well play out in situations that seem to have nothing whatsoever to do with race. They are expressions of the power we've learned to associate with white identity. Sexual harassment, for example, in this context is an expression of racialized white male identity. The "Me Too" phenomenon is not simply about gender.

When our sense of comfort, stability, and safety is linked to the very dynamics that disempower and oppress others, it seems beyond our capacity to seriously consider fundamental change. We experience what some have termed loss aversion. Loss aversion is when the uncertainties of change sabotage the promises of change.[88] The pain of possible loss seems to overshadow whatever we might gain from changing the racial calculus.

In the 2016 election cycle, Donald Trump centered his campaign on the fear of loss that gained traction with many potential white voters. He frequently and dramatically suggested that something has been stolen, or will be stolen, and that he is the one able to recover it.

We are, in a manner of speaking, suspended between the aspirational imagery of our original national vision and the realities of the brutal deeds and processes we have been prepared to tolerate, rationalize, downplay, and ignore that have constituted the actual society we live in. We disassociate ourselves from the brutality of the past and present yet are averse to risking the future. Enfleshing our aspiration is too daunting! This dissociative aversion is the place of our trauma. It is a sign of the damage racialization has wrought.

In order to grasp that the very dynamics that advantage us also hurt and do violence to us, we have to visit our terrain and examine it carefully. Then we can grasp that we are in effect held captive. Our investment in the echo chamber holds us fast. It insulates us from reality. When it comes clear that we are imprisoned and held captive, we can begin to grasp that when things change, we stand to benefit. We gain. And what we gain is our own stolen, traumatized humanity. But we must do our work.

Historical Accountability

Standing in the place of gain rather than loss requires some deep inner work—some soul work. I think of this soul work under the rubric of historical accountability. It is work that we must do collectively and personally. There are at least three way stations in this work of historical accountability; they are direct counters to the interior dynamics that, like psychic rivets, make us vulnerable to the power of the pathologies of white identity. We must learn to remember, to feel deeply, and to claim our space in the racial drama that continues to play out in our daily lives.

Remembering

This is more than simply learning our history (although this is a crucial piece; we all must become historians with integrity). It involves hearing all the stories that together account for how we, as a nation, came to this place. Others' stories may shock us. Many of them we have never before heard. White supremacy insulated us. They will reveal a history that is more nuanced, complex, and substantial than the history we know. It also means being engaged in the work of creating space for those stories to come forth, to be heard, and to be validated. It means becoming historical, in the sense of connecting oneself personally to the ongoing historical drama of this nation and being willing to expose oneself to the whole drama, all that brought us to this point. Existentially, this means being willing to be vulnerable. This sense of historicity is more than an academic or scholastic exercise; it is an existential drama. Our history flows through us; we experience it playing out in our lives.

Feeling Deeply

The willingness to experience our experience is another way of saying what feeling deeply is about. This requires a bit of unpacking. Bob Marley's rendition of Psalm 137 from the Hebrew scriptures is suggestive of the work to be done in this arena. All of us live emotional lives, even when we intentionally craft our lives around ideas and rational processes. Emotions are simply part of who we are. But we often learn how to keep our emotions under the surface, carefully contained. Some emotions are more powerful than others—in effect, deep and foundational. Literary traditions testify to common, fundamental emotions. They are the stuff of great works of literature: drama, poetry, storytelling. Perhaps what makes some literature devotional literature is the ability to capture in poetic metaphor and language the deep, powerful emotions that are common, that knit us together as human beings across culture, language, and time.

The poetry of Psalm 137 conveys the powerful sense of grief that is associated with the experience of captivity and domination. There are many examples of devotional literature, in addition to the psalms, that suggest that grief is, finally, more than just an emotion. It humanizes us even as it wrenches our lives. It intrudes into the deeps of our consciousness and profoundly changes our experience of being human. When white people experience their own helplessness and deep captivity, grief is apt to come front and center. We grieve over our lost humanity; we grieve over what has been done in our name; we grieve over our captivity and our inability to trust the future. This is suffering as a spirit phenomenon. As such, it shapes the foundations of resolve and enhances our capacity to risk. Save we trod this difficult pathway, we lack the ability to stand in solidarity with others; grief gives us empathic resonance. It makes us trustworthy. Grief helps us grasp that our pain, most personally experienced, is not simply about what has been done to others in our name; it is about what white supremacy has done to us. This is grief work; being open to the experience of grief is part of our rehumanization. But we must remember that this is our work; we cannot expect people of color to either do our work or give us some slack because we're grieving.

Lamentation is the expression and language of grief, of deep sorrow. Lamentation is the domain of literature and artful expression, of poetry, storytelling, music, and dance. The literature of resistance that racial hegemony has fostered always contains lamentation. We have witnessed the power of lamentation in the literature and art that has been germinated in communities of color and articulated by sensitive writers, poets, musicians, painters, dancers, actors, and so on. Perhaps the time has come when artful expressions of resistance can convey the lamentation of the white collective.

In her book *Emotional Agility*, Dr. Susan David suggests that helping children learn how to navigate the world of emotions is fundamental to a successful life.[89] In a society that often sublimates emotions or uses emotional appeals to manipulate others, this may also be useful advice for adults. Emotional skills, in her view, are fundamental to a healthy sense of self and the ability to negotiate the stresses of life. Some have termed such skills emotional intelligence. There are four practical steps that Dr. David lifts up that adults dealing with the emotional challenges of white identity might profit from:

- *Feel it.* Difficult emotions can be scary. Our default is to push them away, push them down, and avoid them. Being willing to be where you are emotionally is important.
- *Show it.* We do have some clear rules around emotions that suggest keeping them under wraps, not expressing them. My family is from the South; my mother's side is from the Deep South. Southern gentility is real and is a presumed part of the socialization of cultured folk. Consequently, I was raised with the clear understanding that I was to be nice, regardless of how I actually felt. I can still hear my maternal grandmother saying, "Jamie, shugah, now be nice!"

While this may make civil intercourse more pleasant, it can be emotionally costly. In our society, white cisgender males often learn not to show their feelings.

- *Label it.* Naming emotions is crucial. Rabbi Estelle Frankel suggests that when we name difficult emotions, it provides some psychological space; we can step back, so to speak, and take a self-conscious relationship to that emotion. "Accurately expressing a feeling, liberates us from the unconscious control that the feeling may have had over us."[90] Dr. David suggests that labeling emotions is key to our capacity to empathize. In effect, it enhances empathic resonance, the very capacity racialization sabotages.

- *Watch it go.* Difficult emotions are just that, difficult! But they don't last forever; they pass. And when we risk experiencing them and naming them, we are changed by the experience. We remember them, we can appreciate them in others, and we can create stories that help us move on and gain from their visit.

Claiming Our Space

This is a direct counterpoint to the desperate dynamics of denial. Before we can be in any other space, we must *own* the space that has been the locus of white identity in our history. That is, we must own up to our complicity. This is more than being honest about the reality of racial oppression, yesterday and today. It is more than conceding the role white people have played in this history. It is claiming and being willing to inhabit our own personal complicity in the process as an integral, even if unwilling, participant. Effectively, this is the assumption of personal responsibility, not because someone has guilt-tripped me or because those oppressed by race have found me guilty. Rather, this is about confessing what is. It is about reclaiming my own humanity, which is done in the context of solidarity with all who have been harmed by race.

Because this choosing is about personal and collective responsibility, it is far removed from the discussions about fault. Whose fault is this? When we no longer have to spend vast sums of energy in the drama of denial, we are free to participate in the construction of an alternative vision of society. Then, we no longer experience a personal investment, even if unacknowledged, in the architecture of white supremacy. Rather, we can join with others in the processes of deconstruction and reconstruction. We find our humanity in the dialectic between denial and responsibility. It is in claiming our space in the racial calculus that the identity that was simply our fate becomes an opportunity to shape the new. Fate becomes opportunity. We can be a part of the work of reparation, the reparation of community itself, beyond the pale of our apartheid history. This new place is what is meant by the term antiracism. Antiracism is the praxis of resistance to the dehumanization wrought by race.

This praxis may not be comfortable; initially, it may even feel like we are betraying something or someone. We are. We are betraying, via deconstruction, a collective identity we experienced as normative and, thus, comfortable. It is an identity, frankly, that is fabricated from the suffering of others. Antiracism requires us to become, in effect, race traitors. The website for Race Traitors has an interesting slogan: *treason to whiteness is loyalty to humanity*. The slogan is derived from the work of historian Noel Ignatiev.[91]

Brené Brown, on her Facebook page, has some pertinent commentary: "When we own our history, we have the power to change the present and the future. We must collectively and courageously turn toward our history of slavery, segregation and systemic racism and own the pain, trauma and violence it created and continues to create. This is the first step in writing a braver, more loving and more just story for our children."[92]

I have not intended this chapter to be either a how-to guide for overcoming our racialization or a clinical analysis of pathological behavior and related therapy. Rather, I hope it is a metaphorical exercise that indicates—however roughly—the damage race has done to us as white people. Further, I hope it poetically suggests the pathway we must walk if we are to be a part of creating a future that does not simply repeat our past. This commentary on historical accountability sets the stage for Part 4 and our exploration of reparation as the portal to the future.

PART IV

REPARATION: THE PORTAL TO THE FUTURE

Introduction

The Choctaw Trail of Tears and the Piney Woods of Arkansas

I had originally planned to walk the trail from Philadelphia, Mississippi, to Durant, Oklahoma. The Choctaw Reservation is just outside Philadelphia; the administrative center for the Choctaw Nation of Oklahoma is located in Durant. I understood the walk to be ceremonial. It would be a ceremony of reconciliation and reunion. I was seeking a way to symbolically reunite the descendants of Betty and Joseph Lea with their Choctaw relatives in Oklahoma. The Removal Act of 1830 had split our extended family. The part of the family that I am descended from remained in Mississippi. The ones who migrated were simply lost, at least to our memory.

My youngest daughter, Indira, expressed concern about my safety on such an undertaking. Then, as I conditioned my body for the experience, my feet and knees began to talk to me. "Hold on there, bud! What are you thinking? We can't handle this trip!" I had become an avid biker over the years; biking was less stressful on knees and feet damaged by several years of running on pavement and sidewalks. When my body began to raise doubts about my capacity to walk the trail, biking it suddenly seemed like an exciting and doable alternative.

One of my friends was also an avid biker. Jim suggested he would be interested in biking with me and that we might use his car as a sag wagon. We could alternate: one would drive while the other biked. In short order, the trip came together. We would drive from Chicago to the Choctaw Reservation, stay at the Casino hotel, and get an early start on the trail. We were able to pay a courtesy call on the chief of the Mississippi Band of Choctaws the day before. Phyllis Anderson was the first female elected to head the Mississippi Choctaw Nation. She graciously took time from a busy schedule to chat with us. We presented her with tobacco and expressed our appreciation for her leadership of the Mississippi Band of Choctaw Indians. She, in turn, affirmed our effort and gave us her blessing on the journey.

In fall 2013, as we biked the trail, we passed through the beautiful pine forests of southwestern Arkansas. I distinctly remember the experience. I could have been swept up in the beauty of the moment, tall pines, and roadside waterways. The weather was perfect for biking, not too warm, a gentle, constant breeze. It was mid-October. The deciduous trees were beginning to show color. It was a bright, sunlit day with only a few clouds on the periphery of the horizon. However, something intruded that kept the beauty of the moment at bay.

As I traversed the area between Washington, Arkansas, and the Oklahoma border, I became aware of a strong, palpable sense of presence other than that of the trees and rolling hills. It was the presence, for lack of a better word, of grief. *I could feel their grief!* As I rode, the sense of grief grew until it was almost overwhelming.

Now, this was a strange phenomenon. It was not that I was experiencing grief; rather, I was experiencing a presence that was not me. Indeed, it was palpable! I do not subscribe to supernatural explanations of historical events. I am not suggesting any magic or invisible beings. Had this been a laboratory setting, there would have been nothing measurable beyond me, my bike, the road, and the landscape.

I know there are several explanations for this experience, depending on the interpretive screen one invokes. Perhaps the most accessible for postmodern people is the psychological one. I was simply experiencing emotions evoked by the cumulative power of the history: family, region, and nation that I had pieced together. I was physically tired after several days of biking. I was imagining what it might have been like to walk through these woods in the winter of 1831–32. I'm sure one of my therapist friends could easily and colorfully have expanded this interpretation. "James, you just have a powerful imagination!" Or, others less psychologically oriented might wish to riff on the impact of strong collectively experienced emotions on the space-time continuum. Perhaps I was simply experiencing something akin to reverberations at a subtle, molecular level.

Finally, however, I simply have to confess that I have no explanation for that experience. It was incredibly palpable; that is, it felt like not me. And the only English word I could summon that seemed fitting was grief. As I biked, I was surrounded by grief. I felt as though I had experienced another's intimate emotional reality, as though I was privy to interior realities that were not mine. I almost felt like an intruder; a tinge of embarrassment touched me.

This experience accompanied me for several miles, almost to the Oklahoma border, until it was time for me to drive our sag wagon and my biking partner's turn to ride the trail. The experience put me in a somber and reflective place. I had come to know and experience a lost, hitherto unknown, part of family and national history. I had walked, or rather pedaled, a passage appropriately termed the Trail of Tears. My pedaling did not involve the loss of home, family, or possessions; it did not involve leaving loved ones in Mississippi or along the trail. I was not confronting the challenge of starting a new life in unknown territory, with possible hostile neighbors who might not appreciate my intrusion. Nonetheless, at age seventy-four, I was experiencing a journey that touched me deeply and would alter my experience of my nation and my family. It was a journey that would make new claims upon me and give me new dimensions of accountability. The experience in the piney woods of southwestern Arkansas stands out, even several years removed from the journey. It became central to the entire adventure. Even now, I remember it as the experience of their grief.

For those of us who have been racialized as white, there is some deep and ongoing work we must do. It is powerfully symbolic and ceremonial. It involves the language we use to articulate identity, it involves accountability, and it involves community. I have come to believe that this work, perhaps call it grief work, is fundamental to our ability to be a part of shaping the future.

In Part 4, we will presume the work that has gone before in order to explore its significance for our future as a nation. The first step, in chapter 13, is an exploration of language and its role in helping us imagine beyond the boundaries of the social canon. In particular, we will focus on the terminology of resistance that is relevant to repairing the damage done to the fabric of community by generations of racialization. What is meant by antiracism, and why is it important to use such language?

In chapter 14, we will turn to the matter of accountability. What is the role of accountability in relation to the damage done by racism? What is accountability? How do we use the term in a manner that is life-giving and, therefore, counter to the ravages of race? What is the place of antiracist accountability in the complex fabric of community?

Chapter 15 turns directly to the matter of antiracism and the reparation of community. What is meant by reparation, and what is necessary for it to transpire? We will discuss the importance and limitations of apology and the matters of recompense and atonement. What does it mean to "make it right"? Why is this important when it comes to reparation? Shouldn't we simply forget the past and respond to present-day challenges? Why do we need to rehearse the tragedy and pain of yesterday?

Finally, chapter 16 is an effort to speak provocatively, persuasively, but certainly not exhaustively about transapartheid community. What is a vision of community that is reality oriented, does not deny our past, yet is responsive to the challenges of a dramatically changing world? Dr. Martin Luther King Jr. wrote of our dilemma in his book *Where Do We Go from Here: Chaos or Community?*[93] If anything, the challenges of shaping community life that is humanizing and ecologically responsible are more sharply drawn than ever.

We will conclude this brief exploration of our nation's investment in systemic oppression with some practical suggestions of steps we can take. We'll also note some troubling questions and some hopeful promises.

13

Language, Resistance, and Community

Language, we are learning, plays a paramount role in brain development. Hearing, speaking, reading, and writing create neural pathways that enable us to process information, experience emotions, and imagine the world. Language (in the spoken and written sense) enables us to connect events and fabricate stories that interpret what's going on around us. If a person has a hearing challenge and uses sign language to communicate or learns to read lips, then communication using sign language becomes a visual process. If one is visually challenged, then communication may also be tactile, using the Braille system. It is not unusual for individuals with visual challenges to also have very sensitive hearing.

The centrality of language is clear relative to shaping relationships and mediating our relationship with society and the earth. We begin Part 4 with some brief reflections on the role of language in shaping resistance to racism. Without language, there is no meaning, even at the most basic level—survival. Communication is common among animal and even plant species; however, best we can discern, no other species has developed language to the extent that humans have (or we simply have not yet become adept at reading the utterances of other species). Due to the role of language in shaping relationships and in conveying meaning, how something is *said* or *written* is important. Words and how they are arranged invoke other frames of reference and meaning. Comments that are carelessly framed or hastily shaped easily lead to misunderstanding and misinterpretation. That is why the language of diplomacy is carefully crafted. It needs to take into account cultural differences as well as all the ambiguities around the meaning of words. That is also why the language of legislation involves endless wordsmithing. What is conveyed and not conveyed (or perhaps intimated) is everything. Clearly, communication is more than the meaning conveyed by the selection and sequencing of words. Things such as body language, tone of voice, volume, social context, and timing are all part of the process.

Naming is a crucial part of this process. The names we assign to things and experiences also interpret them and disclose our relationship to them. Naming invokes a frame of reference. John Gall, in the *Systems Bible*, suggests that we should not underestimate the power of naming. It is "literally the power to bring new realities into existence."[94] In this sense, naming is a central part of the process of social creation. Naming weaves a social fabric. Communication makes this fabric a shared reality. In this sense, social discourse creates society. There is no social *isness* outside of the communal discourse that weaves it, interprets it, and even challenges it.

For example, if we speak of "African slaves," we indicate something about fundamental identity: slaves who happen to be African. If we speak of "enslaved Africans," the most fundamental identity indicated is *African*, not slave. We have indicated Africans to whom something tragic has been done; they've been enslaved. Slave is not their central identity. As Africans, they may be Yoruba, Hausa, Efik, Zulu, Igbo, Fulani, and so on, but slave is not an ethnic, clan, or family identity. It is not central to who they are.

Previously, we noted how white Americans learned to associate and even equate slavery and Africans of the diaspora. Slave, in other words, was viewed by white people as a natural condition, a core identity. It was an expression of appropriate status and of individual and group inferiority. Even freedom, manumission, did not alter this fundamental identity. It was a racial feature. Chief Justice Taney expressed this belief when he wrote that Dred Scott did not qualify for citizenship owing to his race. Words matter. What we name phenomena makes a difference. It reveals our relationship to what we've named and also suggests something about the limits of our action. Language shapes our perspectives and constrains our action. This description of the role of language and the importance of naming contextualizes how we use language to substantiate resistance. The term *enslaved Africans* is an example of the language of resistance; it counters the subtle implications of *African slave*.

In this book, I have suggested that the term racism refers to a system of oppression rooted in racial designation. It is a system that has been fundamental to the development of our economic system. It also invokes a mythology about what it means to be human and who is human. It is a system that invokes and strengthens other oppression systems rooted in other social identities. If indeed racism is systemic, then naming the alternative is crucial. We don't stop participating in systemic processes simply by discerning and naming them. It is necessary to imagine and name the alternative that counters the system. Countering the system is more than simply trying to avoid participating in the system. Efforts to be nonracist or nondiscriminatory are insufficient and ineffective. Such language suggests a passive alternative to active participation in racism; in effect, efforts to be nonracist become a form of complicity in racialization. An alternative is the term *antiracism*. It is yet another example of the language of resistance.

The prefix *anti* as it is used in medical science and in therapeutic practice gives us a way to imagine alternatives to racism and other forms of systemic oppression. Let me illustrate. If I wake up one morning with a fever, a sore throat, and a headache, a call or visit with my physician may be in order. After listening to my symptoms, and perhaps ordering some lab tests, she may well prescribe an antibiotic. (We are learning that judicious use of antibiotics is wise; bacteria are crafty and mutate to overcome familiar antibiotics. However, antibiotics, as a class of medicines, have saved millions of lives over the course of the last several decades.) Some bacteria produce life-threatening systemic infection. The prefix *anti* suggests an intervention that counters such systemic infection. In fact, medical science has produced a veritable plethora of therapeutic tools that use the prefix "anti" to indicate a rigorous effort to counter systemic challenges. This includes such classes of medications as antivirals, antioxidants, anti-inflammatories, antifungals, anticoagulants, antiparasitics, antitoxins, antidepressants, antipsychotics, and so on. The list is long. Research has also found naturally occurring plants, such as some spices, that have antibiotic, antioxidant, or antiviral properties.

In relation to racism, the equivalent term is antiracism. Antiracism is an intervention in the systemic processes of racial oppression. The medical profession provides a useful frame of reference and contextualizes the term. Antiracism, when it involves an activity, is like the practice of community medicine. The term indicates interventions that counter the damage to community life done by systemic racism. Racism breaks the bonds of community, sabotages efforts to build community, and undermines community well-being. Antiracism, as an intervention, interrupts the processes of racialization. In this sense, antiracism is active. It does not suggest avoidance or disassociation; it indicates action. It indicates resistance and an intention to intervene in the processes of racial oppression in order to interrupt them, thus creating a space in which we can envision alternative social arrangements.

Some people have difficulty using the term antiracism. It seems too negative! I've actually heard people say, "That sounds so negative. It says what you are against; it doesn't say what you are for!" Such reservations about using the term suggest a couple of things to me. They suggest an unspoken suspicion about complicity (there's something being implied about me if we use this term). Second, it suggests unclarity regarding race and racism.

Whether the term was used in times past is beside the point. In the context of our times, it is a clear indication of resistance to the oppression of racism. Invoking the term places one in the history of resistance. When we risk action that intervenes concretely in the social processes, that decision joins us with others who have risked intervention. It places us in the company of others who have gone before us, as well as contemporaries who risk such action. Antiracism captures this sensibility. It is one example of using language to intentionally challenge the existent social canon. It is an example that we will utilize to explore what intervention is about.

Antiracism as Intervention

In this book, we have explored briefly the processes of racialization. We have investigated how these ongoing social processes impact and shape individual identity. We looked in depth at the terrain of white identity, using metaphor and analogy to describe the impact of race on those of us who are white. We looked at structural racism and the various ways race impacts institutional identity and systemic processes. These impacts produce discriminatory behavior in the dynamics of access and control of institutions. Measurable racial disparities are the footprints that cue us to such institutional behavior. We also surveyed the impact of race in culture, noting the impacts on language, lifeways, performing arts, and our story about being American.

These three poles—individual, institutional/structural, and cultural—engender a kind of racialization synergy. The multigenerational impact of race has produced, in effect, an electromagnetic force field emanating from these three poles. This force field gives birth to a monocultural echo chamber that holds in thrall all who are caught up in the field. People of color tend to be quite aware of this force field; those of us who are white tend to be clueless. A brief story will illustrate the experience of encountering this field.

A few years ago, a friend of mine related her experience of being elected to the board of a local nonprofit in her city of residence. My friend is Mexican American. Her first board meeting, she told me, was an experience she'll never forget. When the meeting started, she realized that she was the only woman of color on the board. As the meeting progressed, it was almost like there was a "force field in the room. I couldn't get in! It was like I was invisible." Finally, she noted, "I simply had to break in. I had to intervene in the force field and interrupt it!"

Her story gave me a new metaphor for describing an encounter with the dynamics of racialization. It also underscored for me the significance of antiracism as an intervention. Rather than a passive nonracist identity, the term antiracism indicates interventions that interrupt the recurring cycles of racialization and the synergy they produce. Antiracism, in this sense, is an action-reflection praxis. It is the movement from an idea to application followed by reflective assessment. Identity is constituted in this movement: intervention and reflection. We do not become antiracist, whether as individuals or collaborative efforts, and then act. Our antiracist identity is enfleshed in the action of intervention. The social critique that gives meaning to our action, the action itself, and the reflective assessment together substantiate identity. This means choosing to risk intervening, personally, in the processes of oppression. This is the stuff of history! To intervene is to be historical, to be part of the historical drama. Intervention, in this sense, is the act of claiming an antiracist identity. We claim this identity by choosing to be involved in the struggles for racial justice.

This was the power and authority of the young women and men who challenged segregation in the South in the 1950s and '60s. It was the power of the organizing done by La Raza Unida in the 1960s and '70s, the Black Panthers in the latter 1960s, the American Indian movement in the

1970s, the Black Lives Matter movement today, and a multitude of other history-shaping movements. Individuals were and are prepared to insert their lives into the processes of oppression, to intervene and interrupt. This has always been the power and authority of social movements that occasion fundamental transformation. They begin as resistance to oppression. Resistance is the context in which an alternative vision can be birthed.

And, I suspect, resistance always begins with those who are directly oppressed. Others may experience the pangs of conscience. And the pangs of conscience testify to a spark of empathy and may indeed lead to action. But the social canon is powerful and exerts authority even over people of conscience. Its thrall is strong. Dominant group members who speak out will be isolated and undermined. The key to their steadfastness and even sanity is accountability. Solidarity and strength in numbers comes from entering into accountability relationships with the oppressed and with other awakened white people.

This brief commentary on the power of language and naming is clearly not an exhaustive exploration of the subject. We have only noted the importance of one term in the process of social change: antiracism. And we have noted the importance of careful, intentional use of language in shaping resistance to oppression. English itself is not always the best medium for expressing the subtle complexities of social dynamics and identity (when I was in college, I recall reading that the Hopi language was much more hospitable to Einsteinian physics than English). My intent is to set the stage for a careful examination of the application of the term antiracism and its relevance for the reparation and restoration of community. The first step in such an examination is an in-depth treatment of the term accountability in the context of our work on racism and the mischief it has wrought in the fabric of community life.

14

Historical Accountability

In this chapter, we will flesh out the notion of historical accountability that was introduced in chapter 12. We will note the way the term accountability is typically used and will spend some time reframing its use in the context of our work on racism and racialization. This chapter will suggest that accountability is fundamental to racial justice and to the reparation and restoration of community. It is central to shaping resilient, sustainable societies. Consequently, it is that without which communities do not survive. We'll set the stage for this exploration of accountability with a short vignette about the marriage ceremony and a recently conducted wedding.

Jumping the Broom

A few years ago, two white people included the ritual of "jumping the broom" in their wedding ceremony. An African American pastor co-led the ceremony and conducted the broom ritual; the community then blessed the couple, and the pastor pronounced them married. This traditional ceremony, harking back to the days of slavery, is part of many African American marriage ceremonies. It is not typically part of marriages involving white people. What's going on here?

My wife and I were married in November 2014. Two longtime pastor friends performed the ceremony—one African American, the other white. At the completion of the formal more traditional Christian ceremony, the African American pastor conducted a jumping the broom ceremony.

At its completion, the community came forward and laid hands on us in a collective blessing. Those who could not touch us directly, as we knelt, touched someone who was touching us. The pastor carefully contextualized the ceremony and its history and significance prior to inviting us to participate.

Here we were, two older white newlyweds, participating in a ceremony rooted in the African past and of special significance for enslaved Africans enduring the American diaspora in the days of slavery. We were not young, fresh-faced newlyweds. Both of us had been here before. Nonetheless, we found the energy necessary to jump the broom and to do so with enthusiasm!

Jumping the broom needs to be seen as a holy ritual, we learned. It is a holy ritual because it was born out of the experience of oppression—the experience of enslaved Africans. It was a direct counter to legally sanctioned oppression. Slavery did not recognize the marriages between enslaved Africans as legitimate. Slavers regularly split marriages and even sold offspring. The ceremony was an act of liberation that bore witness to the spiritual freedom of enslaved Africans. The ritual itself was a community event. It clearly placed the community and its blessing ahead of the rule of the white man's law. In effect, it was saying, "Your law does not determine who has the right to marry. Our community does!"

All who weave this ceremony into their wedding service need to keep this in mind. They are placing themselves in the context of resistance to oppression alongside a particular historic community. They are also entering into an accountability relationship to the historic community that gave birth to this ceremony: enslaved Africans and, by implication, their progeny. Thus, to participate in this ceremony is to link a couple and a community to the history of resistance in this nation. It is to link them to a particular historical context and the community that fished this ritual out of the reservoir of African memory.

This is the difference between cultural appropriation and historical accountability. Cultural appropriation simply takes without attention to historical context and the claims it makes upon us today. Historical accountability connects self-consciously to the historical context and willingly enters into an accountability relationship that continues the significance and deep meaning invoked by the tradition in question (I want to underscore that this illustration is *not* to suggest that others, white or otherwise, need to incorporate this ceremony into their wedding).

What, then, does it mean to be accountable to a particular historical context and community? At the very least, it means standing in solidarity with others connected to the jumping culture. Standing in solidarity is more than being an ally in the usual sense. It means grasping in a deep fashion that one has as much skin in the game as others engaged in the historical drama of resistance. This is not being allied with others in their struggle; this is not lending my assistance. It is linking arms in the same struggle—our struggle. This does not diminish the fact that different groups have different roles to play. Instead, it is to recognize that the struggle for racial justice is our struggle, all of us. It is also to grasp that it is part of a larger struggle that is central to the viability of our future. Racial apartheid jeopardizes this nation's capacity to navigate the challenges of an uncertain future; this is a central thesis in this book.

When we consider the damage done by generations of racism (the misuse of systemic power) to communities of color, an issue that quickly comes to the fore is accountability. The systems and institutions of our society have seldom been required to answer to the communities most clearly damaged by racialization. When legal changes have sought to require such accountability, resolute resistance from dominant society has been typical. This was the case when slavery was ended; it was also the case when the Civil Rights Act and the Voting Rights Act were passed. When treaty rights are upheld by federal courts, furious resistance is predictable, sometimes even violent resistance. One simply has to wonder, "Where is accountability?"

Two of the organizations that have most clearly, consistently, and persuasively made the case for the centrality of accountability have been The People's Institute for Survival and Beyond (New Orleans) and Crossroads Antiracism Organizing and Training (south suburban Chicago). Together, these two organizations have trained thousands of people across the United States over the past twenty years. Each, in its own way, has made the case that tending to the matter of accountability is the primary pathway to a racially just future. If indeed this is the case, a careful consideration of accountability is in order.

Identity and Accountability

Going deeper in this conversation will require an examination of the relationship between accountability and identity. Racialization, we recall, shapes collective identities. Antiracism, hence, shapes a counter identity. We often tend to think and speak of identity as though it involves an interior essence. What is the essence of James? This is to approach the matter of identity as though it has to do with what I am, in myself; what is the isness that resides within me. This is an atomistic view of identity. It regards the self as separate within itself. In this view, my connections to others are almost incidental to who I really am. From this point of view, we might say of others, "I know her; she's not capable of such things! She (or he) would never do this. It's just not within her character—or their character." We presume an interior essence that, in effect, determines what one is capable of doing.

From such a perspective, we find it almost impossible to reconcile the atrocities committed by Nazi Germany with our view of the essential character of a Christian nation. Similarly, we might suggest that the transatlantic slave trade was clearly an aberration and not a mark of our nation's "deep character." We might even suggest that it really had to do with Europe and the colonizing efforts of others. The system that commodified enslaved Africans and sought to force their labor was not, we might add, a true mark of the American spirit. From this perspective, it was a practice of greedy and brutal plantation owners. Similarly, the massacre of Cheyenne women, children, and elders at Sand Creek by the Colorado Militia was likely a misunderstanding or, at worst, the result of a deranged commanding officer. Indian Removal, some might suggest, was done to protect Indian tribes; it was, after all, for their own benefit in the long run. It was not really an expression of a national identity marked by covetousness, brutality, and violence. There may, indeed, be individuals and groups within our nation that are so motivated. However, in the view of many, there is an essential purity in our identity as a nation. We often hear individuals and groups referencing this way of thinking about identity. But there is more to say about identity.

Attempts to reconcile essentialist thinking with actual historical happenings leads to a kind of pernicious dualism. We may speak of individuals controlled by demonic impulses or captured by the power of sin. We may conclude that humanity has an essentially sinful nature and has to be saved from that nature. We may even frame our thinking about such impulses with language taken from the disciplines of psychology or sociology. So and so is driven by neuroses, compulsions, or psychopathy. We may speak of nations that have a "dark nature" or that have been captured by demonic forces. We may even speak of our own national history as a battlefield in which the American character is at stake. Sadly, we encounter some difficulties when we think of identity being lodged in discernible, fixed, essential characteristics. This is a way of thinking about identity, and reality, that smacks of another time. It also suggests a way of seeing reality that previously birthed the idea of race.

If we are to be consonant with the times we live in, we have to speak of identity relationally and dynamically. This is the impact of Einsteinian relativity and quantum mechanics. There is no essential isness that inhabits me that makes me, *me*. My identity is constituted in dynamic relationships. An individual's DNA may provide the instructions that guide the development of one's social being. But it is in relationships that these instructions are activated. And the genetic instructions themselves are simply part of a complex weaving of social and personal forces that make me, *me*. We all are complex bundles of relationships, many of them occurring at the micro level (genetic, molecular, atomic, subatomic). Some relationships are more powerful, more formative than others in constituting me. The mystery of consciousness and the dynamics of decision-making have a role to play in determining the most formative social relationships. I choose the formative relationships, or allow them to be chosen for me by others.

The dynamic locus of my identity is a consequence both of the relationships I may not be fully aware of—like my genetic makeup—as well as those I am aware of and make decisions about (like organizational membership). It is notable that there are some researchers who suggest decision-making in some fashion may even go on at the cellular level; we simply don't understand why some genes *switch on* and other do not. The relationships that are most influential in shaping my identity are the ones I am obliged to *answer to*; that is, they are accountability relationships.

The matter of what essential characteristics make us human or even mark our individuality clearly needs more conversation. For example, all of us inherit a genetic history. Certainly, that suggests predispositions and tendencies, some of which may be quite benign; others may be quite dangerous. I am simply suggesting that for our conversation about accountability, we will find our contemporary worldview more conducive to insight than if we treat identity as if it is a matter of deep essence. The idea of race, when first shaped, was believed to be about fundamental essence. White superiority was believed to be natural. The white race was believed the most advanced, intelligent, and moral. If we believe in essential identity, our history suggests that the white collective may have a quite different essential identity, perhaps one naturally cruel and violent. This perspective is no more helpful than the belief in a superior essence.

Another perspective is that identity, in the personal and organizational sense, is a function of accountability relationships. If we want to understand an individual's identity, we need to know the primary accountability relationships she has entered into. This is also true for an organization. Accountability relationships will tell us more about the individual and the organization than whatever essential characteristics we might discern or are held up as public markers.

However, this is not the way accountability is most commonly understood. We hear the word bantered about frequently during political campaigns. Often the context suggests that accountability is about pinning the blame on someone. "Who's to blame for this mess?" Usually, political opponents are the intended target of such verbiage, especially if they are in the other party.

All of us have encountered accountability in organizations. Organizations typically construct accountability vertically. It goes in one direction, from bottom up. That is, we are accountable to our supervisor, boss, group leaders, and so on. We answer for the performance of assigned work. In this sense, it occurs within relationships of obligation that are defined by delineated tasks. While accountability in this sense may strengthen the organization's capacity to operate efficiently, it does not lend itself to the construction of community. Rather, it promotes a familiar organizational mode of operation: CYA (cover your own ass).

One learns quickly, in many organizations, that you cannot assume others have your back. This encourages a legalistic way of understanding one's job. Boundaries are drawn carefully in order to limit responsibility. This makes answering for one's job easier. After all, no one is quick to answer for work not clearly assigned (there are, indeed, ambitious people who are quick to do work assigned to others when it enhances the likelihood of personal advancement. Typically, they do not have others' backs). Accountability that creates and sustains community is mutual; it is, in effect, horizontal rather than vertical.

Relationships marked by mutual accountability can be termed *covenantal* relationships. Covenantal relationships are not quite the same as *contractual* relationships or relationships of simple obedience. Contractual relationships invoke the force of law; they are laid out in great detail. Contracts are voided if either party to the contract does not fulfill all the terms of the agreement. Purchasing a house or buying a car are examples of typical contractual agreements. It is important to pay close attention to all the details of a contract; indeed, the devil is in the details.

Covenantal relationships are entered into decisionally and are open-ended. We can choose to opt out (some do, indeed, believe that once entered into, a covenant is not open-ended). They are constituted by promises made. The act of entering into a covenantal relationship is also the decision to answer *to* the other party or parties in the relationship. We answer for our participation in the covenant. This willingness to "answer to" one another is fundamental. However, if the answering *to* is one directional, it is vertical accountability. It is an expression of subordination. It is a matter of simple obedience. It is not mutual accountability. In mutual accountability, we have each other's back. We are responsible "for" each other in addition to being willing to answer to each other. One consequence of this way of thinking about covenantal relationships is that they are not invalidated when one party, for whatever reason, chooses to ignore or violate the covenant. To put it more clearly, my responsibility for the relationship is not dependent on your living up to your promises. But because we have both entered into the relationship, each can call upon the other to account for her participation. This way of contextualizing accountability is often most easily grasped when we consider relationship between individuals.

Meat Pies and Cold Beer

Several years ago, an incident occurred that helped me understand this. My late wife, Imani, and I were living in Jamaica at the time. We lived in a small village in the Blue Mountains on the eastern end of the island and were involved in a community development effort. Occasionally, we would go to the city of Kingston to shop and visit friends. On one particular weekend, we were shopping in Kingston and dropped by our favorite patty (meat pie) shop. This was a small restaurant with a few tables. Its primary menu item was a variety of meat pies. We paid for our patties and our bottles of Red Stripe (Jamaica's well-known beer) and seated ourselves at one of the tables. As we took our seats, I noticed an apparently deranged and disheveled man across the room eyeing us.

In the next few moments, a series of events unfolded that I still remember clearly. As I lifted my patty (intending to take a bite), this strange man suddenly moved across the room in long strides and attempted to grab my patty—before I could even take a bite! I was taken aback, even dumbfounded. Almost simultaneously, my wife arose from her seat and stood between this man and me. She looked him straight in the eye and wagged her finger (meaning "no"). For an instant, we were all three frozen in time. Then he turned, mumbled incoherently, and walked out.

Her action astounded me. Without hesitance, she put herself at risk. This man clearly seemed unhinged. Neither of us knew what he might do. Yet, even before I had time to respond, she had intervened and perhaps thwarted what might have been a very tricky situation. What I realized in that moment was that she had my back. I was clear that the marriage covenant meant we both were prepared to answer to each other. What came clear to me in that moment was that she had decided to assume responsibility for our relationship, even as she was prepared to answer to me for her participation in the relationship. It was then that I understood I also could have her back! This incident gave me a deep and abiding understanding of mutual accountability and personal responsibility.

Now, Hold on There … Not So Fast

What I've come to realize is that this sort of mutual accountability can also happen between organizations and communities, as well as between and among individuals. Several years ago, an event occurred in my daughter's high school that illustrates the community having an organization's back. Humboldt High School is located in a neighborhood known as the West Side in Saint Paul, Minnesota. It is in a community that for years has been the heart of the Spanish-speaking community in the city of Saint Paul. At the time of this incident, the majority of the population was Mexican

American or of Mexican descent. This meant that a large proportion of the school's student body was children from Spanish-speaking homes.

The Saint Paul School District, in a clear effort to provide culturally relevant and sensitive leadership, assigned the first Latinx principal to the school (a Mexican American man). He was a longtime teacher and administrator in the district and was quite popular with the community. Several months after placing him at Humboldt, the superintendent's office (with the support of the school board) announced that they were removing him and assigning someone else. The spokesperson stated that there was a serious issue with some very questionable behavior on his part; however, due to data privacy regulations, they were not able to share the details other than to say it was serious.

The community was up in arms. People interpreted this move as an insult and betrayal on the part of the school board. Some community activists suggested the move smacked of racism, even though the district superintendent was an African American. The board was legally required to have a public hearing on the matter in order to provide an opportunity for public input. They were unprepared for the response. The meeting room was packed, and community member after community member rose to advocate for the principal and to call the board to account for its intended action. The meeting lasted until the wee hours of the morning.

The board was resolute and stood by their decision. However, the fact that the community turned out en masse and was provided an opportunity to express strongly held views is significant from the perspective of accountability. The community understood Humboldt to be its school, especially the community members of Mexican descent. Many adults in the community had attended Humboldt themselves. They turned out to stand by their school and to demand their voices be heard. Community members in attendance had a stake in the well-being of the school, and they believed its well-being was diminished by the removal of the principal. In short, the community had the school's back, just as they had the principal's back.

The school board was clear that the community had to voice its concerns and that they had to answer to the community for their intended decision. Answering to the community was necessary. However, answering to the community did not mean the board had to alter its decision. It did mean that it had to submit its decision for review and be prepared to listen to the community. The community's suspicion that the decision smacked of racism sharpened the importance of the board's willingness to listen.

In this instance, accountability was more than "answering to"; it was also "assuming responsibility for." Accountability is often messy and frequently uncomfortable. However, it is the bonding agent of community. It binds people and organizations together. Accountability in the covenantal sense is the glue of community relationships. It is life-giving. This is not a religious idea, even though many religious traditions centralize the notion of covenant. Accountability in this sense is existential. We experience it. It plays out in the relationships that shape our lives and constitute our identities. It sustains community in times of difficult challenges and change.

Accountability relationships can become complex and complicated. While it may be easiest to grasp the dynamics of accountability by examining covenantal relationships between two people, we need to also explore how accountability plays out in large, complicated social structures such as school systems, corporations, nonprofits, and the various levels of government. Scholars have written about the compact that exists between citizens and the state and among citizens of a particular state. The complex legal frameworks that constitute citizenship and that spell out the responsibilities of citizen and the state often obscure the underlying covenantal basis. Historically, the citizens of the United States have spoken of a communal entity that is "of the people, by the people, and for the people."

Our nation's history is replete with examples of violation and even amnesia when it comes to this original vision. Just who are "the people"? For much of our history, it was assumed that there were "the" people, the "almost" people, and the "nonpeople." Race, class, and gender determined which of these groups one belonged to. Originally, white male landowners were clearly *the* people. In spite of this historical hierarchy, we can still discern the underlying sensibility that energized the nation in its youth. We might say that the frameworks of government are a proxy for the people. Further, the underlying context of this framework is covenantal; it is based on a vision of mutuality that includes the dynamics of answering to and assuming responsibility for. Even though this vision has never played out in a fashion that has been reliably and inclusively mutual, we have had our moments. Further, this vision continues to inform our sensibilities today and continues to draw hopeful immigrants to our shores.

Many people in our day feel that the proxy for the people (the various expressions of government) has distorted this original vision and has been captured by social actors with disproportionate financial and political power. Accountability has been corrupted! The original vision has been betrayed! Communities of color might suggest that our history as a nation has always been the history of our struggles to enflesh this original vision.

Many American Indian nations and communities point out that they never made the decision to become part of this nation. Other people made the decision and used political and financial power to enforce it. Covenantal relationships are decisionally entered into. When relationships are shaped merely by the imposition of systemic power, it is challenging to form accountability that is mutual and, therefore, humanizing. This is surely an important clue regarding the strains and tensions between the federal government and tribal governments. Indian nations have generally not experienced willingness on the part of the federal government to answer for previous commitments; in fact, many previous governmental actions have sought to end or limit any "answering to" Indian tribes (the Termination Act being one illustration; the misuse of trust funds by the Bureau of Indian Affairs in times past being another).

Accountability and Recompense

Recompense is to give something to as compensation for a service rendered or damage incurred, or as payment for loss or suffering. *Atonement* is reparation for an offense or injury; making up for an offense or injury.[95]

Sometimes, accountability involves making whole or providing recompense. When one party in an accountability relationship has refused to honor the claims of the relationship, and if that party is to remain in the relationship, reparation must be done; recompense must be made for past damages.

A recent example drawn from the long and difficult relationship between American Indian nations and the federal government is informative. The *Seattle Times* reported on March 6, 2016, that a "federal judge approves an almost one billion dollar settlement between the Obama Administration and American Indian tribes over claims that the government shorted tribes for decades on contract costs to manage education, law enforcement and other federal services. Nearly seven hundred tribes or tribal agencies are expected to claim compensation; amounts will range from $8,000 for some Alaska villages to some $58 million for the Navajo Nation."[96]

This is an example of recompense—repairing some of the damage done. Like all such examples, it will not rewrite the past or satisfy everyone involved. Was it sufficient to repair all past difficulties between the federal government and Indian people? Of course not. There is still a "trail of broken treaties." However, it is an illustration of one party in an agreement answering to injured parties. In the context of generations of being ignored by the federal government, this settlement is significant. Does this settlement indicate growing sensitivity on the part of federal agencies? Perhaps. Perhaps not. Whether it does or not (and many activists may be cynical regarding this and future settlements), by itself, it is an illustration of reparation. Organizers celebrate every victory won, regardless of whether it leads to additional victories. This particular victory is an example of "answering for" promises made but conveniently forgotten in years past.

The US Congress has been involved in a multiyear conversation about recompense to the descendants of enslaved Africans. There is legislation gathering dust that shapes a legal framework for making reparations to African Americans.[97] Once again, the devil is clearly in the details. Members of Congress have been at odds over how to quantify the damages done by slavery and therefore how much compensation is due to the descendants of enslaved Africans. Some have argued that existing federal programs have already made up for the past; nothing more is required. No further accountability exists! Certainly the congressional majority in 2018 has no interest in pursuing this conversation. Hence, Representative Conyers's legislation languishes in the Judiciary Committee.

The point here is not to enter into the conversations about reparations for descendants of enslaved Africans or what the federal government owes to American Indian nations. Rather, it is to make the point that accountability relationships include the need to continually attend to the relationship in order to repair damages done to parties in the relationship, even making recompense when necessary. This willingness to attend to and repair damages can also be termed atonement. Both the terms *recompense* and *atonement* suggest a religious context. Indeed, they are both used in some religious traditions. However, their use in this conversation is to suggest that before they are religious ideas, they are existential realities. They are part of the experience of mutual accountability and covenantal relationships.

When the dual dynamic of answering to and assuming responsibility for take place in concrete historical contexts, then recompense or atonement enters as part of the picture. This is where accountability and reparation of community merge. The damages wrought in the past must be repaired; healing must take place. This recompense takes place on many levels—the symbolic as well as policy and practice. Indigenous communities remember the power of ceremony; ceremony bridges the present and the past and opens the door to the future. Making recompense begins as ceremony and then becomes social policy and practice.

Historical Accountability

I've made the case that accountability is primary when it comes to racial justice. Further, I've suggested that accountability, if it is to be life-giving, must be mutual. It includes the willingness to answer to and to assume responsibility for. I've also suggested that accountability and identity are bound together. Identity, in this sense, is dynamic, decisional, and relational. It is always in the process of being constituted and reconstituted. It is not bound by rules that infer a fixed internal essence. Identity, indeed, is linked to the past. It is, in part, a consequence of past decisions and social and biological processes. But these are constantly being revisited in response to contemporary realities. Previous decisions can be interpreted and reframed as we seek to negotiate the challenges before us.

Such reframing, however, makes demands on us. We have to overcome our socialized historical amnesia, recover the capacity to be moved by primal emotions, and claim our space in the racial equation. For those of us who are white (or, as James Baldwin and Ta-Nehisi Coates have told us, "think" we are white), this means being willing to confess the way it is and has been in this nation in relation to race.

Confess is another interesting word. We also tend to associate it with religious liturgy, psychological unburdening, or criminal proceedings. I am using the term in the sense of simply grasping and stating the way things are. Confession, in this context, is the opposite of denial. It is a human dynamic, rather than simply a religious one. It can be incredibly challenging, especially when people have invested psychic energy in denial. Every time we invoke denial, it is strengthened. Confessing reality feels threatening and fraught with risk. It makes us vulnerable. However, there is no other way through the real racial nightmare of our apartheid society. This is historical accountability.

Due to our history, those of us who are assigned to be white may have to do some standing in the snow. There are some dues to be paid. While it is the case that life-giving accountability is mutual, we cannot require equal and mutual accountability before we venture forth. This is about our humanity and our preparedness to be accountable to our human family. Such accountability is a direct counter to centuries of race-based brutality. It is antiracist accountability.

One of the implications of antiracist accountability is that it involves the willingness of white people to support and follow the leadership of people of color. White people often tend to presume that they naturally take the lead, or at least set the agenda; we must be prepared for others to do so. That does not mean that we do not have contributions to make; it simply means we can no longer assume we set the agenda or are the public face. The presidency of Barack Obama demonstrated that the ship of state will not flounder on the shoals of incompetency when this is the case. Frankly, it is likely more at risk of floundering now than when he was head of state. His presidency is at least a clue; this is not to suggest that during his administration the federal government always responded creatively to our most stubborn social issues or that the basic rules of American politics were transformed.

Generations of oppression-induced solidarity and resistance have given people of color some deep wisdom about negotiating overwhelming social challenges. The willingness of white people to support the leadership of people of color is a recognition of that history. It is not based simply on considerations of one person's particular gifts in comparison with others. It is the recognition that those of us who shaped an apartheid nation may not have the capacity to imagine and risk alternative arrangements. The opportunities for us who are white to support the leadership of people of color are plenteous: local and regional elections, organizational decision-making and programming, local community activities, local church activities, even family life. However, this does not mean taking a leave of absence. It does not mean withdrawing from the social struggles of the day or remaining silent during meetings; it means being willing to risk participation without assuming our voice is determinative. The key to this is antiracist accountability. The humanizing mutuality of genuine accountability keeps people in solidarity and builds trust, even amidst tension and difficult conversations. The historic role of the white collective assures that there will frequently be tension and disagreement among organizers working to deconstruct white supremacy. We who are white must listen carefully to the voices of our sisters and brothers of color and be willing to support and follow their lead.

Empathy, Accountability, and Recompense

The preceding commentary on accountability suggests that it is not an add-on, an idea inserted artificially. It grows out of the fertile soil of empathy/empathic resonance. It is a characteristic of viable community. Communities that endure are marked by active accountability relationships. This is not to say that accountability might be, could be, or should be the glue of community; it *is* the glue of community. Wherever the dynamic of community happens, there is accountability. When communities are riven by conflict, divided by walls of apartheid, dominated by a powerful few, or otherwise dysfunctional, it indicates that the bonding agent, accountability, is weak, has dissolved, or is being applied insufficiently or destructively.

Recompense, as an aspect of accountability, is also, therefore, rooted in the fabric of community, of empathically generated connections. In mutual accountability relationships, we are moved by the sense that we need to "make it right." Recently, I stayed in a hotel near the Seattle-Tacoma International Airport. When the desk clerk handed me my electronic key card, I noticed a small card inside the key-card wallet. It was about the size of a typical business card. On the card was printed the following: "Let us make it right!" The card went on to say that I should notify the front desk if anything was amiss or not to my liking in my room or the hotel. The staff then would "make it right."[98] In other words, the corporation that owned the hotel was stating they were prepared to make recompense, as necessary, to satisfy unfulfilled expectations on the part of their clientele. If corporate America is clear about the necessity of recompense regarding unfulfilled expectations, surely the citizens of our nation should reasonably expect no less. The requirements of community are clear: it is time to *make it right* regarding the multigenerational damage done by race.

15

Antiracism and the Reparation of Community

"There is an evil which most of us condone and are even guilty of: indifference to evil. We remain neutral, impartial, and not easily moved by the wrongs done unto other people. Indifference to evil is more insidious than evil itself; it is more universal, more contagious, more dangerous. A silent justification, it makes possible an evil erupting as an exception becoming the rule and being in turn accepted" (Abraham Joshua Heschel).[99]

I have suggested that racialization sabotages and tears the fabric of community. It breaks the bonds of accountability that bind people together, and it threatens community viability. The thrall that accompanies racialization will indeed capture some; the resulting monocultural echo chambers will insulate the captives from contemporary reality. Echoes of American exceptionalism and imagined threats will strengthen the force field that excludes those who are neither enthralled nor at the centers of power.

Repairing the Fabric of Community

Under the auspices of racial apartheid, we who are white learn (via socialization) to deaden our empathic resonance and build walls of exclusion. We designate some as unworthy and consign them to the margins of society. Various forms of apartheid are the consequence. We do this to groups right in our midst. This is not simply a "natural" response to those "strangers over the hill or across the lake." This is creating destructive power differentials right in the midst of society itself. Historically, the interlinked triumvirate of race, class, and gender has provided the template for marginalization and subordination.

This is pathological behavior when viewed through the lens of community well-being. It is pathological because it normalizes behavior that is contrary to our internal wiring and, consequently, contrary to our own best interest. The ideology of race as a social organizing tool has engendered incredible pathological behavior on the part of those who see themselves as normative and structure community accordingly.

However, the evolutionary forces that gave us the capacity for empathy and the urge to form relationships and build community continue, if only subtly, to undermine apartheid and challenge the thrall of systemic racism. That is the significance of the interventions in community and national life that we can term *antiracist*. They are about the reparation and restoration of community. Such interventions in community life create the space and time in which communal immune responses can repair the fabric of community life. They create the opportunity for rehumanizing relationships. This includes creating and reshaping accountability relationships. Antiracism, in this sense, reframes power relationships; the social forces that marginalize people based on stigmatized social identities are interrupted; horizontal accountability is introduced into vertical (up-down) power relationships.

When we say that community is the foundational focus of our work, we can also say that healthy community is the central outcome we seek. What are the marks of healthy community? Alfred Adler's notion of *gemeinschaftsgefuhl* (community engagement / social interest) is one of the marks—an engaged citizenry that grasps that individual well-being is connected to collective well-being. In such an engaged community, interest in the well-being of others is fundamental to one's sense of personal well-being.[100] In an engaged community (in the Adlerian sense), there is an ongoing bridging of historically imposed isolation. Such community engagement is in sync with the deep neuro-wiring that binds us together.

An engaged community is an activist community. It is a community in which intervention in the status quo is a frequent, perhaps constant process. This is how the marginalization process is constantly relativized. The voices from the margins must be heard, even when they increase public discomfort. An activist community learns to value the voices from the margins. The consequence is a continuing relativization of the dynamics that would strengthen the walls of apartheid and the forces of marginalization. If antiracism is about facilitating healthy community, it is also about strengthening the community's immune system—that is, enhancing the ability to resist disease and community breakdown. It is about shaping local resilience. It is both reparative and preventive. It is about repairing the damage done by racialization, thus strengthening the ability to resist future attacks. In this sense, it is also preventive.

What are the agents that, like the cells in our immune system, accomplish the reparation of community? Some of them are the already existing community organizations that served the aims of apartheid under the old mandate: local churches, community organizations, service organizations, and civic clubs. However, they must see their role differently in order to serve the Geist of reparation. New leadership networks are needed in order for old organizations to see reality differently. Two such networks in the Chicago area are examples of new leadership networks that help existing organizations reframe their life and mission in ways relevant to the recovery of healthy community life.

One is the Chicago Sustainability Leaders Network (CSLN) that has emerged out of an organizing effort known as Accelerate 77. Accelerate 77 was organized in 2012 to link the seventy-seven community areas of the city together in a grassroots effort to identify and strengthen local projects that were about the work of healing community and enhancing local resilience. While not specifically framed as an antiracism effort, the network actively seeks to inculcate the perspective of antiracism and breach the walls of separation that have been part of the history of Chicago. CSLN frames policy initiatives, organizes grassroots planning sessions, provides local training opportunities, and links neighborhood efforts to outside resources.

Another is Chicago Regional Organizing for Antiracism (CROAR). A network of antiracism organizers provides training and organizing services to denominations, local churches, community organizations, schools, and nonprofits. CROAR is a regional partner of Crossroads Antiracism Organizing and Training. It connects local organizations to other efforts, such as Crossroads, that provide resources, tools, and leadership training. CROAR staff also facilitate monthly opportunities for racial identity caucusing (a process that enables individuals to explore the impact of racialization in their lives and begin to rebuild accountability relationships).

In the Kalamazoo, Michigan, area, another regional partner of Crossroads, ERACCE (Eliminating Racism and Creating/Celebrating Equity), plays a similar role and has done so for several years. ERACCE staff also conduct monthly opportunities for racial identity caucusing. Hundreds of individuals and multiple institutions in the Kalamazoo area have participated in antiracism training organized by ERACCE. Many of these institutions have been involved in a long-term leadership development process aimed at shaping an antiracism leadership team. These institutions have been involved in a long-term process of institutional transformation intended to craft a culture of inclusion.

These are only three examples out of a plethora of organizing efforts across the nation that seek to overcome the walls of racial apartheid and restore community well-being. What they illustrate is that antiracism is an activity, not an abstract idea or a doctrine. It is not about absolutes or ideological litmus tests. Any intervention that interrupts racialization and promotes community reparation is antiracist, whether framed thusly or not. This is an example of naming an activity with a term that invokes a set of values. The test of whether or not the use of the term is appropriate is whether the activity so named is indeed intervening in a fashion that interrupts racialization. Such a test does not require that the actors themselves name their action as antiracist. Indeed it may be others who use the term in a manner that interprets the intervention. Any strategic action or protocol that puts a community on the road to healing and sustainability, thereby overcoming the walls of apartheid, is antiracist! Outcomes are finally the litmus; the proof is in the pudding, so to speak.

While individuals may well intervene personally in an effort to interrupt racial dynamics, the interruptions that tend to be most effective and produce lasting social transformation are collaborative and collective. Such collaborative efforts, in turn, foster the storytelling that make the effort part of historical memory. Every time the story is told, the history of resistance is rehearsed. The rehearsal of resistance creates mythology that, in turn, vitalizes community life. That is why it is crucial to remember the local people who previously engaged in the struggles for racial justice, the places they touched, and the events that marked their efforts. It is a matter of community spirit and well-being.

When we imagine that antiracism is about the reparation of community, we can begin to discern the necessary connection between organizing for racial/social justice and caring for the ecosystems of the planet. We can grasp that eco-justice and social justice are not two different works; they are one and the same. Paul Hawken, in his book *Blessed Unrest*, suggests that when environmental organizers get on the social justice bus, they will realize there is only one bus.[101] Clearly, a resolute movement for ecological justice is historically necessary. We all need to be engaged in shaping responses to the eco-crises of our day, with global climate change being at the forefront. But this cannot happen unless the wounds of systemic oppression are tended to. Hawken's insight is that tending to these wounds is part and parcel of responding to the wounds of the planet itself. The violence done at the behest of race and other socially constructed identities is also violence done to the planet. Racism is an ecological challenge!

Leadership and the Reparation of Community

Now, we need to look more carefully at the character and function of the collaborative leadership that accomplishes the ongoing reparation of community. In the context of our racial apartheid history, we can call this antiracist leadership. If we think of leadership as a dynamic response, rather than a role, it helps us gain a functional understanding of the term. We can then use the term to name an activity. In our society, as a consequence of our hyperindividualism, we tend to use the term leadership to indicate individuals who play the role of leader and how they play that role. This is not a wrong view; there is simply more to be said in understanding how we might apply the term. When we view leadership as an activity (a dynamic response), two characteristics that mark those involved in the activity are sensitivity and the capacity to act. Leadership is sensitive and responsive, in the words of H. Richard Niebuhr.[102] Individuals may play a symbolic role and even be seen publicly as the leader of an effort, but leadership is fundamentally a collaborative, collective effort.

For example, we often speak of Rosa Parks as one of the leaders of the civil rights movement and note her refusal to give up her seat on a public bus to a white man. When we individualize leadership in this fashion, we overlook all the planning, strategizing, and decision-making that resulted in Mrs. Parks being on the bus in that place at that time. She was part of an organizing effort, not simply a seamstress whose feet were tired and who made a courageous decision (certainly her deed was a courageous action). She became, in that moment, the face of the movement, albeit a representational face. She was not alone, even in her solitary action. Leadership is being sensitive and responsive; it is collectively engendered and shaped. It invokes ancestors as well as contemporary brothers and sisters.

When we look at leadership through an antiracism lens, there are four marks that stand out. These four are like the locus of leadership (in mathematics, a locus is a set of points; it can also be understood as a place or site where a particular activity occurs). They are the following: calling power into accountability; expressing and generating hopeful engagement; bringing a sense of history; and shaping and ensuring viable community. This way of thinking about leadership was inspired, in part, by the work of Walter Brueggemann, a noted scholar of the Hebrew Scriptures.

Calling Power into Accountability

This is perhaps the easiest mark to illustrate. We are accustomed to speaking of leadership that manifests resistance in this fashion. Historical examples are plentiful: for example, the role that the Southern Christian Leadership Conference or the Student Nonviolent Coordinating Committee played in the South during the civil rights movement. Clearly, the decision had been made to confront and challenge segregation and the states that had legalized it. This was also the power of the Black Panthers, even though their strategy was not framed as nonviolent resistance. Calling the state, in any of its iterations, to account for the exercise of systemic power is never easy, comfortable, or safe. Power differentials always seem to put those who step out at risk, often in frightening ways. Antiracist leadership calls power to account and stands with those who are oppressed by the misuse of systemic power. This also means that antiracist leadership bears witness to reality. This is the secret to the power of speaking truth, which is necessary to effectively call power to account. It is grounded in reality—the real situation rather than what might be or what we wish was our reality. This may well be what Mohandas Gandhi termed "truth power or force (satyagraha)." Truth, in this sense, is equivalent to reality. Speaking truth to power invokes the forcefulness of what is—reality, so to speak.

Racialization enthralls those who are at the center of systemic power. Change is not in their perceived interest. Consequently, those who shape the social expressions of systemic power do so, in part, by fabricating a false view of reality. Events and people who threaten this social canon are met by elaborate fabrications that are a denial of reality and that demonize those who bear the truth. We have seen this dynamic repeated throughout the history of racism and resistance in the United States. Today, we see this taking place in the vitriol expressed in debates about fake news and what is real.

Expressing/Generating Hopeful Engagement

When people believe in the possibility of change and can imagine an alternative to present realities, they will trust and follow those who step out and call power to account. Thus, the rhetoric of leadership poeticizes and imagines new realities. It is not sufficient to point out the shortcomings and abuses in present social realities, or to undermine and sabotage current social arrangements. It is necessary to visualize and believe in alternative arrangements. It is important to generate proposals for getting from here to there. When the resistance calls on power to change but has no vision or proposals for what change might look like, agency remains with the upholders of the status quo. When we beat up on institutions for their behavior but have no alternative to suggest, we become irritants to be marginalized or impractical threats to be pounded down.

Part of the attraction of the 2015–16 presidential campaign of Bernie Sanders was that he painted a vision, albeit in broad strokes, of an alternative society. The vision Sanders articulated generated enthusiastic support across the nation from people who might otherwise simply be disaffected. But the vision of an alternative future that is generated must also be rooted in reality. It must be informed by the lens of struggle and the forcefulness of truth, rather than the thrall of white supremacy. The misuse of systemic power creates clear-eyed lucidity among the oppressed. Pie in the sky simply will not call people forth to challenge the way things are.

Bringing a Sense of History

Historical memory and imagination are critical to effective confrontation with power and reimagining social realities. This is especially crucial in the struggles for racial and social justice. A sense of history brings our ancestors into the present moment. All those who have gone before and whose sacrifices brought us to this moment are present when we call power to account and ask our communities to believe in an alternative future. Antiracism requires us to become historians. Antiracist leadership links us to the past and calls us to assume personal responsibility for the future, even if only for the next step in the journey. Leadership, in this sense, catalyzes a sense of agency. All who are involved become historical actors who have inserted their lives into the breach, the gap between what has been and what is to be. In this sense, personal and communal agency and historical imagination are bound together.

Shaping and Ensuring Viable Community

Finally, antiracist leadership is rooted in the experience of profound community—that is, community shaped by empathic connections and mutual accountability. In turn, it promotes and protects community that humanizes. Perhaps this is what Dr. King meant by the Beloved Community. It is that which we seek as well as that which somehow we remember, even if the experience of radical community is only momentary or now and again. Perhaps it's in the experience of neighborhood solidarity when families require their city to shape schools that are genuine learning communities; maybe it's the experience of a community gathering itself following a natural disaster; maybe it's in the experience of shared struggle on a picket line, street demonstration, or reclamation of land stolen long ago; perhaps in the fleeting victory of legal action seeking voting rights. The realization that this Beloved Community is created out of shared struggle and common vision is central. But this is not simply about enfleshing a noble vision or enduring values; it is about survival itself. It is about choosing life, as the Hebrew scriptures declare.[103] Leadership that stakes its life on this promise is antiracist leadership.

These four marks, together and in dynamic tension, are what I would name antiracist leadership. Together, they are the locus, the moving site of leadership. Together, in the context of this work, we might call them profound or radical accountability. Such accountability is deeply human and is itself a living symbol of deep community. It is the flesh and blood alternative to the social architecture of white supremacy and its interiority, the terrain of white identity.

The individuals, groups, and communities that embody these dynamics are real human beings. We miss the real impact of their lives when we sentimentalize and romanticize them. They are larger than life simply because they chose to intervene, not because they are paradigms of virtue that fit our romanticized images of what great human beings should be. They struggle with the same personal challenges we all do. They may be short-tempered individuals; they may struggle with broken families; they may not be among the pretty people we see in television advertisements; they may not be particularly gifted intellectually or artistically. They simply choose to invest their lives in social transformation. That is their power. That is why they call us forth.

Now we are ready to look more carefully at the dynamics of reparation: the repair and restoration of community. This is the process and the outcome of antiracism and antiracist lives.

Healthy Community is like a Nurse Log

16

Beyond Apartheid: Shaping Resilient, Sustainable Communities

We live in a time of daunting and frightening ecological challenges. Best we can tell, human activity has instigated and strengthened these challenges. While there are individuals and groups who deny the role of human activity, the scientific community has come to a working consensus: human activity is playing a primary role in the ecological crises confronting us, especially the crises of climate change. Naomi Klein, in her book *This Changes Everything*, has suggested that the crisis of climate change challenges every aspect of our globalizing economic system.[104] We can no longer afford business as usual. We must examine and even change the manner in which we do human society.

Modern societies have utilized various forms of social apartheid, some based on class, caste, and gender; those formulated under the auspices of European colonial expansion have placed race at the center of their social architecture. We have to ask whether or not apartheid of any sort is sustainable at this historical juncture. This book has suggested that apartheid is fatal to human community. The stark realities of our moment make that especially clear. Shaping community life that does not threaten the ecosystems of the planet is the challenge before us. This requires moving beyond social apartheid. It requires revisioning life-in-community and reframing the social systems that link us together. A primary question is, "How do we do community in a manner that is sustainable, especially if that requires radically revisioning our social architecture?"

Some practitioners have suggested that the term sustainable suggests resilience. Sustainable communities are resilient communities. The word resilience means being "capable of withstanding shock without permanent damage or rupture; tending to recover from or adjust ... to change."[105] On the way to a radical revisioning of life-in-community, our organizing needs to embed resilience in communities recovering from the damages done by apartheid. Resilient communities will endure the blows and impacts of change; they will thrive in the stresses and strains that will accompany the changes required to address the ecological challenges before us.

So then, what does it mean to shape resilient communities? What makes communities resilient? What are their characteristics? Many thoughtful and experienced practitioners and commentators have documented and written at length about these questions. The proponents of permaculture, for example, lift up twelve core principles that guide their work. (Wikipedia, the online encyclopedia, has a helpful description of permaculture: it is a system of agricultural and social design principles centered around simulating or directly utilizing the patterns and features observed in natural ecosystems.[106]) Those involved in the Bioneers movement speak of human ingenuity wedded to the wisdom of the wild. Bioneers seek to fashion "a framework of interdependence (that) brings together all the parts—and diverse voices—to build connections among many communities across boundaries."[107] Other organizing efforts lift up similar principles, even if articulated differently. I'm not interested in advocating for any particular eco-justice effort. I am interested in how their work informs the challenge of moving beyond apartheid.

I've come to believe that moving beyond apartheid is, in a very deep sense, an ecological challenge. It is more than working for racial and social justice in the sense that community organizers typically understand and frame the challenge. It is imagining and organizing social relations and systems in a manner that is patterned after and in sync with the natural systems of the planet. Among all the principles and characteristics that are features of resilient communities, three, especially, stand out and merit our attention. Sustainable, resilient transapartheid communities are diverse, adaptive, and regenerative. These principles are familiar to many of us; they are not new insights when it comes to understanding ecological health. However, we don't normally see them as central to organizing racial justice. They are not usually part of the conversation about antiracism. I believe they are a necessary part of the conversation and that they represent the conflation of ecological and social resilience. They define, functionally, sustainable transapartheid communities.

Diverse

Diversity is one the marks of a healthy ecosystem. The proponents of biomimicry point out that nature's diversity has a lot to teach us about healthy human communities: they are diverse. One of the clear difficulties with apartheid as a social design is that it contradicts demographic diversity. It creates communities that are monocultural and relatively homogenous. Social homogeneity may, on the surface, seem to lend itself to harmonious communities that have minimal social strife and tension (this was likely one of the guiding assumptions when the Federal Housing Authority crafted a model restrictive covenant in 1938[108]). That appearance, however, comes at a cost.

Such communities are like monocultural agricultural practices; they require continuing attention and expensive chemical inputs to survive. When conditions change, increasing external inputs are required to sustain productivity. Similarly, when social conditions change, monocultural communities lack a sufficient reservoir of creativity and diverse perspectives to respond to a new situation. Social apartheid fosters monocultural communities. Communities that are diverse—demographically, economically, culturally, politically—have a reservoir to tap into that has the potential to enhance community resilience; consequently, they are more sustainable.

One of the curious phenomena that has transpired in small towns across the upper Midwest is rapid demographic change. Even as townspeople bemoan the departure of young high school grads, increasing numbers of Latinx, Somali, and Hmong families are moving in, usually to work in turkey, chicken, or pork processing plants. One of the challenges for townsfolk is responding to this new and dramatic diversity. Understanding it as a gift is difficult. Clearly the newcomers are an economic boon; local industry benefits. However, perceived racial difference and real cultural differences challenge the multigenerational experience of apartheid. Several years ago, a local pastor mentioned to me that his town was quite diverse: there were two kinds of Lutherans and Roman Catholics to boot! Now, his community is struggling to respond to real diversity. Change is difficult, even when it increases the reservoir of creativity and cultural richness.

One dramatic example of our nation's investment in monocultural communities is language. We have come to believe it is necessary to speak only one language: English. Although it is the case that most of us are exposed to other languages in school, most of us live our lives speaking, thinking, and writing only in English. We are one of the most impoverished nations in the world when it comes to linguistic ability. A bilingual person has much more cognitive and perhaps emotional flexibility than a monolingual person. She can think and feel from two perspectives and move back and forth with ease. Someone who is multilingual has an even richer experience of daily events. Bilingualism and multilingualism enhance a community's resilience; it has a deeper reservoir to draw upon in times of crisis. The value of bilingual or multilingual citizens to a community is clear.

This reframes the argument about legal and undocumented immigrants. If we view immigrants as a potential resource rather than a threat, it also changes how we think about immigration policy and how we provide access to green cards. Rather than inflammatory rhetoric about building walls along our borders, we might be organizing immigration summits with our neighbors, Mexico, Canada, and the Caribbean nations. Immigration policy that is informed by the need for resilient communities would have an antiracist impact.

If it is the case that we cannot afford business as usual in terms of how we shape community life, then we must find ways to deconstruct and move beyond the walls of apartheid. Diversity must become a value that we urgently and forcefully inculcate in community life. However, it is more than simply one of the values of sustainable communities, a value that we work to achieve. Rather, diversity is a feature of sustainable community without which there is no sustainability. We've learned to develop communities that are monocultural and that consequently lack the interior resourcefulness to adapt to changing realities. This means, in effect, that antiracism is key to shaping sustainable communities. The apartheid history of this nation necessitates antiracist interventions in order to assure the forceful presence of diversity. Naturally occurring ecosystems demonstrate the necessity of diversity; without it, ecosystems don't survive. They cannot respond to changes, and they are not adaptive. In this sense, biomimicry is required. We need to inculcate the lessons of nature regarding the value of diversity.

Adaptive

Resilient communities are adaptive. When conditions change, resilient communities change, whether economically, culturally, or politically. Change is never easy. It brings tension, stress, and perhaps even strife. When a community has a history of economic dependence on one crop or one industry, it is vulnerable. Economic downturns can be disastrous. It can spell the end of the road for the community. The capacity to adapt to new realities—difficult as that might be—is a key to sustainability.

Social apartheid tends to shape communities that are not only monocultural; they also tend to be economically and politically homogenous. They tend to be ideologically inflexible, to the point of fostering intense partisan divides and intellectual sterility. Individuals and groups that are countercultural are marginalized, perhaps even violently. In this nation, we have a history of reacting poorly to cultural, ideological-political, and even economic diversity. This has negatively impacted our ability to creatively respond to fundamental change.

If we are to imagine human communities that are resilient, and therefore can be called sustainable, it is necessary to do whole systems thinking. Whole systems thinking includes recognizing the role of feedback loops. Reality will constantly provide feedback to our organizing efforts, projects, and even the way we shape communities in general. While it may not be advisable or practical to respond to every bit of feedback, it is important to develop the capacity to recognize and assess feedback. This capacity itself indicates a willingness to change, even when change is difficult.

When a community's self-understanding is bound up in a story of being exceptional just as it is, change is especially difficult. American communities, large and small, tend to be shaped around the American story of being exceptional. We tend to believe that the way we've done things is central to our exceptionalism and therefore must not be questioned. If a community is to be adaptive, it needs to generate and inculcate a story and self-understanding that centralizes the reality of change and a belief in the capacity to change. We are living in a time when larger, global realities are changing dramatically. Communities that do not understand this will not survive. Nations that do not grasp this are in for some especially hard times.

Some of the most dramatic illustrations of the importance of being adaptive can be seen in communities that have developed around the mining industry. Sooner or later, mines close down. The impact on small towns can be disastrous. We are clear that the time has come to move away from our dependence on coal as a primary source of energy. However, moving away from coal means an increase in poverty in coal-mining areas; it also means an increase in desperation as families break apart when the flow of resources dwindles.

I vividly remember the impact on my little mining town in eastern Arizona when the copper mines began to lay off workers as mines shut down. Applications for public assistance, including food stamps and housing assistance, soared. Families moved away as income streams dried up. Businesses closed their doors. School student bodies declined, followed by a decline in state funding. It required years of struggle and near subsistence for my hometown to acquire sufficient adaptability to survive.

Regenerative

Contemporary agricultural practices illustrate both the drawbacks of an extractive economic paradigm and some of the values and strategies that build resiliency in local communities. This is especially dramatic in a conversation about the value of regeneration for local communities.

Practitioners of sustainable agriculture are clear about the necessity for their practices to be regenerative. Regenerative practices protect and restore the ecosystems in their environment. They return nutrients to the soil and enhance the microbiota. Such agricultural practices may sometimes be more labor-intensive; they are not dependent on chemical inputs but upon careful balancing of multiple factors, including integrated pest management, no till cultivation, and rotating cover crops. They also typically are not focused on one crop; they emphasize multicropping rather than monocropping. They may mix crops in the same field.

In similar fashion, resilient communities are regenerative. They have gained the capacity to regenerate themselves and their environment. In this sense, they are probiotic. They are like an aged tree in an old growth forest that has fallen and become a nurse log, feeding multiple biota where they lay. They promote life. Such communities are learning how to minimize their environmental impact, even while learning how to regenerate community life. They typically encourage local agriculture by sponsoring farmers' markets; they may have a number of community-supported agriculture initiatives (CSA). They are likely to encourage community gardens and have effective community recycling programs.

Some communities that are learning to be regenerative have instituted local barter programs. Residents share skills and tools without exchanging cash. Rather, they bank credits by using a skill to assist a neighbor. Then they spend their banked credits to meet their own needs, be it home repair, yard care, or snow shoveling—all without an exchange of cash. Some communities are even experimenting with local currency that functions like official currency.

Once again, mining towns tend to be dramatic examples of communities that struggle with the regenerative challenge. Many are very diverse, culturally speaking. But they are frequently not economically or politically diverse. Cultural diversity alone is insufficient. There is more to being a resilient community. Dependence on one industry — like mining — can become a form of death-dating. Market collapse or resource depletion can turn bustling communities into ghost towns. Cultivating regenerative capacity means always preparing for coming generations. It requires leadership that is imaginative, accountable to the whole community, and future oriented. It requires antiracist leadership!

Therefore

These three features—diverse, adaptive, and regenerative—are fundamental to community resilience. They are not the only principles or features that constitute resilience. But they are central to reparation as an outcome of antiracism. However, resilient communities do not exist in isolation. Resilient communities are connected communities. Their capacity to be diverse, adaptive, and regenerative depends directly on their connectedness to other communities. The governance frameworks that shape and administer the public policies affecting them are also critical. County, state, regional, and federal governance can help or hinder local efforts that repair and restore the fabric of community.

Now, we are ready to return to the earlier conversation about accountability. Antiracism is at bottom about historical accountability. It is about shaping mutual accountability relationships that are grounded in historical realities. Reparation happens in the context of accountability. A skein of accountability relationships sustains the efforts to fashion resilient, sustainable communities. It is mutual accountability that maintains the challenging dynamics of resilience. Governance that is antiracist fosters such historical accountability. One aspect of historical accountability is answering for the grief and trauma associated with past violence and oppression. That means that recompense for the historical damage done by racial apartheid must be a policy priority. It must be because reality requires it. History requires it. The future requires it.

Recompense is not simply about paying money to make up for past mistakes. It is much more. There is no making up for the brutality and theft of slavery. There is no making up for the grief, trauma, eviction, and cultural obliteration visited upon indigenous nations. Recompense is about making whole in relation to the challenges the future poses. Wholeness is not an abstraction. It simply means fashioning a communal fabric that is fit for this historical moment. It is about communities that have the capacity to be what is necessary—and about a nation willing to risk the future, rather than retreating to an imagined version of history based on the mendacity and violence of the past. Some have suggested this is a core insight of the theory of evolution; it is about the survival of the *fit*. Communities that are fit are constantly adapting to the challenges posed by the future.

Previously, we noted examples of monetary recompense that were an effort to "make it right." Modest compensation was paid to Japanese American families who experienced internment; compensation was provided to American Indian communities for misuse of funds managed by the US government. Recompense, in this sense, is not about individuals; it is about communities that were systemically and systematically oppressed in the past as a consequence of explicit government policy, practice, or neglect.

Historically, slavery was permitted, maintained, and supported by our federal government. Following the end of slavery and the collapse of Reconstruction, our government ignored efforts in the South to turn back the clock with the passage of Jim Crow and vagrancy laws. When Jim Crow was challenged legally, the SCOTUS put the federal stamp of approval on our system of racial segregation. Time and again, the federal government either turned a blind eye to racial violence and injustice, subtly encouraged it, or simply ignored the struggle for racial justice in favor of other priorities, such as the New Deal. Consequently, the accountability that repairs the damage done and promotes sustainable community must be demonstrated and promoted at the federal level. The first step is apology; claiming responsibility requires nothing less. Such apology must happen at the highest level. Our government is the people's proxy; thus, our assumption of responsibility for the outrages, brutality, and violations of slavery must be symbolized by the executive branch of government—the office of the presidency.

Similarly, the devastation and violence this nation visited upon indigenous cultures and communities were integral to our development as a nation. The historical record is clear. We can attempt to minimize it or even whitewash it by invoking all the ways we lift up and admire Native traditions and practices. Anyone who has been involved in Scouting will remember how central American Indian metaphors and images are. Many organizations have attempted to integrate Native teachings and sensibilities into their life and work. Many spiritual teachers invoke tribal practices and traditions in their work. The names of states, counties, and even communities invoke their tribal roots: Arizona, Yavapai, Seattle, Chicago, Miami … the list is long. However, if these are to be more than examples of cultural appropriation, they must be accompanied by historical accountability. Such accountability includes recompense that atones for the grief and trauma Indian people have lived through.

Many Native activists speak of the *trail of broken treaties*. Treaties are the highest law of the land. Only the president can abrogate a treaty. A president may indeed seek the advice of the US Senate, but the Senate cannot abrogate a treaty. Indeed, in recent years, federal courts, including SCOTUS, have upheld the terms of some treaties made with Indian nations. Nonetheless, the record is clear. This nation has not honored its treaties with indigenous nations and has defaulted on its promises to Indian people following the end of treaty making. Historical accountability certainly means apology. It means apology that represents the nation claiming its real history. It means apology by the offices that represents the people—the presidency and Congress. It also means being willing to revisit every broken treaty and trust promise. Recompense requires nothing less. Apology must be manifest in policy and presidential decision-making.

Some indigenous nations may not be interested in revisiting past treaties, but integrity requires that the federal government be prepared to do so. The key is listening to the voices of Indian Country, however long it takes to hear consensus from the indigenous nations that have been damaged by our government. Similarly, the federal government must revisit its trust obligations and make good on them. The Indian Gaming Act and the consequent economic vitality on some reservations is not an adequate context for ignoring obligations previously endorsed by the United States Congress.

I have made the case earlier in this work that this nation invested in two separate but deeply related funds in the early years. These two funds were so deeply intertwined that effectively they were one investment. It was an investment in the enslavement of African people, as well as subsequent efforts to maintain racial apartheid, and the subjugation, devastation, and attempted disappearance of American Indian nations. Apology is the first step necessitated by historic accountability. The follow-up to apology is recompense; it must be concrete and substantial. Thus it must be a matter of public policy. Apology, alone, is not sufficient; however, recompense without apology will not take into account the enormity of the debt. Neither will it be trustworthy. Shifting ideological winds and economic realities will take it away. Witness recent attacks upon the Voting Rights Act and efforts to overturn all affirmative action / EEO programs. Some may argue that the case for apology and even recompense is clear but that the nation simply cannot afford to even consider recompense for these two historic atrocities. We cannot afford not to. Our future is at risk. Our viability as a nation is at stake. In addition, our moral authority and integrity as a people are on the table.

But, some may ask, what about other racial groups abused through the misuse of systemic power under the auspices of white supremacy? What about the routine subordination and marginalization of Latinx populations? What about the effort to exclude, restrict, and demonize most people of Asian heritages (thus making them perpetual foreigners)? What about the waves of Islamophobia that demonize people perceived as Middle Eastern or North African? Then there is the history of making invisible the people termed Melungeon, Yellow Hammers, Caramel Indians, and Redbones. And what about the lingering vestiges of anti-Semitism?

The multigenerational impacts of the white-nonwhite binary are many, complex, and continuing. This binary has guided our historical investment in racial oppression. The original dual investment, in effect, became the filter that translated the binary into public policy, thereby generating social apartheid. This original investment—the enslavement of Africans in the service of economic development and the efforts to remove and disappear indigenous nations to gain land—created a Geist and a mind-set that rationalized and sanctioned the oppression and marginalization of every ethnic group perceived as nonwhite.

This binary integrated all the disparate strands of ancient prejudices that crossed the Atlantic from Europe. The long centuries of European anti-Semitism was one of the fertile seedbeds that nourished the white-nonwhite binary and white supremacy. Similarly, today's vehement anti-Muslim sentiment is rooted in European Christendom's centuries of anti-Islam pronouncements and doctrine. It is best understood racially rather than religiously. It's a matter of social identity, not doctrinal difference. The intense anti-Irish sentiment of the English followed Irish immigrants to our shores and assured they would be initially considered nonwhite. In similar fashion, Italian immigrants and virtually all others immigrating from southern and Eastern Europe were consigned to nonwhite identity upon arriving on our shores.

When we dare to burst the walls of apartheid, all of us will gain. We will gain the possibility, even the likelihood, of the reparation of community. Apology and recompense will be the twin maneuvers that undermine and weaken apartheid. They symbolize the intent to make things right. They are substantiated in the policies, programs, and citizen actions that rebuild and restore vibrant community life. These twin maneuvers must, initially, be in the name of those upon whom racial devastation has been visited most consistently for the longest time: indigenous nations and the sons and daughters of Africa whose ancestors were brutally brought to these shores.

The policies and programs that will make it right will benefit all who reside within our national boundaries, including the children of Europe who view themselves as white. They will gain as much as anyone from apartheid's demise. Certainly, all the historic groups that have had to contend with the stigma of being seen as nonwhite, even if only temporarily, will gain from a nation and communities intending to engage in the processes of reparation.

What will be gained and how will we know? To begin with, they will gain equitable access to the systems and institutions of our nation. The evidence of such gains will be ongoing improvement in the measurable racial disparities that mark and shame America. These will not happen overnight, but they will happen. As stated previously, we do know how to fashion equitable access. We also know that creating equitable access will require enduring commitment, assigning sufficient resources, administrative follow-through, and steadfast accountability. All communities will gain when we bridge the gaps that racial disparities reveal. They will gain creative, responsible citizens who are accountably engaged in shaping their community.

Since race invokes all the oppression systems that intersect, intentional repudiation of racism must also include repudiation of all systemic oppressions that scar, disfigure, and put human beings at risk. The social "isms" that we are all familiar with must be intentionally addressed, not simply presumed solved by virtue of our attempt at being antiracist. Gains that have been made under the rubric of inclusivity must not be lost. We do not need to revisit the early 1930s when the New Deal, important as it was to the nation's viability, eclipsed racial justice as a priority, putting it on the back burner. This means protecting commitments to marriage equality, pay equity, gender equity, civil rights for LGBTQI people, inclusive language in the public arena, and all the other interventions that counter social processes that marginalize people based on fabricated social identities.

For those of us who are white, racial justice will feel like surrendering something of value, something so much a part of our lives that it is difficult to imagine living without it. In order to be a part of the process of reparation, we will have to reframe how we imagine the *costs* associated with change. Rather than loss, we can imagine and commit to the gains for communities that come with change. This reimagining cannot happen unless and until we are clear that affairs cannot continue as they are. Our survival depends on fundamental change. The most fundamental change necessary is the deconstruction and dismantling of white supremacy. Its continued existence compromises our viability as a nation, now and in the future.

When our nation chose to enter World War II, we were clear it was no longer business as usual. As a nation, we made sacrifices that made it possible to divert our energy and prodigious economic capacity to the war effort. President Roosevelt even asked automobile manufacturers to forego their usual annual sales efforts and use their manufacturing capacity to support the war effort. (I recall, as a youngster, our family using ration coupons to purchase food. I also recall grade school cafeteria mac and cheese made with surplus cheese—a terrible tasting concoction! Some seventy years later, my taste buds still remember its flavor! We believed the war effort required these and other sacrifices!)

The crisis facing us today is no less a threat than the "good war" of 1941–45. In spite of the mendacious, fabricated denial by elected officials who have decided to ignore the science of climate change, we do have the capacity, as a nation, to respond to these times. Elected officials who decide their primary accountability is not to the people need to be "retired" by their constituencies.

In my view, however, we will not risk fundamental change as a matter of goodwill, personal merit, or perceived virtue. We will construct several iterations of looking-good strategies, so long as they don't involve fundamental change of the racial rules that are embedded in our society. Many of our organizations have become skilled at shaping such looking-good strategies. They publicly value multiculturalism and diversity and spend substantial energy managing diversity. Somehow, the management strategies employed leave the deep racial rules in place.

To put it another way, the white collective will not intentionally work with others to undo, deconstruct, or dismantle white supremacy until it is clear our lives depend on it, individually and collectively. We will not commit racial treason until we are committed to an alternative reality—an alternate vision of social relatedness. Such an alternative vision has power for us when it comes clear, as Janice Joplin used to sing, that "freedom's just another word for nothing left to lose!"[109] Freedom, for white people, means grasping that we have nothing left to lose. The old racial paradigm is a death trap. Our nation has nothing to lose and everything to gain.

CONCLUSION

Organizing Our Way into the Future

I am the welder.
I understand the capacity of heat
to change the shape of things.
I am suited to work
within the realm of sparks
out of control.
I am the welder.
I am taking the power
Into my own hands.

Excerpt from "The Welder," Cherríe Moraga[110]

There is no magic involved in radical social transformation. There are certainly many unknowns and countless variables involved. Organizing is the deep work that is part and parcel of social change. Organizing social transformation includes all the education, training, legal strategies, street demonstrations, and personal soul work that we do, out of necessity. Change never flows from A to B to C in a linear fashion. The terrain is always changing. The unexpected always intrudes. Hence, our organizing must always be reality based, in as much as we are able. This means we must deal with things as they are, not as we wish they were. Save we are adaptive in our organizing, we will not be resilient and will not endure in the work. The new social realities that result from our organizing (as well as the other forces at work) will never be exactly as we envisioned. They will, however, be a costly purchase. They represent an investment of energy, creativity, flesh, and blood that is an intentional counter to the historical investments in systemic oppression our nation made. They are, consequently, the stepping-stones to the future.

Following are a few examples of practical actions that can be carried out locally. When a compelling case is made for reparation, local creativity can generate a plethora of relevant practical actions. Our local organizing needs to value inclusive participation; we must engage those on the margins and those at the center of community life. The whole community must be involved in this effort. However, being inclusive in our organizing does not mean being naïve about white supremacy. People use the phrase *the struggle for racial justice* because it is just that: a struggle. Apartheid is deeply rooted in our history; the white collective is directly and subtly invested in white supremacy. Left to our own devices, we white people will replicate the past, albeit in new clothing. This is not a matter of how well-intentioned or committed we are. Rather, it reflects our captivity. Hence, leadership that is transformative simply does not begin in the center; rather, it is initiated from the margins! In relation to race, it is communities of color that inhabit society's margins. Consequently, it is in communities of color that the vision of a transformed society incubates.

That is why leadership from the margins is especially important. The key is antiracist accountability relationships between those at the center and those on the margins. While it is clearly important to call out and challenge reactionary activism that seeks to maintain the grip of white supremacy, it is also important to avoid being the antiracism Gestapo. So, we need to create pathways to participation lodged in antiracist accountability.

Now, some additional comments regarding the organizing challenge. Antiracist organizers must move beyond the energy-draining competition that is often prevalent among progressive groups committed to antiracist transformation. The ideology of free market capitalism pits us against one another and does unnecessary mischief. Granted, competition can help us hone our message and sharpen our craft. But unrestrained competition undercuts effective collaboration. When we undermine one another and promote ourselves as *the answer*, the only winner is systemic oppression. A helpful exercise is to ask, "What unique contribution do we bring to the table? What gifts do other groups bring? How do we help them fulfill their contribution?" In this moment, we need all hands on deck. Collaboration and collective effort are required. Otherwise, our past will be intractable. Finally, this is more than an ideology that stresses collaboration; it is practical. Those of us working to deconstruct white supremacy cannot match the financial resources used to maintain and strengthen the racial canon. Our primary resource is human; to be effective, it is necessary to link our human capital together.

Many voices from the political camp that supports the current administration will dismiss our efforts as left wing ideology or misplaced liberalism, thus suggesting it has no relevance and is perhaps un-American. We have to make a persuasive case that nothing less will safeguard our passage to the future. More than an "educational task," this is an organizing challenge and task.

Local Organizing—Some Examples

- Learn your local and regional history with regard to race and racial oppression; be sure to highlight the local history of resistance.
- Engage local resources (journalists, higher education, high school journalism classes) to document this history and make it available to the public; utilize libraries, newspapers, and magazines, and so on.
- Press local institutions to develop an explicit antiracism strategy and antiracist institutional leadership; Crossroads Antiracism Organizing and Training is an organization that specializes in helping institutions of all types become antiracist.
- Community foundations can be a key philanthropic partner in this effort. Enlist support for local antiracism organizing by regional community foundations. The Saint Paul and Minnesota Community Foundations are among those that are dramatic examples of leveraging philanthropic resources to address racial challenges. A little research will lead to the discovery of others and resources for your efforts.
- Organize a skein of local accountability relationships that span racial boundaries and link community organizations, businesses, public institutions, and churches in a concerted antiracism effort.

- Build respectful, accountable, antiracist relationships with reservation communities in your area. The first step might include invitations to share tribal history and concerns with churches, community groups, and educational institutions.
- Support the efforts of local Native communities to recover land and protect sovereignty.
- Support collaborative efforts among municipal, county agencies, and reservation communities.
- Support and promote public dialogue about recompense—what is adequate and appropriate recompense for our brutal history of racial injustice: slavery, segregation, disenfranchisement, removal, and disappearance. Such dialogue needs to be locally and regionally relevant, taking into account the actual history of the region re racial justice; it does not need to dismiss the struggles and needs of low-income white families.
- Promote dialogue in your community on the benefits of multicultural, multiethnic diversity; reject commentaries that relate such efforts to left wing ideologies. Instead, frame them as strategies that ensure we have a viable future. Spell out the practical outcomes that will benefit your community.
- Highlight local efforts in other communities that link racial and eco-justice. Invite activists in those efforts to local sharing opportunities and speaking engagements.
- Organize a regional event highlighting efforts across the region that link environmental and social justice efforts (they are there; you may have to search them out). Such an event gives visibility to efforts that may be hidden and will accelerate the efforts.
- Support local and state initiatives that adequately fund public education; adequate funding needs to be determined with primary input from public education entities and from communities of color.
- Similarly, support curricula reform efforts that relate to the real world that students encounter. Encourage and support curriculum changes in public education that present a nuanced and inclusive picture of our multicultural history, beginning in elementary school. (Note there has been important writing for children—both fiction and nonfiction—regarding the Holocaust; similar work can be done regarding the history of racism and resistance.)

- Engage colleges and universities in your area in the effort; help them shape accountable relationships with local communities and organizations of color.
- Reward local entrepreneurs who seek to shape business ventures that are ecologically responsible, take climate change into account, and have an antiracist commitment. Give them business!
- Support local efforts for renewable energy that move us beyond our dependence on fossil fuel.
- Encourage community links with local and regional agriculture, especially those farm operations that are seeking to transition to a more sustainable, organic approach and that value the participation of people of color and women in agriculture.
- Support and elect politicians who are personally committed to racial justice and environmental issues. (We know that an effort to promote apology at the national level will fuel a backlash and resistance. Local support for such efforts is crucial. It will strengthen the voice of elected officials in their respective party caucuses.)
- Support federal efforts to engage with Indian nations and tribes regarding broken treaties.
- Support an apology for slavery by our federal government (with the office of the president taking the lead).
- It is unrealistic to expect Congress or the current administration (much less the Supreme Court) to provide leadership in the struggle for racial and eco-justice without strong local and regional support. In the absence of national leadership, we can organize local leadership to apologize for the brutal excesses of slavery, segregation, Jim Crow, and their contemporary vestiges. We can also press for apology for the local and regional theft of land and the brutal attempts to destroy tribal cultures. Churches can play a critical role in this effort.

Final Words: What Is at Stake?

This book makes the case that our capacity as a nation to negotiate the challenges the future poses is at stake. Save we reimagine and repair the fabric of human community, we will not move beyond our apartheid history. Our survival is on the table. Our capacity to provide leadership in responding to the challenges posed by dramatic climate change and related ecological issues is also at stake.

I have suggested that local communities and neighborhoods are the critical focus for our antiracism organizing. This is the work of reparation—the reparation of the very fabric of community life. It is work that is transapartheid and that creates links between antiracism and eco-justice. It is work that, in effect, is an investment in our future that counters our historic investment in racial oppression.

Troubling questions do persist. Are the racial default settings in our nation intractable? Does racism's ability to mutate and adjust to new social realities mean we will always be struggling with this systemic affliction? Will the forcefulness of free market capitalism and its historic relation to racial oppression contradict our efforts to respond to climate change? Can human community be repaired and restored in the digital age? Can we really devise ways of cooperating that are inclusive and robustly equitable?

Finally, we cannot answer such questions, save by the investment of our lives. What we shall do and who we shall be in the future will be our answer. The society we have, with its history of aspiration and brutality, is a costly purchase. We simply have paid too much to allow things to continue as they are. That means we have no option save to commit to organizing that is reality based and to trust that, as Martin Luther King Jr. bore witness, "the arc of the moral universe is long, but bends towards justice."[111] Or as the Irish poet Seamus Heaney put it, "once in a lifetime ... the tidal wave of justice can rise up and hope and history rhyme."[112]

NOTES

Introduction

[1]   Lerone Bennett Jr., *Confrontation: Black and White* (Chicago: reprinted by Johnson Publishing Co., 1965).

Chapter 1

[2]   Daniel Goleman, *Social Intelligence* (Bantam Books, 2006).
[3]   Jeremy Rifkin, *The Empathic Civilization*, animated video by RSA Animate, YouTube presentation May 2010.
[4]   Goleman, *Social Intelligence,* 43.
[5]   Melissa K. Nelson, ed., *Original Instructions* (Rochester: Bear & Company, 2008), xvii and introduction.
[6]   Octavio Paz, *Return to the Labyrinth of Solitude* (Grove Press, 1985).
[7]   Yuval Harari, TED Talk, June 2015.

Chapter 2

[8]   Dorothy Roberts, *Fatal Invention* (New York: The New Press, 2011), 4.
[9]   Ian Haney Lopez, *White by Law* (New York: New York University Press, 1996), 13.
[10] Lopez, *White by Law,* quoting John Calmore, 13.
[11] Jacqueline Battalora, *Birth of a White Nation* (Strategic Books Publishing & Rights Company, 2013), 33.
[12] Jack Forbes, "The Peoples' Voice," November 27, 2000.
[13] Lopez, *White by Law,* 22–24.
[14] Lopez, *White by Law,* 27.
[15] Battalora, *Birth of a White Nation,* 69.

[16] "Understanding and Analyzing Systemic Racism," workshop designed and presented by Crossroads Antiracism Organizing and Training, Chicago. Used with permission.

Chapter 3

[17] From the workshop "Understanding and Analyzing Systemic Racism," Crossroads Antiracism Organizing and Training.
[18] Michelle Alexander, *The New Jim Crow* (New York: The New Press, 2010), 237.
[19] David Williams, TED Talk, May 2017.

Chapter 4

[20] Nick Hobson, University of Toronto, YouTube, April 2016.
[21] Michael Pina, "The Archaic, Historic and Mythicized Dimensions of Aztlán," from *Aztlán,* edited by Rudolfo Anaya and Francisco Lomeli (Albuquerque: University of New Mexico Press, 1989), 37.
[22] Anaya, *Aztlán,* iii–iv.
[23] Luis Leal, "In Search of Aztlán," *Aztlán*, 7.
[24] Ibid., 7.
[25] Mircea Eliade, *Myth and Reality* (San Francisco: Harper & Row Publishers, 1963).
[26] 26, Lopez, introduction and conclusion to *Dog Whistle Politics* (Oxford: Oxford University Press, 2014).
[27] George Mosse, *Toward the Final Solution* (New York: Howard Fertig, 1978, 1985), xxx.
[28] National Public Radio (NPR), March 4, 2017.
[29] 29 Juleyka Lantiqua-Williams, "Race and Solitary Confinement in US Prisons," *Atlantic Monthly,* December 5, 2016, quoting Judith Reznik, Yale Law School.
[30] Henry J. Kaiser Foundation, "Poverty Rates by Race and Ethnicity, 2016."

Part II Introduction

[31] Jack Weatherford, *Genghis Kahn and the Making of the Modern World* (New York: Crown Publishers, 2004), 247.
[32] Nigel Cliff, *The Last Crusade* (New York: HarperCollins Publishers, 2011), 91.

Chapter 5

[33]   Dietrich Bonhoeffer, *Ethics* (Minneapolis: Fortress Press, 2008), 244.

[34]   H. Richard Niebuhr, *The Purpose of the Church and Its Ministry* (New York: Harper and Brothers, 1956).

[35]   Ibid.

Chapter 6

[36]   Eric Williams, *Capitalism and Slavery* (Chapel Hill: University of North Carolina Press, 1944).

[37]   National Cotton Council of America, www.cotton.org.

[38]   Beckert, *Empire of Cotton*, 108.

[39]   Cole et al., Economic Research Service, Department of Agriculture, "Tobacco and the Economy;" Foreman and McBride, "Policy Reforms in the Tobacco Industry" (Washington, DC: Economic Research Service, September 2000 and May 2011).

[40]   Mathew Perrone, "Big Tobacco's anti-smoking ads begin after decade of delay," Associated Press,   November 2017.

[41]   James H. Tuten, *Lowcountry Time and Tide* (Columbia: University of South Carolina Press, 2010), chapter 1.

[42]   Alan Gallay, *The Indian Slave Trade* (New Haven: Yale University Press, 2002), 7.

Chapter 7

[43]   Sven Beckert, *Empire of Cotton* (New York: Alfred A. Knopf, 2014), chapters 2 and 3.

[44]   Matthew Parker, *The Sugar Barons* (New York: Walker Publishing Company, 2011), 26–27, 48–51.

[45]   *Matewan*, Cinecom Entertainment Group, 1987.

[46]   James J. Lorence, *The Suppression of Salt of the Earth* (University of New Mexico Press, 1999).

[47]   Alfred W. and Ruth G. Blumrosen, *Slave Nation* (New York: Barnes and Noble Books, 2005), chapters 8 and 9.

[48]   Blumrosen, *Slave Nation,* 224.

[49]   Don Fehrenbacher, *The slaveholding Republic* (New York: Oxford University Press, 2001), 46–47.

[50]   Blumrosen, *Slave Nation,* chapter 12.

[51]   Gregory Dowd, *A Spirited Resistance* (Baltimore: Johns Hopkins University Press, 1992), chapter 5.

52 Library of Congress, "Northwest Ordinance, Third Article."

53 Ron Satz, *American Indian Policy in the Jacksonian Era* (Norman: University of Oklahoma Press, 1975), chapters 2 and 3.

54 Philip S. Foner, *Basic Writings of Thomas Jefferson* (New York: Willey Book Company, 1944), IV 248–50.

Chapter 8

55 Lopez, *White by Law,* 133.

56 Satz, *American Indian Policy in the Jacksonian Era,* appendix: text of the Indian Removal Act (also Library of Congress).

57 Roger B. Taney, "*Dred Scott* Decision" (Washington, DC, Library of Congress).

58 Indian Appropriations Act of 1871, Library of Congress.

59 Chinese Exclusion Act of 1882, Library of Congress.

60 The General Allotment Act, Library of Congress.

61 United States Supreme Court, *Plessy v. Ferguson*, Library of Congress.

62 Clara Sue Kidwell and Charles Roberts, *The Choctaws: A Critical Bibliography* (Bloomington: Indiana University Press, 1980), 55.

63 Howard Zinn, Mike Konopacki, and Paul Buhle, *A People's History of American Empire* (New York: Metropolitan Books, a division of Henry Holt, 2008), 53.

64 Asiatic Barred Zone, Library of Congress.

65 Executive Order 9066, Library of Congress.

66 Supreme Court of the United States, *United States v. Korematsu*, Library of Congress.

67 John Gall, *The Systems Bible* (Walker: General Systemantics Press, 2002), 164.

68 68.Vernon G. Carrion, MD, and Shane S. Wong, "Can Traumatic Stress Alter the Brain? Understanding the Implications of Early Trauma and Brain Development and Learning," *Journal of Adolescent Health* 51, no. 2 (August 2012).

Chapter 9

69 Naturalization Act of 1790, Library of Congress.

70 Fourteenth Amendment to the Constitution of the United States, Library of Congress.

Chapter 10

[71] John Gall, *Dancing With Elves* (Walker: General Systemantics Press, 2000).

[72] Tig Productions, Majestic Films International, Allied Filmmakers, *Dancing With Wolves*, 1990.

[73] Randall Robinson, *The Debt: What America Owes to Blacks* (New York: a Dutton Book, published by the Penguin Group, 2000), chapters 7 and 8.

[74] Crossroads Antiracism Organizing and Training, from the workshop "Understanding and Analyzing Systemic Racism."

[75] James Webb, *Born Fighting* (New York: Broadway Books, 2004), chapter 5.

Chapter 11

[76] Joseph Barndt, *Dismantling Racism* (Minneapolis: Augsburg Fortress, 1991), chapter 3.

[77] William Earnest Henley, "Invictus," from *Book of Verses* (1888).

[78] *Merriam-Webster Online Dictionary*, www.merriam-webster.com.

Chapter 12

[79] Everyday Feminism, www.everydayfeminism.com.

[80] James Loewen, *Lies My Teacher Told Me* (New York: The New Press, 2008).

[81] Loewen, *Lies Across America* (New York: The New Press, 1999).

[82] Robin DiAngelo, *Seattle Times* interview, August 9, 2014.

[83] Brené Brown, Facebook page, www.facebook.com.

[84] Bob Marley and the Wailers, "Legend," Tuff Gong International, 1984.

[85] Barndt, *Dismantling Racism,* chapter 3.

[86] *Merriam-Webster Online Dictionary*, www.merriam-webster.com.

[87] LeManuel "Lee" Bitsoi, PhD, presentation at Gateway to Discovery Conference, 2013.

[88] Financial Page, *New Yorker,* June 6 and 13, 2016.

[89] Susan David, *Emotional Agility* (New York: Penguin Random House, 2016), chapter 10.

[90] Estelle Frankel, *Sacred Therapy* (Boston: Shambhala Publications, Inc., 2005), 119.

[91] Race Traitors, www.racetraitors.com.

[92] Brené Brown, Facebook, www.facebook.com.

Part IV Introduction

93   Martin Luther King Jr., *Where Do We Go from Here: Chaos or Community?* (New York: Harper & Row, 1967).

Chapter 13

94   John Gall, *The Systems Bible,* 42.

Chapter 14

95   *Merriam-Webster Online Dictionary,* www.merriam-webster.com.
96   *Seattle Times,* March 6, 2016.
97   Representative John Conyers, US House of Representatives, "HR 40, Commission to study and develop reparations proposals for African-Americans Act."
98   Hilton Hotels, Inc.

Chapter 15

99   Lehrhaus Judaica website, www.lehrhaus.org.
100   *Gemeinschaftsgefuhl: A Magazine for Alumni and Friends of the Adler School of Professional Psychology* (Summer 2013).
101   Paul Hawken, *Blessed Unrest* (New York: Penguin Group, 2007), 190.
102   H. Richard Niebuhr, *The Purpose of the Church and Its Ministry.*
103   "Deuteronomy," in the Holy Bible, NRSV (Iowa Falls: National Council of Churches, 1989), chapter 30, verse 19.

Chapter 16

104   Naomi Klein, introduction and conclusion to *This Changes Everything* (New York: Simon & Schuster, 2014).
105   *Merriam-Webster Online Dictionary,* www.merriam-webster.com.
106   Wikipedia, "Principles of Permaculture," www.wikipedia.com.
107   Melissa K. Nelson, *Original Instructions,* page xvii.
108   Wendy Plotkin, *FHA Underwriting Manual, 1938, 1998.* (The manual listed eight elements that restrictive covenants should contain; number seven noted, "Prohibition of the occupancy of properties except by the race for which they are intended."), www.wendyplotkin.asu.edu.
109   Kris Kristofferson and Fred Foster, "Me and Bobbi McGee," originally performed by Roger Miller.

Conclusion

[110]   Cherríe Moraga, "The Welder," from *This Bridge Called My Back* (New York: Kitchen Table: Women of Color Press, 1981), 219.

[111]   Martin Luther King Jr., graduation address at Wesleyan University, June 8, 1964.

[112]   Seamus Heaney, "The Cure at Troy," 1961.

BIBLIOGRAPHY AND
WORKS CITED

Adams, David Wallace. *Education for Extinction: American Indians and the Boarding School Experience, 1875–1928*. Lawrence: University Press of Kansas, 1995.

Alexander, Michelle. *The New Jim Crow: Mass Incarceration in the Age of Colorblindness*. New York: The New Press, 2010.

Anaya, Rudolfo A., and Francisco Lomeli, eds. *Aztlán: Essays on the Chicano Homeland*. Albuquerque: University of New Mexico Press, 1991.

Anzaldúa, Gloria. *Borderlands La Frontera: The New Mestiza*. 2nd ed. San Francisco: Aunt Lute Books, 2007.

———, ed. *Haciendo Caras, Making Face, Making Soul: Creative and Critical Perspectives by Feminists of Color*. San Francisco: Aunt Lute Books, 1990.

Ariely, Dan. *Predictably Irrational: The Hidden Forces That Shape Our Decisions*. New York: HarperCollins Publishers, 2008.

"The Site That Nobody Knows: Kinishba Reawakened." Tucson: *Archeology Southwest* 30, no. 1 (Winter 2016). www.archeologysouthwest.org.

Baker-Fletcher, Karen. *Sisters of Dust, Sisters of Spirit: Womanist Wordings on God and Creation*. Minneapolis: Fortress Press, 1998.

Baldwin, James. *The Fire Next Time*. New York: Dial Press, 1962.

Banks, Ralph Richard, and Richard Thompson Ford. "Does Unconscious Bias Matter?" Washington, DC: *Poverty & Race Research Action Council* 20, no. 5 (October 2011): 1–2. www.prrac.org.

Baptist, Edward E. *The Half Has Never Been Told: Slavery and the Making of American Capitalism*. New York: Basic Books, 2014.

Barndt, Joseph. *Dismantling Racism: The Continuing Challenge to White America*. New York: Augsburg Fortress, 1991.

Battalora, Jacqueline. *Birth of a White Nation: The Invention of White People and Its Relevance Today.* Houston: Strategic Books Publishing and Rights Company, 2013.

Beckert, Sven. *Empire of Cotton: A Global History.* New York: Alfred A. Knopf, 2014.

Bell, Derrick. *Faces at the Bottom of the Well: The Permanence of Racism.* New York: Basic Books, 1992.

Bennett Jr., Lerone. *Before the Mayflower: A History of Black America,* 5th ed. New York: Penguin Books, 1984.

Berlin, Ira, Marc Favreau, and Steven F. Miller, eds. *Remembering Slavery: African Americans Talk About Their Personal Experiences of Slavery and Emancipation.* New York: The New Press, 1998.

Blackmon, Douglas A. *Slavery by Another Name: The Re-Enslavement of Black Americans from the Civil War to World War II.* New York: Anchor Books, 2009.

Blumrosen, Alfred W., and Ruth G. *Slave Nation: How Slavery United the Colonies and Sparked the American Revolution.* New York: Barnes & Noble Books, 2005.

Bordewich, Fergus M. *Killing the White Man's Indian: Reinventing Native Americans at the End of the Twentieth Century.* New York: Anchor Books, May 2007.

Brodkin, Karen. *How the Jews Became White Folks and What That Says About Race in America.* New Brunswick: Rutgers University Press, 1998.

Brooks, Roy L. *Atonement and Forgiveness: A New Model for Black Reparations.* Berkeley: University of California Press, 2004.

Brown, Dee. *Bury My Heart at Wounded Knee: An Indian History of the American West.* 4th ed. New York: Owl Books, 2007.

Brown, Wilmette. *Black Women and the Peace Movement.* 3rd ed. Bristol: Falling Wall Press, 1984.

Brueggemann, Walter. *The Prophetic Imagination,* 9th printing. Minneapolis: Fortress, 1989.

Camp, Stephanie M. H. *Closer to Freedom: Enslaved Women and Everyday Resistance in the Plantation South.* Chapel Hill: University of North Carolina Press, 2004.

Carr, Nicholas. *The Shallows: What the Internet Is Doing to Our Brains.* New York: W. W. Norton & Company, 2010.

———. *The Big Switch: Rewiring the World, from Edison to Google.* New York: W.W. Norton & Company, 2008.

Cavett, Kate, Hand in Hand Productions. *Voices of Rondo: Oral Histories of Saint Paul's Historic Black Community.* Minneapolis: Syren Book Company, 2005.

Cheney, Glenn Alan. *Quilombo dos Palmares: Brazil's Lost Nation of Fugitive Slaves.* Hanover: New London Librarium, 2014.

Chisom, Ronald, and Michael Washington. Vol. 1 of *Undoing Racism: A Philosophy of Social Change.* 2nd ed. New Orleans: People's Institute Press, 1997.

Cliff, Nigel. *The Last Crusade: The Epic Voyages of Vasco Da Gama.* New York: Harper Perennial, 2012.

Coates, Ta-Nehisi. *Between the World and Me.* New York: Spiegel and Grau, 2015.

Cooper Lewter, Nicholas C. *Black Grief and Soul Therapy.* Richmond: Harriet Tubman Press, 1999.

Cone, James H. *Martin & Malcolm & America: A Dream or a Nightmare.* Ossining: Orbis Books, 1993.

David, Susan. *Emotional Agility: Get Unstuck, Embrace Change, and Thrive in Work and Life.* New York: Avery, an imprint of Penguin Random House, 2016.

Davies, Susan E., and Sister Paul Teresa Hennessee, SA, eds. *Ending Racism in the Church.* Cleveland: United Church Press, 1988.

Davis, Angela Y. *Women, Race and Class.* Random House, 1981; New York: Vintage Books, 1983.

Davis, F. James. *Who Is Black? One Nation's Definition.* University Park: Pennsylvania State University Press, 1992.

Darity Jr., William A., and Samuel Myers, with Emmett D. Carson and William Sabol. The *Black Underclass: Critical Essays on Race and Unwantedness.* New York: Garland Publishing, 1994.

Debo, Angie. *And Still the Waters Run: The Betrayal of the Five Civilized Tribes.* Norman: University of Oklahoma Press, 1986.

Derman-Sparks, Louise, and Carol Brunson Phillips. *Teaching/Learning Anti-Racism: A Developmental Approach.* New York: Teachers College Press, 1997.

Derman-Sparks, Louise, and Patricia G. Ramsey. *What If All the Kids Are White: Anti-Bias Multicultural Education with Young Children and Families.* New York: Teachers College Press, 2006.

DeWolf, Thomas Norman. *Inheriting the Trade: A Northern Family Confronts Its Legacy as the Largest Slave-Trading Dynasty in U.S. History.* Boston: Beacon Press, 2011.

DeYoung, Curtiss Paul. *Coming Together In the 21ˢᵗ Century: The Bible's Message in an Age of Diversity.* Valley Forge: Judson Press, 2009.

Diamond, Jared. *Collapse: How Societies Choose to Fail or Succeed.* New York: Penguin Books, 2005.

————. *Guns, Germs, and Steel: The Fates of Human Societies.* New York: W.W. Norton & Company, 1999.

Diouf, Sylviane A. *Slavery's Exiles: The Story of the American Maroons.* New York: New York University Press, 2014.

Douglas, Kelly Brown. *The Black Christ.* Ossining: Orbis Books, 1994.

Dowd, Gregory Evans. *A Spirited Resistance: The North American Indian Struggle for Unity, 1745–1815.* Baltimore: Johns Hopkins University Press, 1992.

Drucker, Peter R. *The Effective Executive: The Definitive Guide to Getting the Right Things Done.* New York: HarperCollins Publishers, 1967, 1985, 2002, 2006.

DuBois, W. E. B. *The Souls of Black Folk.* Bensenville: Lushena Books Inc., 2000.

Edelman, Marian Wright. *Lanterns: A Memoir of Mentors.* Boston: Beacon Press, 1999.

Egan, Timothy. *The Worst Hard Time: The Untold Story of Those Who Survived the Great American Dust Bowl.* New York: A Mariner Book, Houghton Mifflin Company, 2006.

Ehle, John. *Trail of Tears: The Rise and Fall of the Cherokee Nation.* New York: Anchor Books, Doubleday, 1988.

El-Kati, Mahmoud. *The Myth of "Race" / The Reality of Racism: A Critical Essay.* Minneapolis–Saint Paul: Stairstep Foundation and Challenge Productions, 1993.

Eliade, Mircea. *Myth & Reality.* Translated by Willard Trask. New York: Harper & Row, 1963.

Elizondo, Virgil. *The Future Is Mestizo: Life Where Cultures Meet.* New York: Crossroad Publishing Company, 1992.

Emerson, Michael, and Christian Smith. *Divided by Faith: Evangelical Religion and the Problem of Race in America.* New York: Oxford University Press, 2000.

Eoyong, Glenda H., ed. *Voices from the Field: An Introduction to Human Systems Dynamics*. Circle Pines: Human Systems Dynamics Institute, 2003.

Fairbanks, Evelyn. *Days of Rondo: A Warm Reminiscence of St. Paul's Thriving Black Community in the 1930s and 1940s*. Saint Paul: Minnesota Historical Society Press, 1990.

Feelings, Tom. *The Middle Passage: White Ships, Black Cargo*. New York: Dial Books, 1995.

Fehrenbacher, Don E. *The Slaveholding Republic: An Account Of The United States Government's Relations to Slavery*. New York: Oxford University Press, 2001.

Felder, Cain Hope, ed. *Stony the Road We Trod: African American Biblical Interpretation*. Minneapolis: Fortress Press, 1991.

———. *Troubling Biblical Waters: Race, Class and Family*. 7th ed. Ossining: Orbis Books, 1990.

Forbes, Jack D. *The American Discovery of Europe*. Champaign-Urbana: University of Illinois Press, 2007.

———. *Columbus and other Cannibals*. New York: Seven Stories Press, 2008.

Foreman, Grant. *Indian Removal*. Norman: University of Oklahoma Press, 11th printing, 1989.

Frankel, Estelle. *Sacred Therapy: Jewish Spiritual Teachings on Emotional Healing and Inner Wholeness*. Boston: Shambala Publications Inc., 2003.

Friedman, Thomas. *The World Is Flat: A Brief History of the Twenty-First Century*. New York: Farrar, Straus and Giroux, 2005.

———. *Hot, Flat and Crowded: Why We Need a Green Revolution—And How It Can Renew America*. New York: Farrar, Straus and Giroux, 2008.

Gall, John. *The Systems Bible: The Beginner's Guide to Systems Large and Small*. 3rd ed. Walker: General Systems Press, 2002.

Gallay, Alan. *The Indian Slave Trade: The Rise of the English Empire in the American South 1670–1717*. New Haven: Yale University Press, 2002.

Giddings, Paula. *When and Where I Enter: The Impact of Black Women on Race and Sex in America*. New York: Bantam Books, 1988.

Gladwell, Malcolm. *Blink: The Power of Thinking Without Thinking*. New York: Little, Brown & Company, 2005.

Goleman, Daniel. *Social Intelligence: The New Science of Human Relationships*. New York: Bantam Books, 2006.

Grant, Verlene. *Beyond Racism: A Deeper Understanding of Cultural Diversity.* Minneapolis: Kirk House Publishers, 2004.

Green, Richard L., ed. *A Salute to Historic Black Abolitionists.* Chicago: Empak Publishing Company, 1988, 1993.

Guerrero, Andrés G. *A Chicano Theology.* Ossining: Orbis Books, 1987.

Hacker, Andrew. *Two Nations: Black And White, Separate, Hostile And Unequal.* New York: Charles Scribner & Sons, 1992.

Hadden, Sally E. *Slave Patrols: Law and Violence in Virginia and the Carolinas.* Cambridge: Harvard University Press, 2003.

Hairston, Peter W. *The Cooleemee Plantation and Its People.* Winston-Salem: Hunter Publishing Company, 1986.

Harari, Yuval Noah. *Sapiens: A Brief History of Humankind.* Translated by Yuval Harari, John Purcell, and Haim Watzman. New York: HarperCollins, 2016.

Hawken, Paul. *Blessed Unrest: How the Largest Social Movement in History Is Restoring Grace,* *Justice and Beauty to the World.* New York: Viking Penguin, 2007.

Hooks, Bell. *Teaching Community: A Pedagogy of Hope.* New York: Routledge, 2003.

————. *Teaching Critical Thinking: Practical Wisdom.* New York: Routledge, 2010.

————. *Writing Beyond Race: Living Theory and Practice.* New York: Routledge, 2013.

————. *Sisters of the Yam: Black Women and Self-Recovery.* Boston: South End Press, 1993.

————. *Ain't I a Woman: Black Women and Feminism.* Boston: South End Press, 1981.

Horton, James Oliver, and Lois E. Horton. *Slavery and the Making of America.* New York: Oxford University Press, 2005.

Howard, Gary R. *We Can't Teach What We Don't Know: White Teachers, Multiracial Schools.* 2nd ed. Edited by James A. Banks. New York: Teachers College Press, Multicultural Education Series, 2006.

Howell, Annie, and Frank Tuitt, eds. "Race and Higher Education: Rethinking Pedagogy in Diverse College Classrooms." Cambridge: Harvard Educational Review, Reprint Series no. 36 (2003).

Hyde, Lewis. *The Gift: Creativity and the Artist in the Modern World.* New York: Vintage Books, 2007. (Originally published as *The Gift: Imagination and the Erotic Life of Property* by Random House, 1981.)

Isasi-Díaz, Ada María, and Fernando F. Segovia, eds. *Hispanic/Latino Theology: Challenge and Promise*. Minneapolis: Augsburg Fortress Publishers, 1996.

Jacob, Harriet A. *Incidents in the Life of a Slave Girl: Written by Herself.* Cambridge: Harvard University Press, 1987.

Jaspin, Elliot. *Buried in the Bitter Waters: The Hidden History of Racial Cleansing in America*. New York: Basic Books, 2006, 2007.

Johnson, Charles, Patricia Smith, and the WGBH Series Research Team. *Africans in America: America's Journey Through Slavery*. New York: Harcourt, Brace & Company, 1998.

Johnson, Kevin R., ed. *Mixed Race America and the Law: A Reader*. New York: New York University Press, 2003.

Juettner, Bonnie. *100 Native Americans Who Shaped American History*. San Mateo: Bluewood Books, 2003.

Katz, Judith, and John G. Mentzos, Compas Inc. *Way to the River Source: A Community's Journey to Supporting Diversity in Schools Through Family and Community Involvement*. Saint Paul: Compas, 1997.

Katznelson, Ira. *When Affirmation Action Was White*. New York: W.W. Norton and Company Inc., 2005.

Kellerman, Barbara, ed. *Political Leadership: A Source Book*. Pittsburg: University of Pittsburg Press, 1986.

Kennedy, N. Brent, with Robyn Vaughan Kennedy. *The Melungeons: The Resurrection of a Proud People, an Untold Story of Ethnic Cleansing in America*. Macon: Mercer University Press, 1997.

Kidwell, Clara Sue, and Charles Roberts. *The Choctaws: A Critical Bibliography*. Bloomington: Indiana University Press, published for the Newberry Library Center for the History of the American Indian, 1980.

Kinzer, Stephen. *The True Flag: Theodore Roosevelt, Mark Twain, and the Birth of American Empire*. New York: Henry Holt and Company, 2017.

Kivel, Paul. *Uprooting Racism: How White People Can Work or Racial Justice*. Philadelphia: New Society Publishers, 1996.

Klein, Naomi. *This Changes Everything: Capitalism vs. The Climate*. New York: Simon & Schuster, 2014.

Kolbert, Elizabeth. *The Sixth Extinction: An Unnatural History*. New York: Picador, 2015.

Kozol, Jonathan. *The Shame of the Nation: The Restoration of Apartheid Schooling in America*. New York: Three Rivers Press, Crown Publishing Group, 2005.

Krames, Jeffrey A. *Inside Drucker's Brain*. New York: Penguin Group, 2008.

Leonardo, Zeus, ed. *Critical Pedagogy and Race*. Malden: Blackwell Publishing Ltd., 2005.

Lerner, Michael, and Cornell West. *Jews and Blacks: A Dialogue on Race, Religion, and Culture in America*. New York: Penguin Books, 1996.

Lewis, Mary C. *Herstory: Black Female Rites of Passage*. Chicago: African American Images, 1988.

Loewen, James W. *Lies Across America: What Our Historic Sites Get Wrong*. New York: The New Press, 1999.

———. *Sundown Towns: A Hidden Dimension of American Racism*. New York: Touchstone, 2006.

Lomawaima, K. Tsianina, and Teresa L. McCarty. *To Remain an Indian: Lessons in Democracy from a Century of Native American Education*. Edited by James A. Banks. New York: Multicultural Education Series, Teachers College Press, 2006.

López, Ian Haney. *Dog Whistle Politics: How Coded Racial Appeals Have Reinvented Racism & Wrecked the Middle Class*. Toronto: Oxford University Press, 2014.

———. *White by Law: The Legal Construction of Race*. New York: New York University Press, 1996.

Lorence, James J. *The Suppression of Salt of the Earth: How Hollywood, Big Labor, and Politicians Blacklisted a Movie in Cold War America*. Albuquerque: University of New Mexico Press, 1999.

Maher, Frances A., and Mark Kay Thompson Tetreault. *Privilege and Diversity in the Academy*. New York: Routledge, 2007.

Maina-Okori, Naomi, Jada Renee Koushik, and Alexandria Wilson. "Reimagining Intersectionality in Environmental and Sustainability Education: A Critical Literature Review." *Journal of Environmental Education*. doi:10.1080/00958964.2017.1364215.

Malcomson, Scott L. *One Drop of Blood: The American Misadventure of Race*. New York: Farrar, Straus and Giroux, 2000.

Mann, Charles C. *1493: Uncovering the New World Columbus Created*. New York: A Borzoi Book, Alfred A. Knopf, 2011.

———. *1491: New Revelations of the Americas Before Columbus*. New York: Vintage Books, 2006.

Mathews, Michael Ray, and Marie Clare P. Onwubuariri with Cody J. Sanders, eds. *Trouble The Water: A Christian Resource for the work of Racial Justice.* Macon: Nurturing the Faith, Inc., 2017.

Medina, John. *Brain Rules: 12 Principles for Surviving and Thriving at Work, Home, and School.* Seattle: Pear Press, 2008.

Meier, Matt S., and Feliciano Rivera. *The Chicanos: A History of Mexican Americans.* New York: Hill and Wang, 1972.

Menzies, Gavin. *1421: The Year China Discovered America.* New York: William Morrow, 2003.

Michaels, Walter Benn. *The Trouble with Diversity: How We Learned to Love Identity and Ignore Inequality.* New York: Metropolitan Books, Henry Holt & Company, 2006.

Miller, Robert Ryal. *Mexico: A History.* Norman: University of Oklahoma Press, 1985.

Mirandé, Alfredo. *The Chicano Experience: An Alternative Perspective.* Notre Dame: University of Notre Dame Press, 1985.

Montgomery, David R. *Growing a Revolution: Bringing Our Soil Back to Life.* New York: W.W. Norton & Company, 2017.

Moraga, Cherríe, and Gloria Anzaldúa, eds. *This Bridge Called My Back: Writing by Radical Women of Color.* New York: Kitchen Table: Women of Color Press, 1981, 1983.

Mosse, George L. *Toward the Final Solution: A History of European Racism.* New York: Howard Fertig Inc., 1975, 1985, 1997.

Nelson, Jill. *Straight, No Chaser: How I Became a Grown-Up Black Woman.* New York: G.P. Putnam's Sons, 1997.

Nerburn, Kent. *Neither Wolf Nor Dog: On Forgotten Roads with an Indian Elder.* Novato: New World Library, 2010.

———. *The Wolf at Twilight: An Indian Elder's Journey Through a Land of Ghosts and Shadows.* Novato: New World Library, 2009.

Nelson, Melissa K., ed. *Original Instructions: Indigenous Teachings for a Sustainable Future.* Rochester: Bear and Company Books, 2008.

Newcomb, Steven T. *Pagans in the Promised Land: Decoding the Doctrine of Christian Discovery.* Golden: Fulcrum Publishing, 2008.

Nieto, Sonia. *Affirming Diversity: The Sociopolitical Context of Multicultural Education.* White Plains: Longman Publishers, 1996.

O'Brien, Cormac. *The Forgotten History of America: Little-Known Conflicts of Lasting Importance from the Earliest Colonists to the Eve of the Revolution.* Beverly: Fair Winds Press, 2008.

241

Owen, Harrison. *Wave Rider: Leadership for High Performance in a Self-Organizing World*. San Francisco: Barrett-Koehler Publishers, 2008.

———. *The Practice of Peace*. Open Space Institute, 2002; Circle Pines: Human Systems Dynamics Institute, 2004.

Pager, Devah. *Marked: Race, Crime and Finding Work in an Era of Mass Incarceration*. Chicago: University of Chicago Press, 2008.

Parker, Matthew. *The Sugar Barons: Family, Corruption, Empire and War in the West Indies*. New York: Walker Publishing Company, 2011.

Paz, Octavio. *The Labyrinth of Solitude and other Writings*. Translated by Lysander Kemp, Yara Milos, and Rachel Phillips Belash. New York: Grove Press, 1985.

Perkins, Spencer, and Chris Rice. *More Than Equals: Racial Healing for the Sake of the Gospel*. Downers Grove: InterVarsity Press, 1993.

Pero, Albert, and Amrose Moyo, eds. *Theology and the Black Experience: The Lutheran Heritage Interpreted by African and African-American Theologians*. Minneapolis: Augsburg Fortress Press, 1988.

Peters, William. *A Class Divided: Then and Now*. Expanded edition. New Haven: Yale University Press, 1987.

Pevar, Stephen L. *The Rights Of Indians And Tribes*. New York: Oxford University Press, fourth edition, 2012.

Pobee, John S., and Barbel Von Wartenberg-Potter, eds. *Biblical and Theological Reflections by Women from the Third World*. Bloomington: Meyer-Stone Books, World Council of Churches, 1986, 2012.

Pomeranz, Kenneth, and Steven Topik. *The World That Trade Created: Society, Culture, and the World Economy 1400 to the Present*. 2nd ed. Armonk: M. E. Sharpe Inc., 2006.

Poupart, John, Cecilia Martinez, John Red Horse, and Dawn Scharnberg. *To Build a Bridge: An Introduction to Working with American Indian Communities*. Saint Paul: American Indian Policy Center, 2001.

Quarles, Benjamin. *The Negro in the Making of America*. New York: Macmillan Company, 1971.

Rasmussen, Daniel. *American Uprising: The Untold Story of America's Largest Slave Revolt*. New York: HarperCollins Publishers, 2011.

Rediker, Marcus. *The Slave Ship: A Human History*. New York: Penguin Books, 2007.

Rendón, Laura I. *Sentipensante Pedagogy (Sensing/Thinking): Educating For Wholeness, Social Justice And Liberation*. Sterling: Stylus Publishing, 2009.

Reséndez, Andrés. *The Other Slavery: The Uncovered Story of Indian Enslavement in America.* New York: Houghton Mifflin Harcourt, 2016.

Roberts, Dorothy. *Fatal Invention: How Science, Politics, and Big Business Re-Create Race in the Twenty-First Century.* New York: The New Press, 2011.

Robinson, Randall. *The Debt: What America Owes to Blacks,* New York: A Dutton Book, 2000.

———. *Quitting America: The Departure of a Black Man from His Native Land.* New York: Plume, 2005.

Rodriguez, Victor M. *Latino Politics in the United States: Race, Ethnicity, Class and Gender in the Mexican American and Puerto Rican Experience.* Dubuque: Kendall/Hunt Publishing Company, 2005.

Roediger, David R. *Working Toward Whiteness: How America's Immigrants Became White.* New York: Basic Books, 2006.

Russell, Kathy, Midge Wilson, and Ronald Hall. *The Color Complex: The Politics of Skin Color Among African Americans.* New York: Harcourt Brace Jovanovich, 1992.

Salaita, Steven. *Anti-Arab Racism in the USA: Where It Comes from and What It Means for Politics Today.* Ann Arbor: Pluto Press, 2006.

Satz, Ronald N. *American Indian Policy in the Jacksonian Era.* Norman: Red River Books, University of Oklahoma Press, 2002.

Soros, George. *The New Paradigm for Financial Markets: The Credit Crisis of 2008 and What It Means.* New York: Public Affairs, Perseus Books, 2008.

Steele, Shelby. *A Bound Man: Why We Are Excited About Obama and Why He Can't Win.* New York: Free Press, a Division of Simon & Schuster Inc., 2008.

Suchlicki, Jaime. *Mexico: From Montezuma to the Rise of the PAN.* 3rd ed. Washington, DC: Potomac Books, 2008.

Suina, Joseph H. "Columbus: Discoverer or Disenfranchiser? Eurocentric Schooling and Its Effects on Native Americans." New York: The 1992 Catherine Molony Memorial Lecture, City College Workshop Center, 1993.

Swanton, John R. *Source Material for the Social and Ceremonial Life of the Choctaw Indians.* Tuscaloosa: University of Alabama Press, 2001. Originally published by the Smithsonian Institution, 1931.

Takaki, Ronald. *A Different Mirror: A History of Multicultural America.* Boston: Back Bay Books, 1993.

Tamez, Elsa. *Bible of the Oppressed*. Ossining: Orbis Press, 1982.

Tatum, Beverly Daniel. *Can We Talk About Race? And Other Conversations in an Era of School Resegregation*. Boston: Beacon Press, 2007.

Terry, Robert W. *For Whites Only*. Grand Rapids: William B. Eerdmans Publishing Company, reprinted 1994.

Thistlethwaite, Susan Brooks, and Mary Potter Engel, eds. *Lift Every Voice: Constructing Christian Theologies from the Underside*. San Francisco: Harper San Francisco, 1990.

Tinker, George. *Missionary Conquest: The Gospel and Native American Cultural Genocide*. Minneapolis: Augsburg Fortress, 1993.

Treuer, Anton. *The Assassination of Hole in the Day*. Saint Paul: Borealis Books, 2011.

Treuer, David. *Rez Life: An Indian's Journey Through Reservation Life*. New York: Grove Press, 2012.

Tusmith, Bonnie, and Maureen T. Reddy, eds. *Race in the College Classroom: Pedagogy and Politics*. New Brunswick: Rutgers University Press, 2002.

Tuten, James H. *Lowcountry Time and Tide: The Fall of the South Carolina Rice Kingdom*. Columbia: University of South Carolina Press, 2010.

Vowell, Sarah. *Lafayette in the Somewhat United States*. New York: Riverhead Books, 2015.

Watkins, William H., ed. *Black Protest Thought and Education*. New York: Peter Lang, 2005.

Weatherford, Jack. *Genghis Khan and the Making of the Modern World*. New York: Crown Publishers, 2004.

———. *The Secret History of the Mongol Queens: How the Daughters of Genghis Khan Rescued His Empire*. New York: Crown Publishers, 2010.

———. *Indian Givers: How the Indians of the Americas Transformed the World*. New York: Fawcett Columbine, 1988.

Webb, James. *Born Fighting: How the Scots-Irish Shaped America*. New York: Broadway Books, 2004.

Weems, Renita J. *Just a Sister Away: A Womanist Vision of Women's Relationships in the Bible*. San Diego: LuraMedia, 1988.

Weincek, Henry. *The Hairstons: An American Family in Black and White*. New York: St. Martin's Press, 1999.

West, Cornell. *Race Matters*. New York: Vintage Books, 1994.

West, George Randall. *Creating Community: Finding Meaning in the Place We Live*. Bloomington: iUniverse, 2012.

244

Williams, Delores S. *Sisters in the Wilderness: The Challenge of Womanist God-Talk*. Ossining: Orbis Books, 1993.

Williams, Eric. *Capitalism and Slavery*. Chapel Hill: University of North Carolina Press, 1944.

Wink, Walter. *Engaging the Powers: Discernment and Resistance in a World of Domination*. Minneapolis: Fortress Press, 1992.

————. *Unmasking the Powers: The Invisible Forces That Determine Human Existence*. Minneapolis: Fortress Press, 1986.

Wise, Tim. *Between Barack and a Hard Place: Racism and White Denial in the Age of Obama*. San Francisco: City Lights Books, 2009.

Worcester, Donald E. *The Apaches: Eagles of the Southwest*. Norman: University of Oklahoma Press, 1979.

Wu, Frank H. *Yellow: Race in America Beyond Black and White*. New York: Basic Books, 2003.

X, Malcolm (with the assistance of Alex Haley). *The Autobiography of Malcolm X*. New York: Ballantine Books, 1987.

Ziegelman, Jane, and Andrew Coe. *A Square Meal: A Culinary History of the Great Depression*. New York: HarperCollins, 2016.

Zinn, Howard. *A People's History of the United States: 1492–Present*. 20th anniversary ed. New York: HarperCollins, 1999.

Zinn, Howard, Mike Konopacki, and Paul Buhle. *A People's History of American Empire: A Graphic Adaptation*. New York: Henry Holt Books, 2008.

INDEX

C

calling power into accountability,
  as one locus of leadership,
  200–201
Calmore, John, 10, 11
Campbell, Joseph, 37
captivity, 147–148, 151, 158, 164, 220
Caramel Indians, 21, 98, 214
Centers for Disease Control and
  Prevention, 82
central myth, 43, 44, 45
Charles Martel, 56
Chavez, Cesar, 92
Chicago Regional Organizing for
  Antiracism (CROAR), 197
Chicago Sustainability Leaders
  Network (CSLN), 197
child welfare system/programs,
  involvement in, 32, 49
Chinese Exclusion Act (1882),
  113, 115
citizen, use of term, 17
citizenship
  Choctaws as being awarded, 114
  and Dred Scott decision, 42,
    111–112, 174
  Indian Citizenships Act
    (1924), 17
  as legally equivalent to white
    identity, 42, 131, 132–133
  as open to people of African
    descent in Fourteenth
    Amendment, 17, 98
  through naturalization, 19
Civil Rights Act (1964), 30, 109, 181
claiming space in racial drama, as way
  station in work of historical
  accountability, 163, 166–167
Claire, Arthur St., 103
class
  impact of, 34, 46, 121, 128

intersection of race and, 118
intersection of race, gender, and,
  96, 99, 120, 141, 188, 196
as social construct, 6, 23
Clement VI (Pope), 57
Cliff, Nigel, 58–59
climate change, 199, 205, 217,
  223, 224
Clinton, Hillary, 67
Coates, Ta-Nehisi, 191
cocaine, use of crack vs.
  powdered, 119
coffee, as crop that enriched
  economies of imperial-colonial
  nations, 78–79
cognitive/existential dissonance,
  130–131
collaboration, 220, 221
collaborative leadership, 199
collective denial, 154, 155
collective effort, 199, 221
college enrollment, 32
colonialism, use of term, xvi
color blindness, 108, 139
Columbia exchange, 69
Committees of Correspondence, 100
communication, aspects of, 174
communication technologies, impact
  of on community, 3
community
  activist community, 196–197
  apartheid as fatal to human
    community, 205
  architecture of, 43, 44–45
  changing sense of who constitutes
    ours, 2
  as critical focus for antiracism
    organizing, 224
  healthy community as like a
    nurse log, 204
  impact of globalization on, 2–3

New Law of the Indies (1542), 72
Newcomb, Steven, 37
Nicholas V (Pope), xv
Niebuhr, H. Richard, 64, 65, 74, 199
Northwest Ordinance, 101, 102, 103–104, 105, 111

O

Obama, Barack, 11, 67, 134, 150, 192
Obia, 70
octoroon, 21
one-drop rule, 13, 14, 16, 17, 22
oppression. *See also* racial oppression; systemic oppression
  America's investment in, 7, 107, 117, 172
  internalization of, 35
  of people of color, 31–33
  as theme of Europe's efforts at global expansion, 63–64
Original Instructions: Indigenous Teachings for a Sustainable Future (Nelson), 3
otherness, 136
"out" groups, 66
out-of-home placement rates, 32

P

Parks, Rosa, 199–200
parole and probation disparities, 32
Pax Mongolica, 56–57, 58
payday loan companies, 49, 118
Paz, Octavio, 4, 37
The People's Institute for Survival and Beyond (New Orleans), 181
"the people," 188
philanthropic partners, 221
Picasso, Pablo, 61
Pina, Michael, 39, 46
plague, 57
Plessy v. Ferguson (1896), 114, 116

police
  as example of dividend, 119
  and stress, 120–121
political theater, prison–industrial complex as, 49–53
poverty
  impact of on underlying narrative, 53
  insufficient funding for public interventions in, 49
  as necessary feature of social construct, 47
  persistence of, 46, 48
  rates of, 32, 53
  as rehearsing and reinforcing intimate architecture of white supremacy, 47
predatory systems, examples of, 118
prejudice, 22, 23, 31, 66, 116, 147, 148, 149, 150, 215
prison labor, 95
prison–industrial complex, as political theater, 49–53
pro-life, use of term, 65–66
Psalm 137, 158, 164
psychological violence, 35–36
public assistance programs, utilization of, 32, 49
public education
  failure of in poor communities, 49–50
  as policy effort, 49
public innocence, 144, 148, 150, 151, 152
Public Law 280 (1953), 117

Q

quadroon, 21
Quilombo dos Palmares, 70

R

race
　ceremonial invocation of, 44
　collective character of, 18
　destructive power of, 5–6, 7
　as distorting sense of history, 7
　dividends of for white people,
　　121–123
　interconnection of with history
　　and community, 5–8
　intersection of class and, 118
　intersection of class, gender, and,
　　96, 99, 120, 141, 188, 196
　as more than black–white, xiii
　mythological underpinnings of,
　　37–54
　as never value-free, 44
　no evidence for as naturally
　　occurring biological
　　feature, 13
　persistence of power of, 45–49
　as providing solidarity, 141, 142
　as social construct, 9–17, 19, 23
　and stress, 120–121
　as ubiquitous in our society, 162
　use of term, 9
race card, playing of, 52, 154
race construct, internalization of,
　　35–36
race mixing, 14
race relations, differing perceptions
　　of, 20
Race Traitors, 167
racial apartheid, xviii, 14, 37, 150,
　　181, 195, 198, 199, 212, 214
racial arithmetic, 16–17
racial assignment, 6, 10–11, 17, 18,
　　19, 20, 22, 36, 42, 44, 146–
　　147, 151
racial bigotry, 147, 148, 149, 150, 151

racial buffer zones, borderlands, and
　　margins, 18, 20–22
racial categories, application of, 12
racial classification, 9
racial collectives, 18, 19, 46, 126, 135,
　　140, 141, 146, 147
racial designation, 17–20, 22, 23, 175
racial disparities, 19, 20, 32–33, 34,
　　46, 119, 120, 131, 176, 215–216
racial disproportionalities, 32, 33, 46,
　　51, 52–53, 118, 120
racial distinction, 10
racial dynamics, 3, 14, 20, 28, 198
racial exclusion, 31
racial hierarchy, 7
racial hybridization, 110
racial identity
　　as about social status and
　　　value, 17
　　as collective, 19
　　as couched in law, 10, 11
　　legal mechanisms used to
　　　assign, 13
　　as predictor of how likely one or
　　　one's family is to live in a
　　　poor community, 46
　　role of law in shaping and spelling
　　　out social significance
　　　of, 108
　　as social assignment, 6, 23
racial ideology, 14, 47, 108, 196
racial inferiority, 35
racial justice, xiv, xviii, 159, 177, 179,
　　181, 191, 198, 201, 206, 212,
　　216, 220, 222, 223
racial mongrels, 110
racial myth, 37, 42–43
racial oppression
　　denial of, 153–154
　　free market capitalism's historic
　　　relation to, 224

socialization, 6, 14, 35, 136–137, 146, 161, 165, 195

solidarity, 2, 5, 12, 141, 142, 155, 165, 166, 178, 181, 192, 202

solitary confinement, 50–51

Southern Christian Leadership Conference, 200

Spanish American War (1898), 115

stereotypes, 18, 32, 33, 35, 47, 148, 149

stop and search rates, 32, 119

storytelling, 5

strength in numbers, 178

stress
policing and, 120–121
race and, 120–121

stress hormones, impact of microaggression on, 32

Student Nonviolent Coordinating Committee, 200

subordination, xv, 16, 19, 20, 185, 196, 214

sugar, as crop that enriched economies of imperial-colonial nations, 78–79

superiority. See racial superiority; white superiority

sustainable communities, 3, 205–217

symbols
described, 40, 41
as having negative and positive impact, 41

systemic advantage, 137

systemic change, 119–120

systemic oppression
as consequence of undermining one another and promoting ourselves as the answer, 220
investment in, 172, 220

as theme of Europe's efforts at global expansion, 63–64

systemic power
defined, 28–31
duplicitousness of, 36
iceberg image of, 26
institutions as locus of, 29
misuse of, 34

Systems Bible (Gall), 174

T

Taney, Roger B., 42, 111, 174

Tecumseh, 104

Termination Act, 189

Texas, annexation of, 110

Thirteenth Amendment, 112, 133

This Changes Everything (Klein), 205

three-fifths clause, 101

tobacco
as crop that enriched economies of imperial-colonial nations, 82–84
current use of, 83
history of in US, 82–83

"toxic whiteness," 153

trail of broken treaties, 190, 213

"Trail of Tears," 105, 169–171

transparency, 18

trauma
defined, 159
use of term, 160

treaty making, with Indian nations/ communities, 21, 105, 109, 112–113, 190, 213

Treaty of Greenville (1795), 103

Treaty of Guadalupe Hidalgo (1848), 21, 110–111

Treaty of Paris (1783), 102

tribal affiliation, maintenance of, 20

Triple Alliance (Aztecs), 71

Trump, Donald, 67, 115, 150, 163